THE TRAILBLAZERS

The First English Cricket Tour of Australia
1861-62

DAVID FRITH

Boundary Books

For Debbie, Julie, Peter and John
and all my other Anglo-Aussie mates;
and with acknowledgement to
Marti Pellow,
whose golden voice
helped fuel this effort

First published in Great Britain in 1999 by
BOUNDARY BOOKS
Southlands, Sandy Lane, Goostrey, Cheshire CW4 8NT

ISBN 0 9522070 9 5

Typeset by Eva Press
Printed and bound in Great Britain by Clifford Frost Ltd,
Lyon Road, Windsor Avenue, London SW19 2SE

Contents

METRIC/MODERN EQUIVALENTS FOR LENGTHS, DISTANCES, WEIGHTS AND CURRENCY EXPRESSED IN THIS BOOK ARE:

1 MILE = 1.61 KILOMETRES   1 YARD = 91.44 CENTIMETRES [.914 OF A METRE]
1 FOOT = 30.48 CENTIMETRES   1 INCH = 2.54 CENTIMETRES
1 STONE (ST) = 6.35 KILOGRAMS   1 POUND (LB) = 0.45 KILOGRAMS
£1 = WORTH PERHAPS 100 TIMES TODAY'S POUND
SHILLING = 1/20TH OF £1   PENNY (1d) = 1/12TH OF A SHILLING
FARTHING = 1/4 OF A PENNY   HALF-A-CROWN = 1/8TH OF £1
A SOVEREIGN WAS A GOLD COIN WORTH £1   A GUINEA WAS A POUND & A SHILLING

OTHER BOOKS BY DAVID FRITH

The author, who was editor of *The Cricketer* from 1972 to 1978, and of *Wisden Cricket Monthly* from when he founded it in 1979 until 1996, has also contributed to numerous other books and magazines, and made two video programmes, *Benson & Hedges Golden Greats: Batsmen* (1983) and *Bowlers* (1988).

....

FRONT COVER: The All England XI which pioneered Australian tours: standing - George Bennett, William Mudie, William Caffyn, H.H.Stephenson, George Griffith, W.B.Mallam (promoters' agent), Roger Iddison, Tom Hearne, Ned Stephenson; in front - Charles Lawrence, William Mortlock, Tom Sewell. The 12th member of the team, George Wells, sailed ahead of the main party.

REAR COVER: Excitement in Melbourne, Christmas Eve 1861, as the English cricketers, atop the stagecoach, arrive at the hotel after their nine-week voyage.

PREFACE

NOT ONLY is this the longest-delayed cricket tour book of all time – outstretching the 100 years of *Stoddy's Mission* by 37 years – but, in common with that retrospective on the thrilling 1894-95 Ashes rubber, it is one which should surely have been written long before now. The risky 1861-62 undertaking, which begat the most famous of international sporting sagas, has a profound historical significance that is almost too obvious to need stating. Cricket is blessed with a vast corps of researchers and writers who are constantly at work, so it is little short of a miracle that this important chapter in the game's advance has never previously been dealt with in any great detail or depth.

This particular unfreezing of history was not a straightforward process. Information on the tour – the travelling, the play, the personalities – was scattered over a wide area, with much of it submerged by time. This writer has long been used to the frantic chase, the patient search, the dead-end, and the exultation of finding. But never has an investigation been so demanding. Reconstructing the scorecards alone took the best part of a day's work apiece. The odd discrepancy may never be clarified.

At first it promised to be a book of slight length, but so much elusive material from unlikely quarters began to accumulate that it was soon apparent that something substantial was in the offing. What capped it was a 10-hour session in the State Library of New South Wales on what would have been the fifth day of the 1999 Sydney Test match if Stuart MacGill had not spun out 12 England batsmen. From the building which happens almost to back onto the Domain, where All England played in 1862, sheaves of photocopies of old Australian newspapers were taken back that night to Randwick, thence Queensland, and then to Surrey (the county in which the 1861-62 tour had been conceived). The remainder of the English winter was spent weaving the tapestry, with barely a thought for anything of the outside world. Bliss. It really was like being on tour with H.H.Stephenson.

What a majestic title they gave themselves: the All England Eleven. Those pioneers of '61-62 opened the way for a cavalcade of popular (and the odd somewhat unwelcome) English cricketers: Grace and Shrewsbury, Stoddart and MacLaren, Ranji and Briggs and Richardson, Hobbs and Barnes and Rhodes, Woolley and Hendren and Tate, Sutcliffe, Hammond and Paynter, Larwood and Jardine and Verity, Leyland and Hutton and Compton and Bedser and Evans, Trueman and May and Tyson and Cowdrey, Dexter and Barrington, Knott and Boycott and Edrich and Illingworth and Snow, Botham and Gower, Randall and Gatting, Tufnell and Gough, and a few hundred other privileged cricketers from England who have felt the same excitement, and heard the same kind of raucous barracking and worse, that the adventurers of old experienced as they explored Terra (or was it mild *terror*?) Australis.

The trail blazed by the 1861-62 English cricketers and their backers eventually inspired not just further tours from the old country to the new, but regular two-way traffic. The Anglo-Australian challenge rapidly became the biggest thing in cricket, and if it has been devalued of late because of one side's on-going superiority, it will level up. By the ghost of HH it will!

As the author slips with a certain reluctance back into his own time, he wishes to record gratitude to Frank Tyson for help with the chronicling of the sensational match at Castlemaine; to Warwick Franks likewise concerning Bathurst; to Marylebone Cricket Club curator Stephen Green for permitting sight of the Spiers and Pond tour contract; to Frank Keating for locating the Brunel comment concerning cricket; to Gideon Haigh for finding extra detail just in time, speedily forwarded by David Studham, Melbourne Cricket Club's librarian; to Michael Down and his colleagues at Boundary Books for showing faith when little existed in the once-great publishing houses of London; to my daughter Julianne for her tutorials on the mysteries and vagaries of the computer; and, for what must be the three-dozenth time in terms of projects, to Debbie, my incredibly caring wife.

DAVID FRITH
Guildford
June 1999

CHAPTER 1

An Inevitable Enterprise

WHEN THE brave efforts of the exhausted England fast bowlers Dean Headley and Darren Gough stole one of the most thrilling Test victories against Australia on that longest of days at Melbourne just after Christmas in 1998, few among the squealing, chattering multitude would have pondered on how this everlasting dramatic challenge began. Those who did probably reflected only on the first of all Test matches, on the same ground in March 1877. But the real genesis of Anglo-Australian competition came fifteen years earlier still, on a primitive and rural Melbourne Cricket Ground which bore as much resemblance to the gigantic concrete MCG of today as did the Roman village of Londinium to the great city of London.

Had the 1861-62 tour not taken place – and it might well have been aborted – then the inaugural venture would surely not have been long delayed, for many a professional cricketer and promoter seemed keen to embark on the great adventure. The time was unquestionably ripe for this groundbreaking tour, for the intercolonial matches between New South Wales and Victoria, which had started as recently as 1856, were attracting feverish interest, and there was impatience and eagerness for development of cricket in the farflung territory. It was merely a question of where the money was to come from and who would shoulder the very considerable risk and responsibility.

A concerted effort to set up a tour by English cricketers had been staged in 1857, when a company was floated in Melbourne, with colonial Governors as patrons and prosperous merchants as directors. An alluring prospectus was printed, but no more than five takers for the 2000 shares offered at £2.10.0d each (the figures vary in old narratives) presented themselves at the secretary's office. The poor devil found himself being sued. Then five gentlemen stepped in, prepared to take a risk and share profits; but this bid also fell apart.

It could be argued that the first overseas cricket tours took place in the 1850s when teams crossed to Ireland to play under various flags, MCC and the United All England XI among them. An Ireland side, led by Charles Lawrence, played MCC at Lord's in 1858. Much earlier, in 1789, a team of Chertsey (Surrey) cricketers were bound for Paris as living evidence of Britain's goodwill towards France, a blatant political manoeuvre by the Duke of Leeds, the Foreign Secretary, endorsed by Prime Minister William Pitt and supported by one-time cricket patron, the rumbustious Earl of Tankerville. The peacemaking party of cricketers were to be received by the British ambassador, the Duke of Dorset, once they had crossed the Channel. But at Dover, they encountered the Duke rather sooner than expected. He had fled the wild atrocities of the exploding French Revolution. Cricket's first missionary venture would have to wait a little longer.

The first major overseas cricket tour took place in the autumn of 1859, when twelve intrepid professionals, with George Parr of Nottinghamshire as captain, somehow survived a stomach-churning crossing of the Atlantic to play eight matches in Montreal and eastern USA. (Canada v USA fixtures have been staged, on and off, since 1844 to the present time.) An Australian retired sea captain, Arthur Devlin, while in London, began to wonder why a tour of Australia should not be undertaken, and spoke to a few leading cricketers, H.H.Stephenson of Surrey among them. It soon became apparent that the professionals would need such high financial inducements that the scheme had no immediate chance of fruition. Devlin's dream, however, was not to be shelved for long. He passed his correspondence to a couple of hoteliers in Melbourne, and in due course those businessmen were to write their names into cricket history (and their bank balances even more emphatically into the big league) by committing themselves to the very first cricket tour of Australia.

Christopher Pond and Felix (spelt Phelix on the tour contract) William Spiers had major catering interests in Melbourne, principal among them being the Piazza Hotel, on the corner of Bourke and King Streets, the Café de Paris, and the adjacent Theatre Royal Café in Bourke Street, which became the social focus of Melbourne night-life. Their fortunes, like so many others, had grown dramatically out of the stampedes to the Victorian goldfields: not from finding nuggets but from providing for the hordes of humanity which flooded into the beckoning region. The pair – referred to as 'a cake and pie crowd' by an oldtime Sydneyite known to novelist D'Arcy Niland – had secured the contract to supply refreshments on the Melbourne-Ballarat railway, used by thousands every week. They even looked after 5000 peckish customers when the Volunteer Regiments camped by the Werribee River, an area synonymous a century later with another huge appetite: that of Merv Hughes. A major step was the acquisition of a café under the National Hotel in Great Bourke Street, Melbourne, which Spiers and Pond modernised, converting it into the Shakespeare Grill Room, where a chop and steak, boiled potato and half-a-pint of English beer cost a shilling. From that foundation a commercial empire was to grow.

Pond was English-born, as was Spiers, whose name appears on the passenger list (as an adult) for SS *Great Britain*, ex Liverpool in August 1853, bound for Melbourne. Spiers was described, years later, as phlegmatic, with a cooler judgment than his partner. He was a practical man, with considerable financial ability. Pond, in contrast, was 'sanguine, impulsive and imaginative; his busy mind was continually revolving enterprises on a large scale'.

They had initially been interested in bringing out Charles Dickens for a lecture tour. The greatest of English novelists had already conducted a highly successful readings tour of America, but, if Spiers and Pond's £10,000 invitation in 1861 ever reached him, he failed to respond. When a further letter was sent in 1862, he considered the matter for several months before declining, after which the caterers successfully tempted the actor Charles Kean instead.

It was not the easiest passage of Dickens's life, for he was besotted with Ellen Ternan, the young actress (who played cricket); had separated acrimoniously from his wife Catherine (one of his daughters was to proclaim Dickens 'a very wicked man'); was agonising over a venereal disease apparently contracted on a brief visit with Wilkie Collins to Paris; and had viciously outmanoeuvred the publishers of his *Household Words* magazine after they had shown sympathy with Mrs Dickens after Charles dismissed her. To large and enthusiastic gatherings he was giving extremely lucrative readings of his work in London and the provinces. But the effort involved would not have improved his humour.

Almost all of his classics had now been written, with *Great Expectations* and *A Tale of Two Cities* the most recent, and only *Our Mutual Friend* to come. It so happened that while the ship carrying the first English cricketers to Australia was steaming into the Indian Ocean, Charles Dickens, now in his 50th year,

Charles Dickens: acceptance of an invitation from Australia would have delayed the first cricket tour by years.

was complaining in a letter to a friend that the agents in Berwick-on-Tweed wanted to position him for his readings into a 'little lofty crow's nest of a stone gallery' which was 'high, deep in the wall, into which it was designed to put me!' He protested, threatened to cancel the engagement, and 'terrified local agents glowered, but fell prostrate'. With such apparent dread of confined spaces, he was unlikely to have anticipated nine weeks in a cramped ship's cabin with any real pleasure. Gad's Hill Place, his Kentish spread, was where he could happily wander freely and clear his head. It seems fair to assume, then, that Messrs Spiers and Pond's first invitation did reach Dickens, but that he could not be bothered responding. It was to cricket's benefit.

He was never to set foot in Australia. (Neither, for that matter, was Queen Victoria, whose name, in all manner of application, was honoured in countless monuments, streets and two States.) Instead, Charles Dickens, having sent Little Em'ly to Australia in *David Copperfield,* was to consign his youngest son, Edward Bulwer Lytton Dickens, to the new land in 1868, when he was only sixteen. Father's parting gift was £200, and for a time Edward prospered in outback New South Wales. Drought then ruined everything, and after a brief and unhappy career as a Member of the NSW Parliament, he was faced with another collapsed business, a broken marriage, and the loneliness of life in a hotel, admittedly with plenty of drink on hand, in the remote township of Moree.

Painful tuberculosis killed him in 1902, and today his grave is visited only at twilight by the local giant kangaroos.

Spiers and Pond, having learned of the success of the 1859 English cricket tour to North America, had responded to an enquiry from the tour leader George Parr in January 1860 with a view to setting up the first tour of Australia. Parr had approached Melbourne Cricket Club, but money was the stumbling block. Spiers and Pond offered Parr and his team £2500, which was declined.

Spiers and Pond's genuine interest in cricket seems to have been there from the start, with East Melbourne CC's first president, W.E.Parry-Okeden, recalling the spells cast by the suppers at the Café de Paris after the club's victories in the field: 'What prodigious cricket we used to play THERE! It was in the air! I wonder if that was when the cricket microbe entered into Spiers and Pond, and stirred them so that they had to bring out an English team later on? If so, here is another triumph for the old club.'

There was no shortage of pleading by cricket-lovers for the business partners to risk their money on the cricket tour so widely craved, for George Gibson and Thomas Moody, founder members of Royal Park (later Carlton) CC, also urged the catering partners to capitalise on cricket's surging popularity, while Tom Wills, the prominent sportsman, returned from England in 1858 burning with the belief that Australia's best would hold their own against England's cricketers.

Then, in September 1860, the entrepreneurial English cricketer John Wisden offered to take a team to Australia, prompting William Levey, owner of *Bell's Life in Victoria,* to set up an eight-man committee, with Melbourne CC members to the fore. The club would make the MCG available for three matches. A share offer of 1000 at £5 was modified to 1000 at £1, and, after almost zero response, a fresh sub-committee, in January 1861, sought to sell 2500 shares at £1. They might as well have been asking £1000 per share for all the interest shown. The All England & Australian Cricket Association was dissolved, half its members shirking their obligations to cover the modest costs, and the secretary having to face debt claims from printers and from newspapers which had run advertisements for the share offer.

Vital encouragement for Spiers and Pond came after consultation with Melbourne's leading impresario, George Selth Coppin, 'Father of Australian Theatre', actor, comedian (he had the face for it), manager, promoter, discharged bankrupt, controller of four theatres, Grand Master of the Masonic Lodge of Victoria, later Geelong's representative in the Legislative Assembly (he achieved wondrous things for the community, reforming land conveyancing, establishing street lighting, a fire brigade and a gas-works). Crucially for cricket, Coppin, who had been born in Steyning, Sussex in 1819, inspired Melbourne's leading clubs by setting up the first structured competition in Australia. The Coppin Challenge Cup, contested by Melbourne and Richmond (whose president Coppin became in 1861) and lesser clubs (on a handicap basis), was short-lived because of the squabbles that broke out. But Coppin's influence, brought to bear in the highly topical and expectant matter of whether an English cricket team should be brought out to the Colony, was of extreme significance. In March 1861 he announced his aim to fund such an undertaking – with George Parr over in England still hoping for a deal – while yet another Melbourne syndicate (of which Pond was probably a member) expressed strong interest. Neither it nor Coppin managed to make any significant progress as weeks drifted by.

Spiers and Pond now grabbed the initiative by dispatching their agent, W.B.Mallam (styled as *Barlow William* Mallam on the tour contract), off to England in the Australian winter of 1861, a £3000 draft in his pocket as he boarded ship (*Jeddo*) on June 25. His mission was to entice a group of England's best cricketers to the Colony for £150 per head plus first-class travel and expenses. (The £150 was roughly equivalent to £6500 in 1999 terms, although the buying power of £150 then was very much greater than £6500 today, thanks in part to much lighter taxation then.)

George Coppin: man of influence in Melbourne.

Mallam's was no straightforward task, and a Sydney newspaper recorded that 'in spite of the golden attractions he possessed, he met with many difficulties'. It was unclear whether the 'golden attractions' referred to any qualities of persuasive charm he may have possessed or to the contracts he was empowered to distribute. Already, on July 8, 1861, Spiers and Pond had written to Melbourne CC referring to a minute in the club's books which recorded a pledge that Richmond Paddock may be available to anyone who succeeded in bringing out the All England cricketers. The would-be promoters now wanted to know what were the terms and conditions. They were in for a pleasant surprise: the ground would be theirs free of charge.

Upon landing, Mallam lost no time in communicating with a number of key English cricketers, for it was mid-August already. It seems that his first face-to-face proposals came at the Griffin Hotel, Manchester. There, he had invited some of the players taking part in the North v Surrey match, and put his terms to them. There was no rush to sign up, which will have disturbed Mallam, for the cream of English cricket was taking part in this game. George Parr, his key target, having led the 1859 expedition to North America and having shown such interest only a few weeks before, surprisingly gave a flat refusal, stating that the money was inadequate for such a long absence. Mallam must also anxiously have sensed that Parr's influence was such that no other Notts player, or even any Northerner, could be persuaded to tour.

Comfort came with the reassuring words of William Burrup, Surrey's honorary secretary, who claimed, not altogether reliably as it transpired, that four of his players (Caffyn, Mortlock, Sewell and H.H.Stephenson) together with six others (Carpenter, Daft, Hayward, Jackson, Ned Stephenson, and Tarrant) would be willing to tour, subject to terms. Already, Anderson, Caesar, Grundy, Lockyer, Willsher, and Wisden, in addition to Parr, had firmly declined, so Mallam knew he could not raise the strongest side England might have mustered. With flagging spirits, he asked the rest of the players to think the matter over.

Billy Burrup remained Mallam's best hope. A wealthy London businessman, Burrup had followed his twin brother John into the secretarial seat at The Oval in 1855. He was proprietorial and yet popular, generous to amateur and professional cricketer alike, thoughtful on hot days, when he would send champagne cups out to the perspiring cricketers in the field, always ready to make friendly little speeches, proud to be at the helm of a successful club which boasted just on 1000 members in 1861. When seven Surrey players eventually took off on the Australian tour, Burrup's solicitous attentions extended to taking out life insurance on all for their families.

As August 1861 progressed, however, the sense of urgency tightened about Spiers and Pond's agent, W.B.Mallam. Came early September and he found himself in Godalming, Surrey, where, from the 2nd to the 4th, the star-studded England XI played a Twenty-two of Godalming, Guildford & District on the Broadwater ground. Mallam met with Burrup again – the Surrey secretary by now having been forced to confess that five of his six non-Surrey cricketers would not sign for the tour – and he also met Henry Marshall, Surrey's president. Mallam might have found it difficult to pass pleasantries with Parr and several others who had turned their backs on the offer, as indeed might Billy Burrup, for the Northerners now saw him as manipulative, and will have resented a certain clumsiness – as they saw it – in his attempts at negotiations on Mallam's behalf. Parr must surely have indulged in divisiveness himself as the gulf between the Surrey camp and the Northerners widened bitterly. As he had refused terms, it really ceased to be any of his business. Only jealousy could have sparked his resentment at H.H.Stephenson's eventual appointment as leader.

Ironically, Fred Lillywhite, scorer, printer and chronicler with Parr's team on the 1859 tour, was later to claim that Parr's grievances, whether justified or not, should have been directed at him, for Lillywhite was, he said, the first person approached by Mallam, and he in turn introduced Mallam

Billy Burrup, the Surrey County Cricket Club secretary who gave the tour crucial impetus.

The Oval, Kennington, in the late 1850s, home to many of the finest cricketers in the land.

to Burrup, beyond which Mallam encountered many other cricketing people in various parts of England. The combative Lillywhite dismissed Parr's pique by writing that 'he has wrongly and unjustly fought the honorary secretary of the Surrey club instead of challenging me, as I held the belt for the time being.'

George Parr refused to play at The Oval for years to come, and even in 1866 the matter disturbed cricket-lovers to such a degree that Surrey members at the annual meeting pressed Billy Burrup for an explanation. Parr, he said, had been offensive to Mr Mallam, and had also wrongly believed that he (Burrup) had somehow prevented Parr from going on the tour. Nor, he insisted, had he pushed Stephenson for captain. And he had enlisted the rest of the Surrey players only after it was clear that so many Northerners – and, importantly, some Southerners besides – had turned down invitations. For such a great batsman, Parr seems to have been uncommonly touchy.

The decisive gathering occurred during the North v South match at the new, 'terribly rough, quite unfit for cricket' ground at Aston Park, Birmingham, on September 5, 6 and 7, 1861. Captain (later General) Sir Frederick Marshall (Life Guards, and a future Surrey CCC president), the very tall and imposing former Zulu war cavalry commander, who was playing for the South XI in this match, invited both teams to dinner at the Hen & Chickens Hotel, and there Mallam, perhaps inwardly quite desperate by now, addressed the cricketers. With Parr having made his feelings clear, overtures had continued in the direction of his

Notts team-mate Richard Daft. But Daft remained among the many top names who could not be tempted, though he later claimed that Mallam told him just to name his price. One satisfaction for the Southerners, at least, was that they went on to win this match at Aston Park by 43 runs.

Soon, a full touring party was in readiness, Mallam having travelled to Dublin to sign up Charles Lawrence and jubilantly telegraphed mission accomplished to Victorian cricketer George Marshall's shop in Melbourne, which was a kind of operational headquarters. H.H.Stephenson was chosen fairly automatically as leader of the daring dozen – and not simply because he was the only one to boast two initials before his surname – and arrangements were feverishly made for departure only a little over a month hence. There was to be no physiotherapist, no scorer/baggageman, no coach, no psychologist, no media relations officer, no horde of predatory pressmen; just twelve cricket pioneers – ten of whom had never been away from the British Isles – about to open up the most famous traditional international exchange sport has ever conceived with a tour the sheer significance of which can scarcely be exaggerated. Their names should never be forgotten:

H.H.Stephenson (captain), George Bennett, William Caffyn, 'Ben' Griffith, Tom Hearne, Roger Iddison, Charles Lawrence, William Mortlock, William Mudie, Tom Sewell, Edwin Stephenson, George Wells.

The memorandum of agreement (now in MCC's safe keeping at Lord's) was dated September 25, 1861, and confirmed that Mallam was given power of attorney on June 24, in Melbourne. Stephenson at that stage was cautiously referred to as 'captain for the time being', and the terms were spelt out: £50 upon embarkation (or to be held by John Farrell and William Burrup); £50 after six weeks in Australia; and the balance of the £150 at the end of the tour. The forward funds were to be fed through the Oriental Bank Corporation in London to its Melbourne branch, retrievable against the signatures of Stephenson, Caffyn and Mallam. An extra £5 was to be paid to each player for the use of his name in advertisements, but no player could engage in any independent advert. Any proceeds from testimonials or theatrical benefits would be shared half-and-half between Spiers and Pond and the team, though any individual award for outstanding performance in the field could be kept by the cricketer. It was confirmed that players might also have to act as umpires from time to time, and that no more than 13 matches would be scheduled. They were free to 'bowl &c and instruct in the game of cricket for profit to themselves' so long as it did not interfere with their tour responsibilities. And while the cricketers were bound to give the tour sponsors every facility for writing and publishing their biographies, they remained at liberty to 'dispose of their photographs on their own account'. There was to be an outward passage on *'Great Britain* or other suitable steam vessel', first-class board and lodging throughout and all travelling expenses, and a second-class return passage to London by the overland route via Marseilles. A return in March was guaranteed.

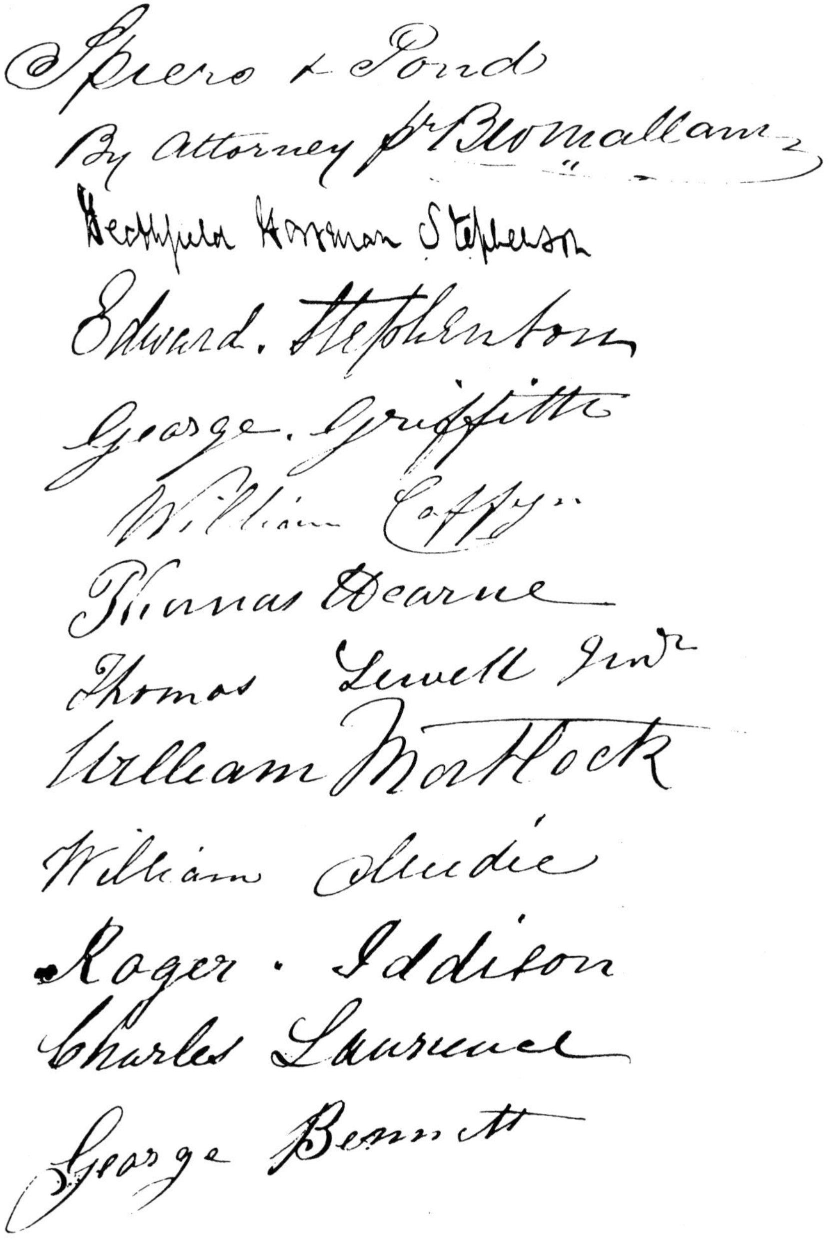

Spiers & Pond
By Attorney for T Bromallam

Heathfield Horsman Stephenson

Edward. Stephenson

George. Griffith

William Caffyn

Thomas Hearne

Thomas Lewell Junr

William Mortlock

William Mudie

Roger . Iddison

Charles Laurence

George Bennett

Historic signatures on the tour contract.   *Courtesy of MCC*

The contract was signed by Mallam and eleven players, Wells, having sailed with his wife a month previously, being already halfway to Australia. The differing styles of their signatures suggest that all were able to write, with no call for the 'mark' or cross so common in those times. Those 'autographs' of the historic first-ever English team to tour Australia would generate an almighty frenzy in the saleroom if ever offered.

The players were fitted out by John Lillywhite, each with a cap, a tie and a belt all in dark blue, and a white flannel shirt, and new pads. The Surrey players were honoured with an evening of entertainment at the Durham Arms Tavern in Harleyford Road on October 15, and two days later the full team, minus Wells, were guests of honour at a dinner staged by Surrey CCC at the Bridge House Hotel, by London Bridge. At this memorable banquet the team's health was drunk with much enthusiasm, and a comic singer rendered a song of tribute to the cricketers, the chorus of which went:

Success to the Eleven of England!
The toast is three times and one more.
May they all meet success o'er the briny,
And safely return to our shore!

Hardly Rodgers and Hammerstein, but it put everyone into an inspired frame of mind, probably expunged all trace of the prolonged agonies of negotiations, and instilled a certain collective patriotic spirit which was inflated by the high-flown words of Henry Marshall, the Surrey president, during his speech. No nation in the world, he said, could touch England at cricket, and he congratulated them on their endorsement of H.H. Stephenson as captain, than whom there was no-one better formed by manner, temperament, and disposition for that office.

The cricketers' last night in London was spent in the Anglesea Hotel, Haymarket, and on the morning of departure they lined up in cricket costume, together with the long-suffering Mr Mallam in ubiquitous stovepipe hat, for a momentous photograph in the stableyard.

The train then took them to Liverpool, Billy Burrup and former Surrey captain F.P.Miller accompanying them, and they boarded the great ship, SS *Great Britain*, on Saturday, October 19, 1861 – theirs was the last boat from the landing jetty – excited unquestionably, anxious perhaps, and inwardly tearful at leaving loved ones for what must have seemed to stretch ahead as an eternity. The customary pandemonium prevailed: passengers, emotions swirling, trying to find their cabins, crewmen shifting luggage and carting victuals, somebody handing out soothing religious tracts to the emigrants, and, while the cricketers and manager Mallam sat with the other first-class passengers for dinner at one end of the ship, the rest jostled for dishes of rice. It was noticed that the many Irishmen on board had brought plenteous supplies of potato, flour and whiskey.

Great anticlimax had overtaken everyone when a cable snagged in a capstan soon after the order to sail had been issued, the tide being high, and, after all the excitement and expectation, departure was postponed until the morning. Thus the

Before entraining to Liverpool, the All England XI (minus Wells, who had sailed ahead) don playing attire and assemble for posterity in the stableyard of the Anglesea Hotel in London. From left: William Mortlock, William Mudie, George Bennett, Charles Lawrence, H.H. Stephenson, W.B. Mallam (promoters' agent), William Caffyn, George Griffith, Tom Hearne, Roger Iddison, Tom Sewell, Edwin Stephenson.

first night was spent immobile under the full moon, Birkenhead to one side of the River Mersey and Liverpool to the other. In the shadows on deck, Irishmen jigged to the wail of a flute, while a gathering of Welshmen sang hymns, and others gambled with cards, and some sat or lay silently with their melancholy and forebodings.

The early sounds on October 20 were of the crew chanting between heaves and grunts as the anchor was weighed, and at 8 o'clock the signal guns fired and *Great Britain* was on her way, easing down the channel. Singing *The Anchor's Weighed* together would have had a 'bonding' and reassuring effect on the cricketers, and thoughts were further diverted by Billy Caffyn's endeavours on the cornet. *Cheer, Boys, Cheer* he warbled. And they did, as the ship headed out to sea, destination half-a-world away, with no dry land beneath their feet for the nine weeks to come.

CHAPTER 2

The England of 1861

THESE trailblazing cricketers knew there would be many 'old chums' in the new land who would make them feel at home. Nonetheless, there was inescapably a sense of travelling not just beyond the horizon out of the mouth of the Mersey, but into such a potentially fearful unknown that it might as well have been another planet. Their advantage over the brave, humble emigrants was that they had each other to confide in, like so many members of a military combination. No-one would be allowed to become dispirited or lonely. And, of course, they were being quite well paid, and were assured a return to their homeland at the latest by the English mail steamer leaving Melbourne on March 26, 1862.

What kind of country were Stephenson's men leaving behind them? Those who lived in or around London knew a city gradually emerging from the depths of depravity and poverty which so often had obsessed the writings of Dickens: 'this compound of sickening smells, these heaps of filth, these tumbling houses, with all their vile contents, animate and inanimate, slimily overflowing into the black road'. By now, one of the vital battles slowly being won was water hygiene. In 1850 half of London's population had relied on water piped from the Thames, into which a couple of hundred open sewers flowed, and upon which floating dead cats and dogs were no unusual sight.

Pavements were crowded with street vendors, muffin-men ringing their bells, urchins, sandwichboard-men, pickpockets, flower-girls and even entertainers, and horse-power was all: hansom cabs, merchants' carts, buses. The smell of equine manure was all about. Shops, offices, the smoke-hazy little pubs and some of the streets were gas-lit, with electric lighting still some years away. Those shops, many of them, were full of rich odours, so many of the offerings being exposed, unwrapped. Magazines were on the verge of a boom period, with *Punch* celebrating twenty years of publication, while the newspaper sellers seemed never to rest their tonsils. The three brass balls outside the pawnbroker's premises seemed, out of necessity, to be assured of a permanent position.

There were surface railway systems, but no underground just yet, and no escalators. Tower Bridge had yet to be built. Holborn Viaduct was several years from completion. Hungerford Market was being demolished, making way for Charing Cross station. There was no Eros statue in Piccadilly Circus as yet. Putney Bridge was still a rickety wooden relic from the 18th Century. And while the Houses of Parliament had just been completed, Westminster, Victoria and Albert Embankments had yet to be constructed. Bristol's pride, the Clifton Suspension Bridge, another Brunel creation, was slowly taking shape.

The iron and glass Crystal Palace, shifted from Hyde Park to Sydenham in 1853, still sparkled and drew rapt attention from all angles, and in 1861 London's first tram had run along Bayswater Road. (Men's top-hats and women's bulky crinolines made movement in and out of public transport no easy matter. Anthony Trollope observed some suffering female travellers as being a 'mis-shapen bulky mass of battered ironwork'.) Nelson's wonderful column had been up since 1842, but Landseer's lions had not yet settled themselves down at the base. There was still a tollgate at Kennington, near The Oval, and old men o'war were still to be seen serving as prison ships anchored in the Thames. Wilton's Music Hall, near Waterloo station, was filled almost every night, the colonies being acknowledged by good-natured taunts from the master of ceremonies, who would invite visiting Australians to stand up and then ask them: 'How does it feel to be the right way up?'

Great Britain was regarded as the richest country in the world, the hub of empire, with a population in 1861 (23 million: 'mostly fools', according to Thomas Carlyle) which had doubled since the start of the century, even while seeing so many of its people emigrating to the New World. Not only was Britain the Workshop of the World, with exports rising more than threefold in the two decades either side of 1861, but this was also the golden age of British agriculture. Domestic servants numbered over a million, twice the number employed in the mills; but, far from the spreading grime of factories and slums, the ranks of the agricultural workers totalled well beyond the million. Stating that he would like to abolish income tax, the Chancellor of the Exchequer, W.E.Gladstone, 51, and with his four premierships well in the future, reduced income tax by a penny to ninepence (just under 4p) in his 1861 Budget, with further reductions to follow, taking the rate down to fourpence (1.75p) by 1866.

Viscount Palmerston charms the House of Commons: Gladstone, middle of trio behind him; Disraeli seated opposite, first beyond the Mace.

Still there were widespread and deeply disturbing problems. Workhouses were overflowing with the sick, the insane, children, hardened criminals, prostitutes, alcoholics, destitute mothers, and the aged and the senile. There the fittest picked oakum all day, earning their bread and soup. Climbing boys spent their days up sooty chimneys, often with disastrous effect, until the ban in 1875, making earlier legislation seem almost enlightened: since 1833 children under nine were not permitted to work in textile factories, and an Act of 1842 banned women or girls from going down the mines; boys were allowed so long as they were at least ten years old. In the darker evil corners of the cities, children drank alcohol, for there was no legal age limit. At least from 1861 nobody in Britain was hanged for any crime other than murder or treason. Previously, 200 or so offences, including stealing sheep or horses, carried the death penalty. As for the elderly without savings, there was to be no old-age pension until 1908.

Viscount Palmerston – 'Old Pam', the Liberal – was in his second term as Prime Minister at the time the first cricket tour of Australia was unfolding. Although the oily Disraeli went on asserting that he was too old and should retire, the priapic Palmerston went on more or less allowing the country to run itself until his death in 1865.

But for the monarch, 1861 was the worst year of her life. Queen Victoria's mother, the Duchess of Kent, died on March 16, grief precipitating the 42-year-old queen's nervous breakdown. The failing health of her dearly beloved consort, Albert, was also weighing heavily, and she was seen by staff and visitors as being often in a 'morbid melancholy'. When the ailing Prince Albert lost his close friend King Pedro of Portugal, he too descended into depression. In the November, news broke of an amorous escapade with an actress at the Curragh Camp in Ireland involving their eldest son, the Prince of Wales, the future King Edward VII (who, by way of appropriate aside, had seen Billy Caffyn score a century for Surrey at Fenner's in the May of 1861). Then the American Civil War spilt more tension into Victoria's life as two Confederate envoys were intercepted by a Federal vessel, causing Palmerston seriously to consider war.

Everything paled into insignificance for the Queen when Albert died from typhoid on December 14. His black-garbed widow was to see out the remaining 39 years of her life in unremitting grief. Victoria's heyday ended in 1861.

Britain's soldiers and sailors were the paramount heroes of the time – perhaps on a par with today's grossly overpaid footballers. Nelson's death at Trafalgar 56 years before the first cricket team sailed to Australia was still

Albert, Prince Consort.

Queen Victoria, symbol of an age – from an 1859 painting by Winterhalter.

remembered personally by the elderly, as was the Battle of Waterloo ten years later (the commanding figure of the Duke of Wellington, the most famous profile in Europe, lived on until 1852). The Crimean War was over and done with, and Florence Nightingale was now presiding over a training school for nurses at St Thomas's Hospital. Chloroform had been introduced to anaesthetise patients, but antiseptic was as yet unknown. The bloody Indian Mutiny, another dramatic chapter in the thick annals of the British Empire, was ostensibly over. Speke had found the source of the Nile, while David Livingstone was still pursuing his extensive African missionary work and explorations.

As for the American Civil War, it remained touch-and-go for some time as to whether Britain might become embroiled in another full-scale conflict. Early sympathy had been with the Union (Northern) States, but the main consideration was always going to be financial. Britain had lost over half her export trade to the USA, but since exports to France had doubled, a neutral stance was maintained, even though the loss of American cotton badly hit the Lancashire mills. Specifically in 1861, since the Union forces had fled from Bull Run, Virginia in July after Confederate reinforcements had stormed in from the Shenandoah Valley, the rest of the year was quiet as both sides prepared for all-out conflict that was to last until 1865. This was one war from which Britain was to be excused all-out participation.

In gentler fields, 1861 afforded art to please the eye, from the brushes of Millais, Hunt and Rossetti, the Pre-Raphaelites, while Ford Madox Brown's *The Last of England* touched all who were about to emigrate, or knew someone who already had done. Forever hovering, it seemed, was the complex, influential and abrasive critic, John Ruskin, who was also an early environmentalist. Turner and Constable were now dead, but William Powell Frith, his fame already assured with *Ramsgate Sands* and *Derby Day*, spent most of 1861 on one of the last of his famous giant canvases, *The Railway Station* (set in Brunel's Paddington station), for which he was paid £5250, almost three times the total fees paid to the dozen English cricketers who sailed to Australia.

The other Frith, Francis the photographer, was making up for lost time by photographing everything that didn't move, as were so many others to whom posterity owes such a vast debt. Wet-plate photography had been in use for only ten years, but now experiments in colour and stereoscopic pictures were being conducted.

Henry Irving was as yet perfecting his art in the provinces, learning his lines in the early hours of the morning, soothing towel around his head. The troubled Dickens, meanwhile, was scarcely relishing the challenge to his reputation by the work of the 6ft 4ins William Makepeace Thackeray. Up on Yorkshire's broad and bleak acres, the remarkable Brontë sisterhood had diminished. Emily had died in 1848, a year after completing *Wuthering Heights,* and Charlotte had followed her to the grave in 1855. George Eliot's *Silas Marner* was published in 1861, and Charles Kingsley's *The Water-Babies* was soon to appear. Charles Darwin's *Origin of Species*, published in 1859, continued to generate heated debate, and it was around the time that the cricketers sailed that Mrs Beeton's *Book of*

Household Management first came out, a volume which, well over a century later, still sells 50,000 copies a year.

Keats, Shelley, Wordsworth, Coleridge, Byron, Scott and Hood were all now gone, but their delicate verse was still much cherished. Robert Browning was distraught at the loss of his beloved Elizabeth; and Tennyson's stirring stuff was recited in many a drawing-room.

Away from the tearful ditties and the vulgarities of the music-hall, the great music of the now-dead Chopin and Haydn and Mendelssohn and Schubert could be heard in the concert-halls, together with Strauss waltzes, Liszt's heavenly piano works, Offenbach's elegant compositions, and Brahms's 1861 creation, his *Piano Concerto No.1*. Much of this was to be heard from the numerous bandstands which were springing up in England's public parks.

In the world of opera, there was the Queen's favourite, Gounod's *Faust*, and Wagner's pounding productions, besides Verdi's range of offerings, with Rossini's *Barber of Seville* proving timeless. Jenny Lind, 'The Swedish Nightingale', was widely worshipped, and around this time the long career of Adelina Patti commenced with an imperious performance at only nineteen of Gilda in *Rigoletto*.

Religious faith was strong in the second half of the century, but a Royal Commission on education (1858-61) found that under half of the 3½ million children in England and Wales went regularly to school, and only a tenth of these learned reading, writing and arithmetic. Unlucky were they who were unable to read the imminent classics of Lewis Carroll (Charles Lutwidge Dodgson), the 'sad, creepy, emotionally-retarded, stammering, partly deaf bore' whose *The Adventures of Alice in Wonderland* was to be published in 1865. In 1861, the 29-year-old mathematics teacher was ordained.

For cricket devotees who could read, there was a choice of sorts, though nothing as compared to the heavyweight publishing industry of the late 20th Century. Aside from the papers *Bell's Life* and *Baily's Magazine*, *Lillywhite's Guide* had been available each year since 1849, though John Wisden's first *Almanack* was not to appear until 1864. The Revd James Pycroft's *The Cricket-Field*, first published in 1851, came out in 1862 in the third of what would amount all told to nine editions. The classic *Tom Brown's Schooldays* was ever popular, having appeared in 1857, while an earlier (1833) classic which would still have had a keen readership was *The Young Cricketer's Tutor* by John Nyren. For a few pence the earliest instructional books, such as William Lambert's manual, would have been available in secondhand shops. *The Cricket Bat and How to Use It* by An Old Cricketer (Nicholas Wanostrocht) came out in 1861, to engross men and boys. Just over a year from now would appear the first four volumes of Fred Lillywhite's (really Arthur Haygarth's) fact-packed *Cricket Scores & Biographies*. Wanostrocht's *Felix on the Bat* and William Denison's *Sketches of the Players*, both originally published in the mid-1840s, were in circulation. But most topical interest must surely have been in Fred Lillywhite's book on the 1859 tour of North America, even if its graphic descriptions of the Atlantic crossings threatened to put anyone off maritime travel for life.

By modern standards, sport generated a narrower and quieter interest. Football had yet to be formalised, with the overdressed participants for school and club playing to their own sets of rules, a chaotic situation that would soon ease with the formation of a central control body, the Football Association, in 1863. Notts County had become the first professional club in 1862. Boxing's bareknuckle era still had almost 30 years to run, before the notorious three-hour scrap in New Orleans in 1889, when John L.Sullivan battered Jake Kilrain to pulp, drew a blessed curtain over raw barbarity in favour of more civilised mayhem in gloves and over lesser distances. Australians, for their part, were reluctant to see Sullivan as world champion since he seemed intent on avoiding their own Frank Slavin and the brilliant adopted West Indian Peter Jackson.

Back in April 1860, the big fight was that between England's Tom Sayers, who weighed less than 11 stone, and the giant American champion John C.Heenan. It was the first world heavyweight title fight, of necessity a clandestine affair. The fighters met up at London Bridge, big Heenan disguised in a beard. They took a train to Farnborough, Hampshire, and before a distinguished gathering which included Lord Palmerston, Dickens and Thackeray, they belted the daylights out of each other for 37 rounds, the marathon struggle ending in confusion and mob violence as the American tried to strangle the Englishman on the ropes. For years afterwards the police made the promotion of fights almost impossible anywhere in England. Adoption of the Marquis of Queensberry's code in 1867 saved the sport, though in the USA it never wavered from its wild and corrupt course, while the Civil War halted any serious progress for cricket in Britain's great former colony.

Meanwhile, in June 1861, Jem Mace from Norfolk became British heavyweight champion (and later became world champion). Perhaps the greatest of English glovemen, the swarthy Mace once, through his battered lips and teeth, tendered a compliment to Ted Pooley, Surrey's tough little wicketkeeper: 'I would rather stand up against any man in England for an hour than take your place behind the stumps for five minutes.' The much-travelled Mace, the first truly scientific boxer, reached his 80th year, while Pooley, who made his Surrey debut in 1861, somehow lived into his 70th before he died in Lambeth workhouse.

The new guttapercha ball made golf a slightly cheaper game to play, but it was still, on the whole, a relaxation for the better-off, or at least their snobbish province. The first tournaments were organised by the Prestwick club in the late 1850s, followed by the first Open championship in 1860. Sculling was popular, and the Oxford-Cambridge eights challenge and the Henley Regatta were already well established. Lawn tennis as recognised today was unknown, but took off after the first Wimbledon tournament in 1877, and croquet was enjoying a boom. In Melbourne, Australian Rules football was proving addictive, while it was already nearly 40 years since William Webb Ellis – or was it Mackie a few years later? – had shocked everybody by picking up the ball and running, thus sowing the seed for the English Rugby code(s), which blossomed during the 1860s.

The ancient game of hockey was also spreading in popularity. A Blackheath club minute book for 1861 survives. Athletic events, amateur and professional, excited wide interest, but cycling was as yet held back by lack of technology. The 'bone-shaker' was for masochists. The traditional sports of fencing and archery were being kept alive by select groups of enthusiasts, and so many other pursuits remained to be devised as the world moved on a further 100 years and more, with more leisure time at the disposal of the working man. In 1861, it was cricket that held sway every summer, and there was no call for marketing men to sell silverware that was not really theirs in a frantic quest for what some see today as excessive prosperity.

While Stephenson's pioneers were on tour in 1861-62, two towering figures faded away back in the homeland, 'Silver Billy' Beldham, from the Hambledon era, at the age of 96, and Alfred Mynn, at 54, a gentle behemoth who was a hero to many of England's current best when they were but lads. To place matters in even sharper perspective, in the winter of 1861-62, a number of the future first wave of noted Test cricketers were still only children: Lord Harris, Ulyett, Midwinter and R.G.Barlow were ten, Shrewsbury and Scotton five, Abel and Peel four, and A.G.Steel and William Gunn three. Johnny Briggs and C.T.B.Turner were conceived about this time. Over in Australia, Charlie and Alick Bannerman, Billy Murdoch, Fred Spofforth, Blackham, Garrett, McDonnell, Massie and Giffen ranged from ten years to two. And W.G.Grace? He was now a strapping 13-year-old nearing the threshold of the greatest career of all.

MCC's president was the bewhiskered fifth Earl Spencer (an ancestor of Diana, Princess of Wales), who presided over a club boasting 641 members, not a few of dubious character (and with a £3 annual subscription unchanged for years in a time of nil inflation). The premier club presided over a game in which overarm bowling was a thing of the near-future. Revolution was just around the corner. In August 1862, in a match at The Oval, Edgar Willsher, the Kent left-arm bowler, was to be no-balled time and again for bringing his arm through above shoulder height. He stormed off the field, but the problem had come to a head, and the inevitable progression was acknowledged in June 1864 by the rewriting of Law 10. Bowlers were no longer to be restricted to bowling roundarm or underhand. They were now permitted to deliver the ball with whatever sweep of the arm they chose, and the modern game of cricket was launched – coincidentally in the summer when the teenaged W.G.Grace entered the national consciousness.

Regular and properly organised competitive county cricket that drew big crowds was still some years away. For the time being, the travelling professional elevens were the major drawcards, and their matches against often rustic opposition had little appeal to anyone outside the immediate locality. Thus, as historian Rowland Bowen observed in his controversial 1970 *magnum opus*, 'It is a strange period of cricket, this, and it is more difficult in many ways to get the "feel" of it than much older periods . . . Money-making maybe, and that is perhaps the only part of it which the present day can understand, with its acquaintance with commercially financed teams of great players touring about the country playing minor teams on Sundays, or about the world in the winter playing not so minor teams. But there was no competitive cricket . . . and there was no acknowledged controlling body. Even the MCC was being challenged as the premier club by the up-and-coming Surrey Club . . . The game at all its levels was loose-knit.'

That it undoubtedly was. But times were changing. The four-ball over was to remain in force only until 1889, when it was raised to five-, and also declarations were first permitted. Not for much longer would batsmen have to run out all their runs, with the first major ground to institute boundaries being Canterbury. A covered scoreboard on wheels was first used at The Oval in 1861. Also to come were widening of the bowling crease by 2ft to 8ft 8ins early in the new century, and, between the two world wars, a reduction in the size of the ball and an increase in the size of the wicket. Amendments to the lbw law came with regularity, as did provisions for the new ball. And then came covering of pitches, protective helmets, coloured clothing, black sightscreens and white balls, marked changes in conduct, deviant forms of the grand old game, and the disfigurement of architecture and cricketers themselves with advertisements. By the end of the 20th Century even the sacred turf and sightscreens had been desecrated. Money, which built Victorian cricket, also corrupted it, but only to a negligible degree against the cash obsession of today.

Yes, it is no straightforward matter to get the feel of cricket in the 1860s. No television, no automobiles, no computers, no aeroplanes, no telephones, no faxes, no antibiotics, no movie films, no typewriters, no X-rays, no Aids, no Pill, no plastic, no strangulated political correctness, no female doctors or politicians (or voters). Were Stephenson and his comrades to manifest themselves at a major cricket match around the end of the millennium, they would surely have to sit down quickly and sink a serving of good strong punch. Not that they were short of intestinal fortitude, for let us reflect that in the summer of 1861, Surrey beat England at the unpretentious old Oval in spite of the fact that Caffyn was lame, Sewell had a dislocated thumb, H.H.Stephenson had diarrhoea, Mortlock had a bad thumb, Mudie was hurt, and Burbidge's hand had been split. It was referred to as 'the Cripple Match'.

Stephenson, with only eleven other cricketers with him on his long and arduous Australian tour, was assuredly praying that there would be no serious injuries.

CHAPTER 3

The Trailblazers

THE DOZEN trailblazers who opened up Australia's cricket frontier were all from the south of England, apart from the Yorkshiremen Roger Iddison and Ned Stephenson. All were professional cricketers.

HEATHFIELD HARMAN STEPHENSON
Born May 3, 1833 in Esher, Surrey

Rather like Captain James Cook, the man who claimed Australia (New South Wales) for King George III just under 100 years previously, H.H. Stephenson was admired for his integrity and innate dignity. These qualities, together with a dry humour, made him the ideal cricketer to lead the first team ever to venture across the thousands of miles of ocean to Australia.

Six feet tall and well-built, he was among the best allround players of his time, his bat straight in sound defence or eager attack – with a distinct preference for the leg side and forward play – and a bowler 'of genius', according to team-mate William Caffyn. He was a bowler who, even prior to the 1864 legislation to permit overarm bowling, brought his arm through well above the shoulder, with a peculiar wrist movement which produced a speedy breakback of sometimes as much as a foot. Had he not also been a high-class wicketkeeper, deputy to Surrey's supreme Tom Lockyer, he would have taken many more than his 302 wickets. His best return was 8 for 28. As a keeper, he held 152 catches and made 25 stumpings – 'Throw straight at my nose!' he would cry to erring fieldsmen – and in a match against Twenty-two of Walsall in 1861 he made five stumpings.

HH has several imperishable distinctions in cricket history, for apart from skippering the first English cricket team in Australia and, nineteen years later, standing as umpire in the first Test match on English soil (on his old home ground, The Oval; it was the only Test he was to umpire), he also has his name enshrined in the derivation of the term 'hat-trick'.

In the early 1850s it was customary to reward meritorious performances with gifts: a new ball for batting or bowling feats, and later a bat – for ornamental use only. Professionals were more likely to be given welcome cash. When Stephenson dismissed the last three Kent men (lbw, lbw and bowled) while bowling for England at Lord's in 1858, the deed apparently brought nothing but applause. Such was the case again soon afterwards when he bowled the third, fourth and fifth batsmen in the Eighteen Veterans' line-up with consecutive balls at The Oval. So when he managed three-in-three for the third time, this time for the All England XI against Twenty-two of Hallam and Staveley at Hyde Park, Sheffield in September 1858, it was felt that something special should be done to mark the event. So he was presented with a brand-new white hat. Although it was years before the expression was launched (probably the first mention of 'hat-trick' was made in *The Sportsman* in August 1878 after 'Demon' Spofforth had taken three in three for the Australians at Hastings), it was H.H. Stephenson's almost habitual 'trebles' that established one of cricket's famous terms, one of those too which have been adopted by other sports.

HH was also known as 'Surrey' Stephenson by way of avoiding confusion with Edwin ('Ned'), who was known as 'Yorkshire' Stephenson. As if this was not enough nomenclature, HH's Nottinghamshire contemporary Richard Daft, who thought very highly of him, bestowed 'Spurgeon' on him, for he often wore a long black frock-coat like that made popular by the renowned Baptist, Charles Haddon Spurgeon, who preached on Sundays and Thursdays to a congregation of up to 6000 at the Metropolitan Tabernacle (opened in 1861), less than a mile from The Oval.

Stephenson's father was a doctor, and his birthplace was 3 Myrtle Cottages, which survives still on the outskirts of Esher, just past Sandown Racecourse, at the opposite end of the town to where Clive of India's house stands. As a toddler on the lawn, HH dabbled at cricket, inadequate against the roundarm bowling of his mother's female servant. As he grew, he played for local clubs, and rose to first-class ranks with Surrey in 1853, catching Alfred Mynn, the Kent immortal, off the fiery Tom Sherman at Kennington Oval in his first match.

A year later, he was invited to join the famous touring All England XI, run by William Clarke, the hard-headed Nottingham entrepreneur. Stephenson was required principally as a replacement for the ageing wicketkeeper Tom Box, but his wider skills were quickly appreciated – a swirling catch he took at long leg was described by Clarke as the finest he had ever seen – while he soon won respect as a professional with the bearing and means of expression of one of the more impressive amateurs. After Clarke's death in 1856, HH became a member of the organisation's committee, which supplanted the dictatorship. He, George Parr, Edgar Willsher, George Anderson, Clarke's son Alfred, and HH's Surrey team-mate Julius Caesar were all now charged with the responsibility of making the AEE's activities profitable.

For the first overseas tour, when an English team sailed to North America late in 1859 (the year his nephew, J. Maurice Read, of Surrey and England, was born), H.H. Stephenson was a key inclusion. So too was William Caffyn of Surrey. Only these two were also to take part in the inaugural expedition to Australia two years later, their bond battle-hardened when they were flung down the ship's steps together during an Atlantic gale.

HH and Caesar had the temerity to ask for more money from the Surrey committee in 1855. The request fell on barren ground, and they were dropped from the side. It mattered little, however, for they played in 24 of the 25 All England XI matches that summer.

HH and 'Julie', who was from Godalming, were great friends. They skylarked and sang duets in the dressing-room, and when Caesar danced to Stephenson's whistling, the tempo would increase almost hysterically, until Caesar was close to collapse. When decorum was restored, HH would turn to an

Heathfield Harman Stephenson, urbane leader of the Trailblazers.

old party trick of pulling his thumb out of joint and pushing it back with a crack like a rifle-shot.

He suffered for his art. His hard work with the ball and his wicketkeeping eventually cost him the feeling in his fingertips, and with it went his accuracy and pace. The rough, crude pitches of the time and the minimal protection worn by batsmen and wicketkeepers would scarcely be understood by modern cricketers, and Stephenson took as much punishment as anybody either side of the stumps. Keeping for All England on a deplorable surface at Lord's in the 1863 Whitsuntide match against the rival United All England XI, he was knocked flat by a ball from John 'Foghorn' Jackson, the terrifying Notts fast bowler, and had to be helped off, his head spinning. It was a lively introduction for the new telegraph board (scoreboard) which the enlightened MCC committee had introduced this year. The imagination is stretched further by the fact that Stephenson was once given out for kicking the ball.

HH went on to play some of his best cricket that season and in the one following. In 1864 he came second in the national averages (so detested by the sporting diehards: 'In every sport under Heaven the unselfish man is the best man,' Fred Gale was to thunder) with 824 runs at 39.23, and his three first-class centuries all came around that time, all at The Oval: 119 for Surrey against Notts, and 117 for Players against Gentlemen, the blue riband fixture in those pre-Test days, along with the AEE v UAE contests; and in 1865 he scored 110 for his county against Hampshire.

He was modest, but no unduly so. It excited him to hear spectators discussing in flattering terms the innings of 51 he had just played at Lord's for the AEE against the UAE, and he tried to introduce himself to them as the omnibus clattered down Baker Street. They dismissed him as an impostor, and when they alighted, the driver added his own reprimand. 'At this,' the deflated Stephenson later wrote, 'I slipped down from the knifeboard and walked the rest of the way.' Mr James Dark's daily serving of 'the old English fare of roast beef and plum pudding' during the match might have repaired Stephenson's morale.

During the winter of 1864-65, he joined the newly-formed itinerant United South of England XI, which sprang from the ever-deepening discontent between North and South. It meant a little more money. Then came closer acquaintance with the sensational teenager from Gloucestershire, William Gilbert Grace. In June 1865, before he had scored, WG's first innings in first-class cricket was terminated by a smart piece of stumping by HH as the 16-year-old toppled forward in playing at a slow from 'Farmer' Bennett, the Kent bowler who had been one of Stephenson's team on the maiden Australian tour three years earlier.

In 1866, Stephenson and the rest of the Surrey side were helpless to prevent WG (batting for 'England') from making his first first-class century, extending it to an unbeaten 224 and becoming the youngest scorer of a double-century. It was surely an exquisite pleasure for the older man to stand as umpire at his beloved Oval some years later, to see at close quarters The Greatest Cricketer scoring 152 in the first Test match on English soil, against Australia, the young country which had played host to H.H. Stephenson's pioneering tour eighteen years before.

Other touring bands were formed as England's appetite for big-name cricket expanded, and one perceived vacuum was filled in 1864 by Stephenson and Ned Willsher. But their 'English Eleven' was short-lived. HH had to make do with his living from Surrey and the spasmodic engagements he could pick up elsewhere until he reached his late thirties.

Having been orphaned when quite young, he had secured employment from exiled members of the French Royal Family who resided nearby, and later had served as whipper-in and huntsman on the Worcestershire estate of the Duc d'Aumale. He had vague plans beyond his final match with Surrey in 1871 to set up a business in London, which he hoped his fame would sustain. He had been granted a benefit in his last Surrey season, WG ensuring its success after making a duck. He comforted the beneficiary with an assurance: 'Keep up your heart, HH. I shall take care that it does not occur in the second innings.' He then scored 268, rendering the match memorable, and HH showed his gratitude with a gift of a gold ring, probably acquired in Victoria.

HH was not the first or last cricketer to harbour chilling fears that he would be forgotten. Hence his hesitation at accepting the offer of Essex businessman C.E. Green to finance a one-year coaching engagement at Uppingham, the public school in Rutlandshire. (He had already coached at Rossall.) Stephenson took up the offer in the spring of 1872 and was to stay until his death in 1896.

He married in 1873 and took up residence in Uppingham High Street. He fathered three children, but in a broader sense he was responsible for the well-being and advancement of hundreds of boys, for he was more a master, a father figure, than a mere cricket coach. He was soon invited to join the school's board of governors, the blend of authority and compassionate instincts which had made him such an ideal member of the committee of the charitable Cricketers' Fund Friendly Society again being recognised. The walls of the sports shop he presided over in the High Street were lined with framed photographs and scorecards.

His word was law among the pupils, who venerated him for his 'good manners, a high sense of honour, and a generous heart', as W.S. Patterson put it in *Sixty Years of Uppingham Cricket.* At one time there were seventeen elevens at Uppingham, and as the talent was spotlighted and polished, so the school very rarely came to be beaten.

HH taught orthodoxy. 'To the batsman, the straight bat. To the bowler, the good length. To all cricketers, enthusiasm.' The *Badminton Cricket* was still expounding his text in 1920.

He disapproved of lofted hits and preferred forward play from a natural, easy stance: a method that would ring true to most modern ears. Patterson describes the reaction to an ungainly shot: 'the deep shrug of the shoulder, the writhing of the body, the inward weeping, the outward groan, in fact the intense disgust of HH when someone had pulled a ball from the off stump round to square leg, even although a resultant cheer had wreathed the offender's face in smiles of triumph. Our coach knew the day of reckoning was not far off.'

The 'Uppingham stroke' – with a straight bat, through midwicket – was a marked feature of the stream of fine young cricketers who emerged from the school, MacGregor, Christopherson, C.E.M.Wilson, T.L.Taylor, Patterson, A.P. Lucas and D.Q. Steel chief among them. The three last-named together with H.T.Luddington and S.S.Schultz (a Test player soon afterwards) all played for Cambridge in the 1877 Varsity match, which made HH a very proud man. There was a slump in Uppingham cricket in the 1880s, but it revived in the 1890s.

Stephenson never got down to writing his memoirs, but the notes he made on his early copy of Pycroft's *The Cricket-Field* were incorporated into an edition published sixty years later. Some of his observations reveal his sharp originality of thought and his concern that the game should be played thoughtfully. Bat-handles, he suggested, should be oval rather than round, as with swords, in order to prevent slipping. He worked out the 'centre of percussion' of a bat, using the same method as swordsmen in estimating where it was to be found. He plotted a batsman's 'blind spot' for both slow and fast bowling, and advocated standing 2 feet in front of the crease when facing fast bowling with the keeper standing back. As for advancing to the ball, you might as well be stumped by a yard, he said, as by six inches. The toe, not the heel, is the pivot on which the back foot turns, he claimed, in contradiction of Pycroft's assertion of so many years earlier. Vividly, HH recalled that William Clarke pitched 4½ feet in front of the crease, Hillyer five feet, and John Wisden, who was the fastest, 5½ feet. He further analysed the art of bowling in some detail, even explaining how one could deliberately bowl a shooter along the ground (without stooping to rolling it). He recalled how, in the old days when umpires did not wear white coats, the batsman could lose sight of the ball against a dark waistcoat. And he stated that all fieldsmen, not only long-stops, should put their heels and legs together as a back-up.

HH was described as an 'extremely interesting soul and most hospitable withal' who 'served excellent ale'. But the theory and practice of cricket were paramount. So determined was he to get his boys to bowl with high arms that he made them practise in a narrow alleyway. The price of a low arm was skinned knuckles.

Stephenson might not have been out of place as a between-overs pundit in today's commentary-box, though as an umpire he may have ranked among the legions whose shortcomings are revealed by television scrutiny. Tom Horan thought little of his umpiring qualities, citing bad decisions against himself (caught off his sleeve) and Spofforth in the 1882 Australians' match against Cambridge University (won by the undergraduates).

Cricket, Stephenson proudly preached, was 'the chosen sport of a great and free people'. The purist in him was always in evidence. When the hitter C.I.Thornton and the stylish I.D.Walker both made fifties against the school, he presented Walker with a bat. When Thornton asked why he was not given one, HH told him: 'Mr Walker played cricket. You didn't.' How fortunate were the boys of late-Victorian years at Uppingham to have such a paragon as their guide and mentor. Not that he was alone in upholding cricket's function as a pastime which stood for honour and all the other virtues. Uppingham's own great headmaster, Edward Thring, wrote: 'Mark me, cricket is the greatest bond of the English-speaking race, and is no mere game.'

HH had at least one confrontation with the autocratic head. The coach wanted the boys to have a sleep-in before their match against Repton. Delivering a sharp crack in the ribs as he spoke, Thring told Stephenson, 'Certainly not. I won't have it – get out!' HH stuck to his guns, and won him over. The boys got their extra sleep, and one of them scored a century in the big match. HH's quest for a top-class young lob bowler, however, was never to be fulfilled.

H.H. Stephenson died, aged 63, on December 17, 1896 (a few months after Thomas Hughes, author of *Tom Brown's Schooldays*) and was buried in Uppingham churchyard. (The last of his descendants died in the early 1970s.) HH had given almost a quarter-of-a-century of loyal service to Uppingham, and had declined at least one tempting offer from a bigger school. He had built character as well as cricket knowhow into generations of pupils, who mourned him en masse. He was a sterling individual. He was England's first international cricket captain against Australia.

GEORGE BENNETT
Born February 12, 1829 in Shorne Ridgeway, Gravesend, Kent

George Bennett may have been fortunate to escape transportation to Australia as a youth. He was, it seems, imprisoned for burglary, though at the time of his honourable voyage to the Great South Land he had long been considered a respectable fellow. They called him 'Farmer', but only because of his rustic appearance. Outside cricket, he earned a living as a bricklayer, before taking employment as a gardener at Cobham Hall, seat of the Darnleys (one of whom led England on the historic first Ashes tour of 1882-83). He also coached, serving five years at Brighton College and ten at Eton.

Just over 5ft 9ins tall and weighing just under 12 stone, Bennett was a fine outfielder, with a long throw. But as a bowler, he shunned athleticism, delivering one of the slowest teasing balls ever seen, allowing the batsman to seal his own doom by indiscretion. It takes nerve.

His most fruitful outing came one day in June 1871, when he finished with 9 for 113 against Sussex at Hove – though his depleted Kent side lost by an innings. As for remarkable overs (which consisted of four balls in his time), there were two: for England against Surrey at The Oval in 1863, when H.H. Stephenson was stumped for 45 off the first ball; Billy Caffyn was run out for 0 off the next; Dowson was bowled by the third; and 'Ben' Griffith was caught off the last. Bennett finished with 7 for 39. In stark contrast, the same Griffith hit all four balls of a Bennett over out of the ground at Hastings a year later.

His crafty roundarm bowling reaped him over 600 first-class wickets at under 17 apiece, but to this and his fielding was added competent batsmanship, perhaps ungainly and somewhat stiff in style, but ideal when some defensive middle-order resistance was called for. Only a few months before the English team sailed to Australia in 1861, he scored 160 at Maidstone for Players of Kent against Gentlemen of Kent, with Alfred Mynn, Fuller Pilch and E.G. Wenman among the spectators. It was a huge score for the period, even against moderate bowling. But he proved himself against mightier stuff four years later at Lord's when he made 100 (47 singles) for the South before being run out. This time the Prince of Wales, Queen Victoria's eldest son, was in attendance, and the bowling of the North was all-professional and of a very high order: 'Tear 'em' Tarrant, George Wootton, Jem Grundy, Cris Tinley, George Atkinson and Alfred Shaw. It was Bennett's innings of a lifetime.

Like all batsmen, he had oscillating luck: 66 and 42, both unbeaten, in a worthy performance for Kent against Surrey at Maidstone in 1861, and in his next match, for Fourteen of Kent against England at Canterbury, a pair of ducks. His career with Kent stretched from 1852 to 1873, and additionally he played for the All England and the United All England XIs. He earned a benefit in 1873 – Kent v W.G. Grace's XI, at Gravesend – and died on August 16, 1886, aged 57, in Shorne Ridgeway, where he had been born, which was no unusual thing in the 19th Century. In his later years he, like most of his team-mates on the 1861-62 Australian expedition, probably enjoyed most talking about that great adventure.

WILLIAM CAFFYN
Born February 2, 1828 in Reigate, Surrey

'Terrible Billy', sometimes also known as 'The Surrey Pet', had the unique distinction of membership of the first three English cricket tours overseas: to North America in 1859, Australia in 1861-62 and again (this time embracing New Zealand too) in 1863-64. He stayed after the last tour, engaged as coach by Melbourne Cricket Club and pursuing his career as a barber, a craft learned from his father and uncle back in Reigate. His fiancee followed him and they married in Melbourne before transferring to Sydney, where they set up as hairdressers to men and women in a George Street shop. However, his wife was repeatedly ill and found the heat oppressive, and although Caffyn added to his lucrative business earnings by coaching at the Warwick Cricket Club for four years (he also played for New South Wales), the outcome was not merely unhappy. It was tragic. Three sons and a daughter were born to the faraway couple, and two of the boys died. The depleted family returned to England in the spring of 1871. Five more children were born in his native land.

Caffyn had enjoyed coaching the keen and potentially impressive young Australian club cricketers, several of whom went on to play big cricket. The best of them were Murdoch, Spofforth and Charlie Bannerman, who scored 165 in the first-ever Test match, at Melbourne in March 1877. But, profitable though his Australian years were, the heartache of infantile loss lingered. Yet, like so many returning migrants, Caffyn somehow never seemed totally at home in England ever again, though he lived to 91, and had a £39 annuity from Surrey.

At the age of 65, he reflected in a letter to Thomas Padwick on the disruption his wanderings had caused: 'I got into hot water for stoping [*sic*] out in Australia. I can see now I made a mistake. I lost my benefitt [*sic*] ... I have nothing to thank Australia for they have not given one fair thing to me.' A tad ungrateful perhaps.

Caffyn's book, *Seventy-One Not Out,* ghosted by R.P. Daft and published in 1899, is one of the most instructive records of pre-1900 cricket. He describes how he became 'passionately fond' of cricket while a pupil at Reigate Grammar School, playing in Castle Field, with a wicket chalked onto a tree-trunk. Playing for Reigate, Croydon and Mitcham clubs, he finally attracted the attention of some of the professionals, and took up a post in Suffolk in 1849. Playing for the local Eighteen against the awesome All England XI at Bury St Edmund's, he bagged a pair, but covered himself in bowling glory with the illustrious wickets of Mynn, Joseph Guy, Pilch, Box and Hillyer. Even his disapproving father must have glowed at the news.

He soon became a prolific player for Surrey, batting stylishly in the middle order and bowling medium-pace roundarm, usually contributing effectively with both bat and ball. Clarke swiftly signed him up to the All England wandering team of stars, and although the young Surrey man did not take too readily to the great entrepreneur, he was later to look back with admiration for 'this glorious veteran', ranking him among the key figures – WG included, of course – who popularised the national game of cricket.

So Caffyn's career was launched and word of his brilliant cutting backward of point and his marvellous fielding at cover soon spread. (He once cut a full-toss so sweetly that the ball burst through a bandsman's bass drum well beyond the perimeter.) Clarke paid him £4 per match, big money, though he had to pay his own expenses. A thinking cricketer, Caffyn became an outstanding coach, serving, as the years passed, such establishments as Oxford, Winchester, Eton, Clifton, Wellington, Brighton and Haileybury.

Always, though, his work in Australia towers in importance, for it helped forge a new nation's emergence as a power in 'the English game'. At the start, he was well paid by Melbourne CC: £300 annually. He bowled tirelessly to members in the nets, and detected a distinct upturn in skill year by year. The reasons were plain to see: 'I never saw such painstaking cricketers as the Australians were in those days.' Having seen so little good-quality cricket, the average colonial enthusiast batted in what Caffyn saw as an 'automatic' style. But they were willing to learn, quick to correct errors, and, crucially, never took offence at having errors pointed out and *were never jealous of one another.*

Caffyn was proud of Surrey's role in developing Australian cricket, for the club had given impetus (and seven of the dozen players) to this first of all tours, and beyond that had provided the first two significant 'instructors' (Caffyn and Lawrence) to work with the best of the 1860s crop in Melbourne and Sydney. He delighted in England's success in Australia fifty years on, in the Ashes series of 1911-12, by which time only he and Charlie Lawrence of the 1861-62 tour were still alive.

Billy Caffyn, 5ft 7ins in height, was affable company. He sang, played the cornet and the harp, and could dispense practical jokes, always an essential of life on tour and in the dressing-room – even if his goodwill was tested when one of the players concealed a decomposing dead mouse in Caffyn's best silk top-hat. It was some days before he opened his hat-box, and the stench overpowered him.

Five of the strong Surrey team of 1861: Billy Mortlock, Tom Lockyer, H.H.Stephenson, Billy Caffyn, and 'Ben' Griffith. Lockyer did not tour Australia until 1863-64.

On the field, he was sometimes sent reeling at Lord's, which was by no means his favourite ground. St John's Wood was, in general, a pleasant place to be, leafy and well away from The Great Stink that oozed out of the Thames. But in the 1857 grand match between the All England XI and the United All England (to which Caffyn had defected two years earlier) he was hit explosively in the ribs by one of 'Foghorn' Jackson's most evil deliveries, 'which made me feel very queer'. A few seasons on, in the same showcase fixture, and on an equally underprepared pitch at Lord's, he was hit again, this time excruciatingly on the elbow, 'which took all the play out of me'. This was the same match in which H.H. Stephenson was struck on the head while keeping wicket. Both men must have been relieved to get back to their own true surface at The Oval.

Caffyn was an automatic choice for years in the Players v Gentlemen matches, and his record in 200 first-class matches of almost 6000 runs (average 18) and 601 wickets places him near the top in the statistical scale of the period.

His centuries for Surrey against England in 1858 (taking pride of place as the first Surrey hundred) and Cambridgeshire in 1861, both at The Oval, were gems to behold, and his highest score outside first-class cricket was 157 against Sixteen Cambridge Undergraduates in 1859, when he felt he might have reached 200 had there not been so many fieldsmen. But his best innings, he considered, was a 91 at Trent Bridge in 1860, against Jackson and Grundy, which he followed with figures of 6 for 36 to squeeze a 30-run victory over Nottinghamshire.

His best figures came in Surrey & Sussex's match against England at The Oval in 1857, a spectacular 9 for 29. Five years later, at the St Lawrence ground, Canterbury, he secured 7 for 7 in Surrey's match against Kent.

Towards the end of his long life, Caffyn acknowledged that cricket had become 'much livelier and more interesting', though he wanted to make it clear that 'we used to get knocked about a bit'. He said: 'There were not the number of nicely levelled pitches that there are now, and I have known players wear pads on their elbows to protect them from the effects of swift bowling on bumpy ground'.

Caffyn's form in 1861 left no doubt that he must be one of the first chosen for the Australian tour: a 98 for Surrey against The North at The Oval, after having been 97 overnight; 5 for 34 against Yorkshire at Bramall Lane; 7 for 21 against Notts at Trent Bridge; 11 for 31 for the United against Twenty-two Gentlemen of Hampshire at Southampton's Antelope ground. And yet the fearsome memories of the gales which came close to tossing the ship upside-down both outward and homeward on the 1859 expedition to America must surely have caused him to hesitate for at least a few seconds before he signed the 1861 contract. He had been heard to vow never to leave England again after the experiences of ocean gales, fog, icebergs, snowstorms and seasickness on the 1859 trip, though the hardships of Australia were unlikely to include the need to wear greatcoats in the field, as happened in Rochester.

The last survivor of the 1861-62 tour, Billy Caffyn died 57 years after it, in his native town of Reigate, on August 28, 1919, in his 92nd year. He was buried in the local churchyard, not far from the grave of Thomas 'Shock' White, who had strolled out with a bat of enormous width, forcing the Hambledon men of the late 18th Century to legislate a maximum dimension. Both departed souls claim unusually significant places in cricket's vast history.

GEORGE GRIFFITH
Born December 20, 1833 in Ripley, Surrey

George (known widely as 'Ben') Griffith was just under average height, but had a frame which proclaimed immense strength, which he liked to use at every opportunity while batting. He was a left-hander, a species that would seem to have been less common in Victorian times.

Caffyn, who knew Griffith so well, described him as one of the hardest hitters that ever lived, and the best left-hander since Felix; somewhat stooped in posture, with a short neck, it sometimes seemed his head was partially buried between his great shoulders. His most famous feat was powering all four balls of an over from Bennett out of the Hastings ground while batting for the United All England XI in 1864, his on-drives carrying roughly 120 yards, a phenomenal distance for the basic willow of that era. One hit landed on the roof of a house. The UAEE were unhappy to lose him and so many other disgruntled Southerners soon afterwards, the schism driving the rebels into forming another touring troupe, the United South of England XI.

Born in the Talbot Tap in Ripley, near Guildford, Griffith was a stablehand before making his first shillings as a professional cricketer. This living he augmented with work in a bakery, and when his cricket skill began to leave him as the 1870s unwound, he gratefully received the tidy sum of £400 from a benefit granted him by Surrey. He umpired, and he ran a small grog-shop in Brodie Road, Guildford, and he coached at Oxford, Rugby, Winchester, Harrow and Cheltenham College. But life was fast losing its joy, and he was headed for dark times.

His first match for Surrey had come in 1856, and he was popular not only because of his willingness to belt the cover off the ball but he was also an awesome sight in the field, catching well at slip and fielding athletically in the deep, throwing long and accurately. As a bowler, Griffith was very effective as a fast left-arm roundarm exponent, later switching to slow underhand. In that debut match, against Kent at Tunbridge Wells, he took 4 for 20 and 5 for 15.

He was a certainty for the 1861-62 Australian tour, and not merely because he was a team-mate of the captain's. During the summer before departure, he crashed one ball right out of The Oval. It pitched in the roadway and bounced into a garden. His 45 was a crucial innings in a match at Lord's which raised almost £140 for the Cricketers' Fund; after which he showed how he could dominate affairs for the United in their match against a local Twenty-two in Portsmouth, taking 9 for 15 and 14 for 49, and top-scoring in both innings with 38 and 28. And still the locals won. In the more serious Surrey v Kent encounter at The Oval, he top-scored twice again, with 55 and 28. For Surrey v The North in Manchester, he made a valuable 69; and then took 11 for 17, including a hat-trick, for the United at Leamington. He was a huge asset to any side which employed him.

His best batting and bowling performances came after the Australian tour. In 1863, at Brighton, he scored 89 in about an hour, followed by 142, his highest-ever score, which included one blow that landed the ball a measured 119 yards away. His other first-class century – and they were just about as rare then as double-centuries today – was 117 against Kent at Gravesend in 1867, in which season he returned his best bowling analysis, 9 for 130 against Lancashire at The Oval.

Small wonder that he was throughout most of his career that rare cricketer: a crowd-puller. He was narrowly the leading runmaker on the historic tour of Australia, and was very successful in the grand opening match. The locals dubbed Griffith 'The Lion Hitter', and he was equally popular on his other overseas tour, with Willsher's side to America in 1868.

Age and injury brought an unwelcome end to his powers. In a match in Dublin he threw his left arm out, and then sprained his broad back while playing at The Oval. Thereafter it had to be umpiring and coaching – and a rather bitter frustration. At 45 he had become morose, a steady drinker, unloving as husband to Eliza and father to their five children. (He also had an early illegitimate child.)

In the spring of 1879, he entered a carpenter's shop just outside Guildford, looking dishevelled and unwashed and ill. 'I want to come and look at you to amuse myself,' Griffith croaked. 'I don't know what to do with myself. I feel very ill from diarrhoea.'

They drank some beer, and 'Old Ben', horribly beset by demons, then announced that he would like to have some of the cord that hung on the wall. The carpenter told him to take what he wanted. As he left the shop, Griffith said he intended to hang himself. And on May 3, he was as good as his word. His small daughter discovered the body. The once-mighty cricketer, cheerful and keen, shy hero of the first tour of Australia (to which land his young brother James had emigrated in 1864), was buried in the churchyard at Stoke-next-Guildford.

THOMAS HEARNE
Born September 4, 1826 in Chalfont St Peter, Bucks

At 35, Tom Hearne was the oldest member of the 1861-62 touring team. He was a tailor by trade, with a shop in Ealing and a ready clientele among cricketers, for whom he would readily cut a pair of flannels. Tall and sparely-built, he had a calm and serious demeanour, an early version of the ideal senior professional. To him fell the honour of making the first century for Middlesex, soon after the club was founded in 1864. Having made 50 and taken 14 wickets against Sussex in the first match, and later seen the county rolled over for 20 by MCC at Lord's, Hearne put together 125 in the return match against MCC at the old Cattle Market ground in Islington, with none of the runs coming on the leg side if contemporary accounts are to be believed. Tom Case scored 116 and Middlesex totalled a staggering 411, the partnership amounting to over 200.

Having been engaged by Harvey Fellows in Rickmansworth from 1849 to 1859, during which time he represented Hertfordshire, Hearne played for the United All England XI, besides serving MCC in the field for twenty seasons. Cricket was his life, and absorbed him and his thoughts days seemingly without end.

Hearne was a leading member of a vast clan of cricketers, with three of his nephews and a great-nephew going on to play Test cricket, and two cousins – J.T. and J.W. Hearne – winning a number of international laurels. 'Old Tom', a villager by birth, kept a level head, and even when approached by a reporter in later years, when he was still head of the ground staff at Lord's, he was reluctant to talk about himself: 'I'm not much of a man for newspapers, and whatever you do, don't you advertise me.'

By now, it was nearly all over and done. 'I don't want to be advertised,' he made clear, while maintaining an innate politeness, 'for I've been here a long time, and I hope in the little time that's left to me that I shan't want another place. There's lots of people that have advertised me and put me in papers and photographed me and what not, but I keep going on in the same old way, and though I'm friendly with everyone, I don't care a [mild profanity of the time] for anyone.'

Some thoughts on his Australian tour thirty-odd years earlier – even though he had done himself little justice – would have been of much interest; but his memory was failing him: 'To tell you the truth, when I come to think about bygone times, the reminiscences, as you call 'em, get so mixed and muddled up in my old brains that I can't clearly call 'em to mind at all.'

He was middle-aged in cricket terms when fame came his way. County cricket was a thin, irregular affair, and anyone from a lesser county, such as Hearne's Buckinghamshire, had to look further afield. His chance came through Fellows, who recommended him to John Walker and his six brothers at Southgate, Middlesex. Hearne went on to play for the United All England XI in the great match of 1858, handling the firepower of 'Foghorn' Jackson bravely and with poise, his 54 not out taking the United to a relishable victory. His fortunes as a professional cricketer had suddenly taken an upturn when he was already into his thirties. He had married Charlotte in 1849 (she was to die sixteen years later), and when he embarked on his Australian adventure in 1861, he left behind two sons and a daughter. H.H. Stephenson wanted yeomen cricketers about him for this demanding campaign, and Tom Hearne was one who filled the bill.

He was one of the last batsmen to play the 'draw', a stroke executed with the bat-face angled to leg, steering the ball between legs and wicket. He preferred to hit hard, and was never daunted on the roughest pitches when confronted by the fastest bowlers. There was, too, a marked absence of show about his batting. Natural strength, a strong heart, and a genuinely professional attitude were his virtues. And he had patience. His 62 on a nasty Lord's pitch in 1859, when he posted 149 for the first wicket with Bob Carpenter, earned him enormous respect.

His best scores came beyond his 35th birthday: 134 for MCC against Sussex at Hove in 1862; the 125 at Islington in 1864, and 146 at the same ground in 1866 for Middlesex against Surrey; and a celebrated 122 not out in 5½ hours for Players against Gentlemen at Lord's in 1866, the season when his 392 runs (35.7) and 46 wickets (13.7) helped Middlesex to become 'champion county'. It was odd that he should have failed to impress in Australia, apart from not-out thirties in Hobart and Ballarat – although he did captain the World XI to victory over Surrey at Melbourne.

As a bowler (he did the hat-trick for Middlesex against Kent at Islington in 1868), Hearne had started as a fast underhand, switching later to roundarm, while in the field he was a skilful long-stop and sometime wicketkeeper. His throw was good too, as he demonstrated memorably in a match at Islington in 1866. As he was about to bowl, he spotted a pigeon flying over the pitch, perhaps 50 feet from the ground. Letting fly at it, Old Tom scored a direct hit. His son George ran onto the field, gathered up the feathered corpse, and took it away to have it stuffed.

Tom Hearne was employed by MCC as a ground bowler from 1861, succeeding Jem Grundy as head bowler in 1872. His authority was broad. Often he was seen with a bat-gauge, checking the width before a batsman strode to the

Tom Hearne in later years. He was part of Lord's for decades, but he claimed his recollections of his early exploits were 'mixed and muddled up'.

crease. Fred Gale saw him as 'the Field-Marshal of the professionals', so identified with MCC that Gale felt he must have been hung on the knocker at Lord's as an infant.

Hearne umpired with authority and insight, and the earlier benefit which had been 'no benefit at all' in 1863 (United South of England v Twenty-two of Ealing – ruined by bad weather) was compensated well by the benefit awarded to him by MCC in 1876. This was the year he suffered a stroke. Was this the end? Not a bit, for he served Lord's for over twenty years further, retiring on a fairly comfortable pension of £30 per annum in 1898. In 1884, upon the death of John Wisden, Hearne had taken over as secretary and treasurer of the Cricketers' Fund Friendly Society.

The family tradition remained much in evidence, for his younger son George had been pavilion clerk at Lord's since 1872 (and had registered the first century for Cross Arrows, in 1886), while elder son Thomas Arthur joined the staff at 'Headquarters' in 1898 as head groundsman. And years later, J.W. Hearne, the prolific Middlesex and England allrounder, took over his late cousin's sports shop – named MCC House – in West Ealing.

'Old Tom' Hearne, who used to think nothing of walking eight miles in his youth to play cricket, died on May 13, 1900 at his Ealing home, after ten days of semi-consciousness during which he surely visualised his greatest cricketing episode, the trailblazing tour of Australia nearly forty years before. He was buried in St George's Cemetery, Hanwell. His second wife, Annie, who had given him another daughter, lived on beyond her 96th birthday, dying in 1927.

ROGER IDDISON
Born September 15, 1834 in Bedale, Yorkshire

It was many years before England sent to Australia anything like the strongest team available. The rift in mid-Victorian times between professional cricketers of the north and the south of England deprived this first-ever 'missionary' team of certain strengths. But at least they had as one of their number Roger Iddison, an honest-to-goodness chunk of old English roast beef if ever there was one.

Beyond the 1861-62 tour, his northernness intensified. When the United South of England XI was established halfway through the decade, he condemned the move in forthright manner, saying: 'I consider that by trying to break the United England XI up they are taking the bread out of our mouths.' When the United North team was set up in 1870, Iddison was its secretary.

He had captained the fledgling Yorkshire County Cricket Club since 1863, genial, thick-set, ambitious, shrewd. Earlier a butcher in his native Bedale, in the North Riding, Iddison became an auctioneer, a dealer in cricket goods, and agent to Lord Londesborough. As a player, manager, coach and match organiser, he spread around his ample shape an imposing sphere of influence.

A 'red-faced, healthy-looking man, a true type of the old-fashioned Yorkshireman', as Caffyn saw him, Iddison sported expansive muttonchop sideburns, and was usually seen on the field of play wearing any of an array of headwear: a dark hat with a flat top, or a light-coloured one with a round crown, or, in more subdued mood, a plain cap. His defence was rocklike, but when he chose to attack, his strokeplay could be brutal. He had a fondness for the off-drive, 'manly in style' as Lillywhite recorded it, with the ability to 'hit like a horse kicking'. Memorably to outsiders, he spoke with the richest of Yorkshire accents, in typical no-nonsense style, an image that was sure to appeal to the settlers in Australia who flocked to see the cricketers from the Old Country.

'Why doan't you keep your eyes open, you bludy great ostrich?' the intolerant Tyke once growled at a fieldsman who had missed a simple catch. And after the 1861-62 tour, when asked for his opinion on the standard of Australian cricket, Iddison gave a pointed and famous reply: 'Ah doan't think mooch to their plaay, but they're a woonderful good lot o'drinking men!'

At that stage of his career he was more the bowler, a convert from fast roundarm to cunning slow lobs which started with the ball coming from somewhere near his armpit, tossed up 'just as one would chuck a penny to a beggar'. The turn from leg was often extravagant. His heavy harvest on the tour of Australia was sealed with 22 wickets in the match against Twenty-two of Victoria, and he sailed home, reputation enhanced, a contented man. 'We are made a great fuss of,' he had written. 'The Queen herself could not have been treated better.'

At 5ft 8ins and weighing over 12 stone and rising, Roger Iddison had the profile of a Great Britain Rugby League hooker of 100 years later. But there can have been few more acquisitive sportsmen in any era. He was forever looking to make money – even crossing the Pennines into 'enemy' territory, taking up engagements at the Broughton and then Whalley clubs in Manchester, in which city he and his brother opened a sporting-goods shop. He even scored the first century for Lancashire in a county match, 106 against Surrey at The Oval in 1866.

Back in Yorkshire, for whom he had returned his best bowling figures (7 for 30 against Notts at Bradford in 1863), he now made his highest first-class score (112 against Cambridgeshire at Hunslet in 1869). In 1872 he had the best of his benefit games, a lucrative match at Bramall Lane, Sheffield, in which the Gloucestershire champion W.G. Grace obliged with a characteristically dominant and watchable 150.

So it was a well-rewarded lifetime of cricket application, from showpiece matches down to the most ordinary of contests, with percentages gleaned from all manner of activities, and coaching assignments wherever Iddison could locate them: Marlborough, Uppingham, Harrow. As all good things do, it came to an end, and the rotund Yorkshireman was to be denied an old age. Beset by diabetes, he then fatally contracted tuberculosis – 'consumption' as the Victorians referred to this common killer disease. He died in York on March 19, 1890, aged 55, and was buried in York Cemetery.

CHARLES LAWRENCE
Born December 16, 1828 in Hoxton, east London

Charlie Lawrence was truly an internationalist, a seeker and wanderer, who made a good ongoing living out of cricket. Early ambition to be a sailor withered with a severe bout of seasickness on a voyage to Dundee in his younger days, but he still covered more miles, surely, than any of his contemporaries.

Although born in Middlesex, the young Lawrence picked up the rudiments of cricket on Lord Nelson's Field, in Merton, which gave him a Surrey qualification. He became a printer's block-cutter, but such was his rapport with cricket that he was coaching at seventeen. He worshipped England's premier batsman, Fuller Pilch, and once walked many miles to see him bat at Lord's – only for Pilch to suffer a first-ball dismissal, his disappointment nothing to that of the young Lawrence, who wept.

In Edinburgh in 1849, Lawrence, now professional coach to Perth CC, took all ten wickets of the powerful All England XI for 53. Representing Twenty-two of Scotland, he bowled Felix, the dapper left-hander, with a fast roundarm shooter that uprooted all three stumps, and also dismissed Parr, Guy, Wisden and the mighty Alfred Mynn, on whom he tried to model himself as a bowler. Felix gave the beaming youngster half-a-crown, and a collection for him raised £20.

Two years later, Lawrence, having been recommended by the shrewd William Clarke, was engaged by the Phoenix club in Dublin, and in time he became founding secretary of the United All Ireland XI. He was now widely regarded as an excellent judge of the game, and was one of its most renowned practitioners: perhaps 5ft 8ins tall, wirily built, with a somehow authoritative goatee beard. And his ambition and vision drove him on.

A missed opportunity came when he umpired a match at Dublin's Vice-Regal Lodge. Queen Victoria's eldest son, the Prince of Wales, played, and Lawrence decided he would like to be his coach. So he put out discreet enquiries through Captain Marshall and the Earl of Carlisle. Events were overrun by his 1861 Australian tour, but he often mused that he would have liked to have returned to England to pursue this possibility.

As with Caffyn, this regret was undoubtedly linked to the awful grief of losing children – with the added tragedy for Lawrence that his first wife also died in Australia. They had married in 1850, when both were twenty-one. He came into some money about that time, and by the 1861-62 Australian tour he had established himself well as player and coach. Their two daughters and one son had all been born in Dublin, and when Lawrence stayed in Sydney to open a sports shop in George Street and to coach the Albert club for a handsome salary, all seemed bright and promising.

But the sky was about to fall in on Charlie Lawrence. In November 1866, Anne Elizabeth died at their residence, the Pier Hotel (later Hotel Manly), and five days later their five-week-old daughter Maud breathed her last.

Always sympathetic to the Aboriginals, after selling the business in Sydney before the move to Manly, he now went down to Lake Wallace, Victoria and threw himself into organising a tour for them to Britain. He duly led the black cricketers in 1868 on the quaintest of expeditions, paternal throughout to his wards, among whom he had lived, sharing many an adventure, and on the UK tour he was personally successful to an extraordinary degree: 1156 runs at 20.16 (second to Johnny Mullagh) and 250 wickets at 12. His skills went further, for the crowds marvelled at his ability to arrest a ball on the blade of his bat and keep it balanced there after someone had thrown it towards him from a distance. Yet further tragedy intruded as one of his players, King Cole, died in London. Lawrence was at his bedside in Guy's Hospital to the last.

Returning to Australia, Lawrence settled in Newcastle, NSW, and began a 24-year term of employment with the Railways, retiring on health grounds at 63. He had married again in 1871, Yorkshire-born Emmaretta being fourteen years his junior, but much further sadness lay ahead. Daughter Minnie was to die before her fifth birthday, and a second girl lived only fourteen months, before Millicent came late in 1877 and survived the perils of infancy.

Lawrence remained close to Anglo-Australian cricket. Soon after settling in Australia he was made captain of New South Wales, and played against the second English team, that of 1863-64, led by Parr. Lawrence pleased himself by taking 10 wickets in the match, though England won by one wicket. In the previous season, he had shattered Victoria with figures of 7 for 48 and 7 for 25 for his adopted State in the intercolonial match at Sydney's Domain ground. His second-innings figures might have been even better, but George Marshall and W.H. Greaves had walked out following a run-out dispute, leaving Victoria with nine men.

Ten years after the 1868 Aboriginal tour of Britain, Lawrence helped sponsor the first white Australian team's English tour. And at the age of 54 he played for

Eighteen of Newcastle against Ivo Bligh's Ashes-chasing England team of 1882-83. With a white beard trailing down, Lawrence was still fit enough to take to the field when in his 70th year, marking his retirement as Melbourne CC coach with a determined innings of 7 in 48 minutes on a treacherous MCG pitch in a farewell to the famous ground he had first trodden in 1862, 36 years earlier. Tom Horan saw the old Lawrence as 'sprightly as a 40-year-old'.

Few veterans had a richer store of memories or breadth of travel. Among his proudest recollections was his 8 for 32 at Lord's for Ireland v MCC in 1858. But his accomplishments were much more broadly based than upon individual feats. A modest man with an alert mind and a feel for the game, Lawrence had greatly helped develop Australian cricket by his coaching in Sydney and later in Melbourne (where Vernon Ransford was among his charges). He had overcome daunting official obstruction to steer the historic 1868 Aboriginal tour of the UK, and helped make the 1878 tour a reality. Not least, though, was his part in making the first-ever English tour of Australia a success.

Charlie Lawrence lived on until December 20, 1916 (a date only recently ratified). He died in Nurse Sutton's Hospital, Canterbury, Melbourne four days after his 88th birthday. Doubt remains over the spelling of his name. Often in contemporary accounts it appears as 'Laurence', a version seemingly supported by his signature on the tour contract.

WILLIAM MORTLOCK
Born July 18, 1832 in Kennington, south London

Solid Billy Mortlock ranked among the reliable yeomen cricketers of his time, one of so many eminent players from Surrey. The young Mortlock, who first played for the Surrey club when only sixteen, was a stodgy, tedious batsman who owed his place in the side as much as anything to his brilliance in the key position of long-stop, the busy, runsaving post beyond the wicketkeeper. He and 'Ducky' Diver, without gloves or pads, were as renowned at long-stop as Jonty Rhodes or Ricky Ponting at point-gully in modern times.

Known as 'Stonewall' – probably after the Confederate general who perished in 1863 – more for his skill at long-stop, Mortlock found liberation as a batsman after his decision to abandon middle-stump guard in favour of leg. Thereafter his strokeplay blossomed, and at his best he hit strongly and stylishly, developing leg-side shots. His top form was never better displayed than in an innings of 106 against Middlesex at The Oval in 1866. As either opener or middle-order batsman, he was much valued.

And then came his bowling. From medium-pace, he switched to slow lobs – 'slow underhand rubbish' chronicler Arthur Haygarth observed – his calm persistence paying off dramatically in Surrey's contest with Kent at The Oval in 1863, when he took 7 for 54 and 6 for 73.

Known as 'Old Stonewall' upon the advent of young Harry Jupp, who liked to sit on the splice, Mortlock was as Surrey as they came, having been born in Clayton Street, abutting Kennington Oval. His father umpired Surrey matches.

Billy grew into a cheerful, sociable and good-natured chap, 5ft 9ins in height and weighing 12 stone. He became a cricket ball-maker, and also coached at Wellesley House, Dr Scale's school in Twickenham. In due course, having declined a place on the second tour of Australia in 1863-64, he set up in business as a supplier of cricket equipment in a shop adjacent to Waterloo station. He endeavoured to expand his profits by hiring Lambeth Baths in the winter of 1867-68 in an early experiment with indoor cricket nets; but the venture was a failure.

He was granted a benefit in 1870, his final year with Surrey, H.H. and Ned Stephenson, his companions on the 1861-62 Australian tour, standing as umpires, though Mortlock himself did not play. W.G.Grace did, scoring 42 and 51 not out to help safeguard the duration of the match, while Jupp lingered 4½ hours for 54 in a drawn encounter between United South and United North. Such was Mortlock's popularity that despite heavy rain on the opening day and dark clouds on the second and third, 16,000 Ovalites paid to watch, ensuring a tidy return for the beneficiary. An oddity of the match was Harry Charlwood's fate off one ball: he hit it high, was dropped, ran a single, then a short run, and was then run out.

Mortlock himself had done something at Lord's that merited a place in the game's imperishable annals when, during an innings of 65 in which he had a stand of 86 with Iddison, he ran a seven after the ball had bounced through the gates, which had just been opened to let in a carriage from St John's Wood Road. What fun was lost when the administrators eventually introduced enclosed boundaries.

For ten years Mortlock was a professional with the United All England XI, before joining the United South. But not always were his pockets lined. After one match with an itinerant eleven in Scotland, he and the disreputable Surrey wicketkeeper Ted Pooley reached Elephant and Castle with a farthing between them.

Billy Mortlock's career embraced 191 matches adjudged first-class, in which he made 5528 runs at 18.73, with three centuries. And he averaged an impressive 25 for Players v Gentlemen. He took 147 wickets (best bowling 7 for 42) and held 85 catches; and his skill at long-stop was best assessed by a statistic of only three byes throughout two whole seasons at The Oval (12,000 balls). As *Badminton's Cricket* (1888) made clear, long-stopping, especially up at Lord's, 'in 1861 and 1862 was no laughing matter'.

At the age of 50, Mortlock became seriously ill, and was confined to his room for the final twelve months, dying there, at 8 Solon Road, Brixton, on January 23, 1884, at the age of 51. He was buried in Norwood Cemetery, widely mourned.

WILLIAM MUDIE
Born April 26, 1836 in Kennington, south London

The youngest of the dozen pioneer tourists to Australia in 1861, William Mudie was a tall, plain-looking man, known as 'The Surrey Shadow'. His impact on the game was slight. He was recognised as a 'useful' middle-order batsman and no more, and as a good slow roundarm bowler who reverted to slow underhand lobs.

He had some success with the ball in 1861, which, doubtless supported by a clean character reference and a good singing voice, persuaded H.H.Stephenson to enlist him for the great Australian expedition. At The Oval in July 1861, Mudie took 6 for 78 for Surrey v The North, Daft, Carpenter, Parr and Anderson being among those he teased out. Any boost to his confidence was probably cancelled out by his experience while batting for Surrey against England that summer, also at The Oval, when the terrifying 'Foghorn' Jackson hurt him badly with one of his thunderbolt deliveries.

That autumn, Mudie's stocks rose again in a minor match when he hit 127 for Colchester Garrison against Braxted Park. Clearly he had cricket in him, though he never made it to the top rank – and, sadly for him, never played in a significant match at Lord's.

Born, like Mortlock, very close to The Oval (in the street parallel: Bowling Green Street), Mudie was employed by Surrey CCC as a practice bowler from 1856 to 1865, when he resigned in the hope of earning a crust as an umpire. Briefly he was a racquet-marker at The Oval, before picking up a job with Cubitts of Gray's Inn Road, at the Bank of England. He had been a messenger before becoming a cricketer.

With tragic irony, the youngest of Stephenson's brigade of 1861-62 was also the first to die. On January 25, 1871, in Loughborough Street, close to his birthplace, Mudie succumbed to 'paralysis of the brain'. He was only 34. He was laid to rest in Tooting Cemetery.

THOMAS SEWELL
Born March 15, 1830 in Mitcham, Surrey

First in the long line of English cricketers who have amused Australian crowds by their antics or even simply by their shapes, Tom Sewell was short (5ft 4½ins) and plump, though a contemporary comment of his being 'as broad as he was short' was rather an exaggeration. Within his less-than-ideal physique lay great strength and surprising agility, and his happy disposition made him generally popular.

He was known as 'Busy Tom', and, in wider terms, as 'Tom Sewell junior' since his father had already earned fame as a player and umpire. It was through his father's term as an innkeeper in Sevenoaks that young Tom played his first important matches for Kent. Lillywhite classified him as a busy batsman, like his father, and altogether an energetic cricketer, while his fastish bowling, delivered with a roundarm slinging action, was generally pretty straight. 'Sewell's bowling was wonderfully fine' has been scrawled on a page of *Scores & Biographies* which records his 4 for 5 as Fifteen of Kent beat an England team by an innings at Lord's, his victims including Carpenter, Caffyn and H.H.Stephenson. This was in July 1861, and probably aided his selection in Stephenson's touring team.

Tom Sewell, fast bowler and one of the irritants in Surrey teams that took on northern counties. He did well in Australia. At Geelong he bagged 15 'rabbits' for 27 runs.

A carpenter by trade, Sewell threw in his lot with Edinburgh's Grange club, the premier cricket club north of the border. There, at the old Grove Park ground, he worked for four summers until 1860, when he picked up an engagement with Surrey that was to take him into the big time.

Essentially an uncomplicated seeker after runs, with no great defence, Sewell was recognised by Caffyn as a 'clean, hard hitter', though his first-class average was just under 12 (equating to perhaps 25 today?). He was one of those late-order batsmen who occasionally turn matches around in just a few overs.

One such occasion was the midsummer match at The Oval between Surrey and Nottinghamshire in 1865. It was against a background of mutual antipathy between the Surrey cricketers and those from the North, and Sewell went in as last man with 14 needed for victory. At the other end was H.H.Stephenson, who was 75 not out. The Notts players believed Sewell to have been lbw first ball, but the umpire disagreed. The new batsman then sneaked eight runs before he was beaten by 'Foghorn' Jackson, and the wicketkeeper, Sam Biddulph, courageously standing up at the stumps, flicked off the bails with Sewell well out of his crease (Oscroft of Notts later stated that he was out by a yard and a half). Biddulph put the ball in his pocket, and there was jubilation all round as the Notts men began to leave the field. But umpire George Lee, a Surrey man, gave Sewell not out. With ten minutes remaining, Tom Sewell thumped a five to steal a one-wicket victory and was carried from the field shoulder-high by near-hysterical spectators, while the incensed Notts players stood around dumbfounded. After this, the two counties avoided each other for three years, deepening Surrey's bad odour, for five Yorkshire players – Anderson, Atkinson, Iddison, Rowbotham and Stephenson – refused to play against Surrey in either match that season, the fixture finally being suspended for two years.

There was to be no long life for Tom Sewell. On June 13, 1871, only a few months after Mudie's death, Sewell was taken by heart disease while in St Johns, Sevenoaks, the paternal hometown. He was buried in Sevenoaks, where his father lived on as a retired publican on annuities from MCC and Surrey until his death at 82 in 1888.

EDWIN STEPHENSON
Born June 5, 1832 in Sheffield, Yorkshire

Lugubrious of expression but capable of the droll remark, Edwin Stephenson was one of two Yorkshiremen on the 1861-62 Australian venture, both having bottled their developing grievances towards Surrey, whose provocative behaviour on the field and in the politics of the all-professional touring troupes was beginning to enrage many of the cricketers from the North.

He was known as Edward, or more commonly Ned or Teddy, or even, to distinguish him from HH, as 'Yorkshire' Stephenson. Like his Surrey namesake he was a wicketkeeper who also bowled and was a batsman of some skill, if not in the same class in any of these departments as HH. The Yorkshireman's dour defence was founded on a particularly long forward reach, but sometimes he surprised by unleashing powerful blows. His preference for scorning risk was probably no more than the natural manifestation of one who played cricket for a precarious living.

His first patron was James Wilson Rimington Wilson, of Broomhead Hall, Sheffield, from where Stephenson went as professional to Whitehaven, Edge Hill (Liverpool), St Helens and Warminster (Wilts) in successive seasons. He was serving Christchurch, Oxford when he secured a job as bowling professional with MCC at Lord's in 1857. Further security came when he took over the Newcastle Arms in Portobello, Sheffield, moving about ten years later to run the Cambridge, also in his native town.

In 1856 had come the major leap into the All England XI as well as the United All England XI after he had done well against both outfits while playing for local sides. But in 1859, he became a pawn in the ever-present background of animosity between Surrey and the Northerners when playing for the North against Surrey at Broughton, Manchester. His finger was damaged while he kept wicket, and George Parr, his captain, asked the equally temperamental Surrey leader, F.P.Miller, if a substitute could bat in Stephenson's place. Miller flatly and rightly refused. When Stephenson gallantly walked out at the fall of the ninth wicket, intending to bat one-handed, Parr stormed out after him and forced him back into the dressing-room. The North lost by 34 runs, and the schism widened.

Ned felt strongly about the Southerners' moves to destabilise the established itinerant teams by setting up the United South of England XI, and spoke (in 1865) of the wage-earning Northerners as having 'been most cruelly ill-treated by the Surrey men'.

So sensitively balanced was his dignity that when his partner ran him out – apparently deliberately – in a North v. Surrey match in 1863, Stephenson walked out on the remainder of the game, the entry in the scorebook in the second innings reading 'absent, shamefully and disgracefully'. There is no doubting that he had a mind of his own.

About 5ft 8ins tall and solidly built, Stephenson had a long career, serving Yorkshire for a dozen seasons beside his other professional commitments (he never earned selection in a Players v Gentlemen match), and in 1870 becoming the first to be awarded a benefit match by Yorkshire. The return was small, United North beating United South at Bramall Lane by an innings in two days. He did not play himself, but his old team-mates on the 1861-62 trip, Iddison, Griffith and H.H.Stephenson, all took part.

They will have reminisced. They might have recalled Ned's naive remark when their ship entered the Red Sea: that it was no redder than any other waters he had seen. And they probably laughed again at the recall of Ned's annoyance at the blaring trombone on deck, a problem he overcame by stuffing a towel down its outlet.

'He was always saying something to put a roomful into a roar of laughter,' wrote Caffyn, though whether it was always by design or sometimes by gauche accident is not altogether clear. Stephenson seems to have been a little gullible at times, as when he took a ball that had passed George Freeman's bat as the batsman sailed well down the pitch. For a wicketkeeper who had completed numerous stumpings – many off the crafty Notts slow bowler Tinley – he now displayed extraordinary dimwittedness as Freeman foxed him by strolling calmly to within the safety of the crease. 'What are you coom here for?' asked Stephenson in amazement. 'Because,' said the urbane, nerveless Freeman, 'you forgot to put down the wicket, my friend.' He went on to a lusty century.

Then there was the time, in 1853, when Ned had just made a name for himself, when a challenge notice appeared in *Bell's Life* to the effect that a single-wicket match between young Stephenson and a John Buggins was set down at the Cricketer's Arms, Little Sheffield, for a stake of £25. Stephenson and his backers travelled six long miles on the appointed day, but it was all a hoax. Perhaps it could have happened to anybody.

Even in the early days, it was noted that Ned Stephenson could usually be found at the Plough Inn, Hallam, and drink must surely have played a major part in his descent into a miserable middle age. He had even been forced to leave the field during a match at Wirksworth, having sunk some antique whisky from the local inn which made him feel very bad. Soon, as he lay in the tent all alone, he began to choke and went black in the face. Only the chance arrival of the scorecard-printer saved him.

He died in obscurity and 'very poor circumstances' on July 5, 1898, aged 66. By now he was living in Tue Brook, Liverpool, and *Cricket* and *Wisden* remained unaware of his death for some time.

The great Yorkshire allrounder George Ulyett had also recently died, and a week after Stephenson, Michael Ellison, the principal figure in the founding of Yorkshire CCC, passed on.

Laughing Teddy Stephenson, who had proudly top-scored with 67 in Yorkshire CCC's first match after its 1863 foundation, and again in 1867 with 54 in the first-ever Roses match, and who had scored England's first run off Australian bowling, had simply faded quietly away while scarcely anyone noticed.

GEORGE WELLS
Born November 2, 1830 in Whitechapel, east London

The only Sussex player in the party, 'Tiny' Wells was also the smallest at 5ft 2½ins. Known by some as 'Punch', he weighed nine stone and was no weakling. Although born in Whitechapel, he was taken to Wisborough Green at three months and baptised in that village, where he was to live for some years.

He had a most peculiar style at the crease, taking guard no more than an inch or so in front of the stumps before moving forward as the bowler approached, bat menacingly over shoulder. He was more comfortable with slower bowling, but his bat packed a punch on his better days. At Brighton, though, in 1860, in playing a ball from Caffyn, Wells had the misfortune to see a piece of his willow torn off and propelled into his wicket.

Caffyn recorded that Wells was a first-rate shot, so good that he beat Caffyn, who prided himself in his skill with a gun. They shot at sparrows released from flower-pots, and winner Wells took home a case of wine.

He played for Sussex from 1854 to 1869, and turned out in a few matches for Middlesex in that time too. In 1855 he made his first appearance for the United All England XI, where his batting, his bowling of roundarm medium-pace and lobs, his excellent fielding at point and ability to keep wicket made him the ideal travelling pro. Twice he carried his bat through an innings for Sussex: for 38 out of 81 against Kent at Brighton in 1858 and for a remarkable 55 out of 73 against MCC at Lord's.

During the 1850s he pursued a livelihood from cricket with engagements successively in Horsham, Stourbridge, Brighton CC and College, Oakley (Hants), Shoreham, Sandhurst Military College, and, in 1860 and '61, at Lord's.

Wells and his wife chose (or it was possibly his personal decision) to emigrate to Australia, and with an agreement in his pocket to assist H.H.Stephenson's team during the tour, he and Mrs Wells sailed from Plymouth on board *Yorkshire* on August 27, 1861, reaching Melbourne on November 26. He soon took up his responsibilities with the emerging Richmond CC, occasionally captaining the side in the absence of the legendary Tom Wills. But on that grassless ground and in away matches, Richmond won only one of their thirteen matches. There was little the professional from England could do to raise the standard.

Disillusioned, having also failed to distinguish himself in Stephenson's tour matches, Wells returned with his wife to England in June 1862. He tried running a tobacconist's shop, reassuring himself, perhaps, that he could always fall back on his early training as a carpenter. But when the bankruptcy court beckoned, he sought further cricket employment, this time in the realm of public schools. The pupils of Eton, Harrow, Brighton, Tonbridge and Lancing (where he worked for 32 seasons on and off) benefited from his guidance. At one point he found a wage at Woodham's cricket ball factory in Southborough.

'Tiny' Wells was a 'nearly' man: never quite made it to the top, never quite reached a century in first-class cricket (highest 90), and fell just short of taking

The Trailblazers: Bennett, Mudie, Caffyn, H.H.Stephenson, Griffith, Mr Mallam, Iddison, Hearne, E.Stephenson; front – Lawrence, Mortlock, Sewell. Wells sailed ahead of the main party.

all ten when he secured 9 for 105 for Sussex against Surrey at Brighton in 1860. Basic subsistence seems always to have been a struggle. His failure in business, as he explained to the court, came about simply through 'scarcity of business, and the expenses thereof exceeding my profits'.

One of his sons, Fred, went on to play for Sussex a couple of times in 1891, but by then George was dead. At the age of 60, he had an epileptic seizure at his home in Commercial Road, Shoreham-by-Sea, on January 23, 1891. He was buried in Old Shoreham Cemetery.

CHAPTER 4

The Proudest Thing Afloat

THE VESSEL which conveyed the first English cricket team to Australia is as much part of history as the distinguished passengers themselves. The SS *Great Britain* is regarded as the Flagship of the Steam Revolution, outstanding among the numerous engineering triumphs of Isambard Kingdom Brunel (1806-59). Son of a French father – an engineer of repute – and an English mother, Isambard was born in Portsmouth but educated mainly in France. Linking with his father, Marc, who had been in financial straits, together they designed and built the Thames Tunnel at Rotherhithe. Eighteen years in the building, the tunnel opened in 1843, and Queen Victoria, having knighted Brunel senior, walked ceremonially through it.

By then, young Isambard's career had boomed. The daring concept of the Clifton Suspension Bridge had taken him to Bristol, to which the Great Western Railway now stretched from London (consulting engineer: I.K.Brunel), terminating at his imposing Temple Meads station. And soon he was planning a great oak-built paddle-steamer, *Great Western*, which made it to New York in 15 days in April 1838, regaining Atlantic supremacy for Britain.

With the advent of screw propulsion, Brunel incorporated this into his next major venture. Four years in the building, and having cost £117,295, SS *Great Britain* (originally intended to be called *Mammoth*) was launched on July 19, 1843, watched by Brunel's proud parents. A champagne bottle was smashed across her iron bow by Prince Albert, Victoria's cherished Consort (Mrs Miles, wife of one of the owners, having missed with the first attempt), and the world's very first ocean-going propeller-driven iron ship – prototype of all modern ships – was soon easing into the Avon, watched from on high by thousands of excited townsfolk lining Brandon Hill.

After successful sea trials, the 3675-ton vessel, 322ft in overall length excluding bowsprit, made her first Atlantic crossing, with passengers, in 1845, strong, fast and efficient under five masts of sail as alternative to steam-power. Later, the five masts were to be reduced to three. Ringed with a five-bar railing, and with the innovation of iron lifeboats, *Great Britain* was the proudest thing afloat, with new levels of consideration for passengers, and enough modern features to inspire confidence in all but the most nervous of sea-goers. For some years she powered across the Atlantic and back, until her new owners, Gibbs, Bright & Co, refitted her and switched to the Australian run in 1852.

With new engines, sail area increased to 27,000 (later extended to 33,000) square feet, and a new 300ft deckhouse for increased passenger comfort, she could now accommodate 730 passengers, 50 (later increased to 85) in the first-class section. Fares ranged from 14 guineas down in steerage to 70 guineas for first-class.

By her final voyage to Australia, in 1875, *Great Britain* had carried some

15,000 passengers to the promised land. She had also, when commandeered for more pressing service, conveyed 44,000 soldiers and horses to the Crimea in 1855-56 and thousands more to India to quell the mutiny against British rule in 1857-58. It was during the jittery time of the Crimean war that the seaboard citizens of first Merseyside and then Melbourne had their nerves shredded by the sudden explosion of guns and rockets. In the first instance, it was merely Captain Matthews' way of celebrating *Great Britain*'s speedy return to England with passengers plus quantities of gold, wool and cotton. In the second, still in 1854, it was his successor, Captain John Gray, merely expressing relief that the ship was cleared for disembarkation at long last after a three-week period of quarantine following a minor smallpox outbreak. In both cases, those on shore thought the Russians were attacking. It brought out the entire Melbourne militia, and a complaint went to the Colonial Office.

Captain Gray was skipper of *Great Britain* for eighteen years. A Shetland Islander of considerable bulk, he was genial and popular, a reassuring master whose physical prowess was demonstrated with regular climbing of the great tree-trunk masts and whose commanding presence showed him to be stoutly undaunted by any of the upsets inevitably caused by rough seas or accident-prone or even dying passengers. His voice, it was said, could be heard above the storm, and one appreciative passenger wrote that 'he always seems to be looking out for something to make his passengers more comfortable'. He once told a passenger that he loved 'every plank' of *Great Britain*: 'I pat her sometimes, and I've promised her a rest if she will only get home in less than seventy days.'

Gray, who was master when H.H.Stephenson and his cricketers journeyed to Australia, generated one of the most tantalising of nautical mysteries when he disappeared thirty days into the homeward voyage of late 1872. One of the square transom windows in his cabin at the ship's stern was found open. Was it suicide or was he murdered for his money?

Brunel now lay in Kensal Green Cemetery, having long since smoked his final cigar. He died from a kidney complaint in September 1859, just as his huge *Great Eastern* – over twice as long as *Great Britain*, with paddles, propeller and sails – was undergoing sea trials.

A certain satisfaction springs from the fact that Brunel and cricket are linked specifically by means of a letter he wrote, just before his death, to an engineer he wanted involved in a new railway line from Temple Meads to Ashley Down: 'the country immediately north of the city I should think a delightful one to live in – beautiful country – good society near Bristol, Clifton, etc. – I can't vouch for any cricketing, but I should think it highly probable.'

There was already concern at *Great Britain*'s condition, and in 1876 she was laid up in Birkenhead and put up for sale. Just as breaking-up seemed unavoidable, she was bought and converted into a coal-carrier, plying between Cardiff and San Francisco, and braving the terrors of Cape Horn – until disaster struck in 1886. She somehow stayed afloat, listing and leaking, fore and main top-gallant masts gone. Into Port Stanley, in the Falkland Islands, she limped, and there she pathetically lay, sold for £2000 and now used as a wool store.

SS Great Britain, *now a three-master, at the time of her Australian voyage when she carried the first English cricket team. Below: Captain John Gray, the much-respected skipper of the ship. His disappearance will forever be a mystery.*

Isambard Kingdom Brunel, most famous of British designer/engineers of the Victorian era.

Into the 20th Century she survived, now a coal store, and fuelling British ships before the Battle of the Falklands in 1914. By 1933, unwanted by anybody, the hulk of the once-proud *Great Britain* was towed across to Sparrow Cove and beached, her sides holed so that she would never float again.

The beginning of the happy ending came in 1968, when the SS *Great Britain* Project was formed. Naval architect Ewan Corlett, having examined the hulk, declared it to be surprisingly sound structurally. It was his strong belief that the 'forefather of all modern ships' ought to be recovered. As with the first cricket tour of Australia, money was the problem. Then British patriot Jack Hayward came to the rescue, and the massive task began of bringing the vessel home and restoring her.

In one of the most dramatic rescue acts in maritime history, the ruin was slowly heaved onto a pontoon and drawn by a gallant little tug, soon encountering a Force 8 gale, and battling 7000 miles home, via Port Stanley and Montevideo, at just over five knots.

What was left of *Great Britain* arrived at Avonmouth Docks on June 24, 1970, to be freed from the pontoon a few days later, and towed 'floating on her own bottom' up the Avon to Bristol Harbour, not without some last-minute drama. She then passed under the Suspension Bridge which had only just begun to take shape the last time *Great Britain* passed this way. And on July 19, precisely 127 years after her launch, the famous ship, now unrecognisable, returned to her birthplace. The Prince Consort had been the guest of honour in 1843. Now, Prince Philip, Duke of Edinburgh, a true naval man, witnessed the emotional events.

In the years that followed, the restoration of SS *Great Britain* became one of the most admirable and thrilling (and expensive) operations seen by the nation. Now, it is possible to walk the relaid deck, descend to reconstructed cabins and saloons, and examine the pictures and the memorabilia – even step down into the dry-dock and pat the hull, as Captain Gray used to pat the deck. The spirit of that strong-willed, friendly, diminutive genius, Isambard Brunel, is all around. The replica engine is awesome, and when alone, one might imagine its great rumble and hear the cracking of the gigantic sails, and perhaps even the voices of the pioneer cricketers as they strolled along the deck, remembering home and loved ones, anticipating things to come in Australia.

CHAPTER 5

Non-Stop to Melbourne

TOM SEWELL and Tom Hearne were the worst of the seasickness cases, though from start to finish the voyage was classified fairly smooth. Alternating engine-power and sail, and sometimes utilising both, *Great Britain* ploughed her way down the Atlantic, taking full advantage of the trade winds before being thrust eastwards by the Roaring Forties towards her destination. Brunel's magnificent iron steamship, now owned by the Black Ball Line, had 687 souls aboard, comprised of 143 crew members, 456 adults, 80 children and eight infants. Few can have failed to appreciate that they were passengers on a very special ship.

The frustration of the false start had been eased for the cricketers when some of their acquaintances bobbed across the Mersey in rowing-boats and came alongside, performing a 'pantomime' which was an 'inexplicable dumb show' to those not in the know. Few fellow travellers, it seems, knew or much cared that there were famous cricketers on board, though Caffyn appreciated chatting with a woman about their hometown of Reigate. While it was a relief to him that this voyage was so much less turbulent than the 1859 trips to and from America, he now fell prey to mosquitoes: they 'tormented the life out of me', he wrote, and he was forced to see the medical officer. Only by swathing muslin around his head and covering his arms with stockings was he able to escape further attacks. The volume of laughter this generated among his team-mates may easily be imagined.

The ship's journal, *The Cabinet*, which was published in four issues during the voyage, was edited by Alexander Reid, and he and his committee kept their material light and jocular wherever possible, though it was necessary to chronicle the deaths of two Cornishmen soon after crossing the Equator. One died of apoplexy, the other, described as having been worn out with previous experiences in Australia, at home and in South America, left an 11-year-old son, to whom Captain Gray became guardian for the rest of the voyage. Even more poignant was the death of one of the children travelling in steerage. Each of the bodies was consigned to the deep, in the presence of the ship's company, with Dr Morland Hocken reading the funeral service.

There was nearly a fourth fatality when a seaman was flung 20 feet from the main royal mast during a gale, but he managed to cling to a rope, thereby saving himself. Lucky too was the cricketer ('Farmer' Bennett, as Caffyn revealed in his book) who lost his grip on the belaying-pin he was using as a bat in one of the deck games arranged by H.H.Stephenson partly to keep his men in shape and partly to allay boredom. The heavy pin smashed into the face of a saloon passenger, breaking his nose and lacerating him bloodily. He survived, so no manslaughter charge transpired.

Without naming her, *The Cabinet* referred to a mature woman, renowned in the field of social reform and for her eccentricity, who was a kind of supernumary to the cricket team, by their own invitation. She would have gone on the 1859 tour 'but for the antipathies of our American cousins to women of colour'. She suffered grievously during the rough crossing of the Bay of Biscay, not only being forced to shun food and drink but finding it impossible to smoke her clay pipe. Curled up in agony on deck, wearing her scarlet robe, she became so ill that one of the cricketers nobly picked her up and took her below to her cabin.

The Cabinet remarked on the cricketers, complimenting them on 'their honest English faces, by the heartiness and geniality of their manner . . . jolly good fellows' – even if it had become known that several of them had branded 'Aunt Sally' (the camp follower in the scarlet robe) as a 'duffer'. The journal conveyed a message, too, from Australia, assuring the cricketers that 'they will receive a welcome which will prove to them that Victoria has not degenerated from the parent stock in her notions of hospitality'. It pointed out that Melbourne now had 21 cricket clubs, while Ballarat, the largest of the inland towns, had four or five, as well as a ground a mile from the township which was the equal of most English country grounds. Then, as if fearing after all that the English cricketers might face strong opposition, a few excuses were itemised in advance: while they paced the deck and played quoits, missing three months of practice, their Australian counterparts would be practising and playing. The tourists, too, would be facing the hottest weather they could ever have known. Good luck, chaps.

The ill-fated Wardill.

Matters were already moving fast in Melbourne, where Spiers and Pond wrote on October 25 to Melbourne Cricket Club secretary Dick Wardill requesting approval of the plans for the spectacular grandstand which was to be erected before the opening match some nine weeks hence, and for sundry other necessary improvements. About 700ft in length, the grandstand would hold 6000 spectators and would be probably the biggest sporting stand in the world. Approval was given without delay. As for Wardill, a Liverpudlian by birth, he was to play in the opening tour match, and he was, five years later, to score the first century in Australian first-class cricket. The best batsman in the country at that time, he was a prominent administrator and businessman too. But greed and irrationality overtook him, and he was identified as an embezzler from the Victoria Sugar Company. Arrested in 1873, he slipped his escort and drowned himself in the Yarra.

Sustenance for *Great Britain*'s passengers was fairly lavish, except for the steerage people, whose

Cricket on deck on ocean-going ships bore little similarity to the real thing.

staple was preserved meat and plum pudding. There were thefts of bread from the stores, and it was not the well-fed cricketers who perpetrated them. For their part, after vermicelli soup, they had succulent choices of mutton, pork, geese, veal, duck, chicken, turkey, lamb, beef, ham, or tongue (only the most distracted of passengers could have failed to notice the huge array of livestock taken on board in Liverpool) with a range of vegetables, followed by any of rice, batter or custard pudding, gooseberry or blackcurrant tart, jam tart, omelette or macaroni and cheese, and orange, ginger, raisins, almonds, walnuts and Barcelona nuts to choose from, if there was room. The cricketers cannot have reached Melbourne in peak condition.

In the worst of the tropical heat, sleep was impossible. The cabins were like Turkish baths, and many chose to sleep on deck, woken only as the boatswain sluiced the decks at dawn. Beyond the railings, the monotony of the water was broken up by sightings of all sorts of aerial and ocean life: stormy petrel, gulls, albatross with 12ft wingspan, porpoise, sharks, flying fish, whales, even the occasional turtle. Such sights must have hypnotised the likes of Mortlock and Iddison.

Things became more relaxed as the days ticked by. Collars, ties and waistcoats were voted a 'nuisance' and discarded during leisure hours. But *The Cabinet* warned, per medium of a letter signed 'Observer', that shipboard romances should be avoided, for 'nice-looking, young, respectable, amiable females are eagerly sought after by influential men of all descriptions' once they reached the colonies. Souls were cleansed on Sundays with divine services on deck in the fresh air.

A letter from Captain Gray in the edition of December 3 expressed disappointment at the absence of stiff breezes, though he still felt confident of getting his ship to Melbourne for Christmas. Alongside was a missive from Aunt Sally herself, telling how cricketer Mudie had gone to her cabin and sat himself down. 'Good morning, Madam,' he said. 'Good morning, Mudie,' she said. And he then proceeded to read to her the *Cabinet* article about her. When 'my dear boy' had finished, she was overwhelmed with pleasure and gratitude at what she saw as an editorial compliment, and now wrote asking to make the editor's acquaintance – and also requesting a clean cutty pipe, for she could not obtain cigarettes on board, a shortcoming 'which don't suit my taste'.

More serious by miles was a three-column article, *How I Became A Cricketer*, by 'One of the Eleven'. He wrote of being little interested in the game while at college, and of having poor health while living in a villa in Kennington. He began to practise cricket with the old college tutor, and gradually advanced from hopelessness to a certain level of efficiency. We are left to guess . . . .

The ship's doctor was to report that the general health of passengers was good, and attributed this to the agreeable weather and the great attention being paid to cleanliness. Less fortunate were the canaries and linnets hung out in cages on deck, on their way to Australia for breeding. Many were found dead.

The weather continued fine as they rounded the Cape of Good Hope, averaging a much higher 260 miles per day now. The excitement was tangibly rising. Instructional notes for new arrivals in Australia incorporated tempting descriptions and impressive statistics, balanced by warnings not only about the weather but against the 'baneful influence' of intoxicating drink. A sad poem from 'TS', who was badly missing England, could have been by Tom Sewell, though he would have known well enough that he had a return passage guaranteed in a few weeks' time.

'Conundrums' embraced an item on Republic or Monarchy? Answer: Monarchy certainly, for they leave one good sovereign, in Victoria, at home, hoping to find hundreds of sovereigns in Victoria abroad. In the second week of December, the band played on deck daily.

The captain's farewell message in *The Cabinet* expressed gratitude that the ship's regulations had been adhered to – 'far exceeding the experience of past voyages' – and now that they were off the coast of Australia, he wished all well who planned to make this country their future home. The passengers would not quickly forget their doomed captain, with his marvellous smile, his hawk-like eyes, and his graceful manner in dancing the quadrille. 'He has none of that durty pride about him,' remarked one of the Irish passengers. The saloon passengers collected a testimonial for the commander which amounted to £82, and the ship's doctor was given 50 guineas.

Farewell soirees, with music, helped waft them across the Bight, and the non-stop voyage of 65 days drew to a close with the cry 'Land on the weather bow!' Cape Otway and its lighthouse came sharply into view in the early afternoon of Monday, December 23. Passengers of fragile disposition will have offered thanks for a trouble-free voyage, Caffyn, the mosquitoes' favourite provider, surely among them. (On the next tour, 1863-64, he and a much stronger English team were shaken when SS *Wonga Wonga*, taking them from Sydney to

Many a mile was walked on deck during Great Britain*'s 65-day voyage.*

Melbourne, hit and sank a sailing boat. 'Foghorn' Jackson, who had indulged himself at the farewell function, slept through the pandemonium, but Tarrant was in such a panic that he jumped into the boat put over the side to rescue those flung into the sea from the small vessel.)

In the evening the pilot boarded, bringing news of the dreadful fate of explorers Burke and Wills. (John McDouall Stuart, a Scot of iron resolve, had just set out in a new attempt to cross Australia from south to north. It was a successful venture, though he returned to Adelaide on a stretcher, and died a year later.)

Great Britain eased her way into Port Phillip Bay. As the night advanced, none could sleep. If there were any doubts about the excitement of the moment, the din on deck dispelled them. There was singing and hurrahing, and the ship's tin buckets came in useful as drums.

Health and customs officials came aboard, followed by a delegation to welcome the cricketers, and at last the great vessel nosed into Hobson's Bay and anchored off Sandridge Pier, within sight of the city, as ships all around hoisted their colours in recognition. Long-lost friends greeted each other, battling for composure, and quaking newcomers with no such luxury as a familiar face to welcome them tightened their grips on baggage and their children's tiny hands.

As for the cricketers, privilege came into its own that early morning. They adopted uniform, the grey felt hat with blue ribbon, supplied in Liverpool, and shook hands with the advance cricket delegation before listening to match committee representative G.W.Rusden's speech of welcome by the mizzen mast. The speaker was a former Surrey man himself, and was clearly thrilled at the sight of the English cricketers. 'We wish you to feel that you are stepping, as it were, from one county to another,' he said, 'although, certainly, at a great distance apart – that you are coming among countrymen . . . .'

When the cheering had ceased, H.H.Stephenson made a 'short, sharp,

Melbourne's Sandridge railway pier, 1860s, free of the clamouring thousands who greeted Stephenson and his fellow cricketers.

decisive' reply, teasingly referring to the 'licking' he and his men intended to dish out to the colonials on the cricket field. Another quick drink, then, with three cheers from those lining *Great Britain*'s railings echoing in their ears, the little steamer *Lioness* took them across to the Railway Pier, at Sandridge, where thousands of animated locals cheered and shouted at the sight of the cricketers from 'home'.

First ashore was Heathfield Harman Stephenson, though Caffyn denied himself the honour only out of courtesy. He followed his captain, and then came Mortlock, Sewell, Hearne, Wells and the rest, quickly swallowed up by the stampede. The players pressed their way through the crowds into the sanctuary of Garton's Hotel, but the hubbub continued as four, perhaps five, thousand (Caffyn thought as many as 10,000) adoring fans called for the cricketers' appearance. They complied, of course, fortified by more sparkling Moselle, and stood on the balcony to acknowledge the masses below. And already the team was complete, for 'Tiny' Wells, in Melbourne for the past month, had lost no time in joining his team-mates. The cheers from the street had made the *Argus* reporter's blood tingle, and moved Mudie, 'The Surrey Shadow', to remark: 'Well, we expected a good reception, but nothing like this!' The *Melbourne Herald* waxed lyrical that there had been no such welcome since the Athenians arrived in Corinth.

Also there to greet them on board had been Felix Spiers and Christopher Pond, and they, with the Englishmen's 'shepherd' W.B. – or B.W. – Mallam, took bow after bow until it was time to clamber not into the 'puffing, grunting rattle-trap' which ran on the first steam traction railway line in Australia, the 2½-mile stretch from Sandridge (now Port Melbourne) to Flinders Street, but instead up onto the outside positions on Bevan's 'monster' coach, which was drawn by eight superb grey horses. It was the largest coach in the colony, and usually ran along the Murray to the New South Wales South Coast and back.

The welcoming committee and a bevy of newspapermen squeezed into the coach, which now headed for the city. The cheering continued as they dashed along the Sandridge road, men and boys running alongside. Amazed at the noise, the visitors threaded their way into Melbourne, where a triumphal arch had blown over, but flags and bunting hung all about. Over the new Prince's Bridge (opened 1850; replaced 1884) and up Swanston Street they clattered, across to Elizabeth Street, thence right into Bourke Street, and three blocks down to the Café de Paris complex, which stood on the northern side, between Russell and Exhibition Streets, with Parliament House solid and reassuring at the far end, facing down Bourke Street. More people milled and jostled outside the Café de Paris, women waving handkerchiefs, males swishing their hats in the fresh morning air of Christmas Eve, draymen pulling up their carts and grinning and waving too. 'The

Comfortable beds at last: the Englishmen reach their new home in
Melbourne after the frenzy of the welcome and over two months at sea.

town reception,' wrote Charlie Lawrence years later, 'made us feel the great honour for we were suppose [*sic*] to represent England.'

Police under the command of Senior Sergeant Kelly guarded the entrance to the two-storey building, having cleared a little space for the arrival, and a few of the English cricketers atop the coach were photographed by Davies & Co of Bourke Street, an historic image that prompts an instinctive wish that there had been more.

Further hospitality followed inside, with speeches of welcome from local dignitaries at the Theatre Royal, before the party transferred to the Piazza Hotel, where they were to stay. Some of the players strolled down to the Melbourne Cricket Ground that afternoon and watched the match between a United Victorian XI and Sixteen of the County of Bourke, a trial game for selection of the Victorian combination that would face the English Eleven in the grand opening match on New Year's Day, eight days hence. They uttered diplomatic remarks about the standard of cricket being played before them, and expressed delight at the greenness of the new turf and the magnificence of the new grandstand. Afterwards, the Englishmen sampled the field for themselves, indulging in half-an-hour's 'skylarking'. 'Perhaps the most amusing part of the afternoon's programme on the Melbourne ground,' wrote the *Argus* man, 'was watching them "play" for the first time on colonial ground.' They were merely bowling to each other, six pairs of them, a stump for each, and having a gentle loosener with the bat, not bothering to remove their coats.

The Englishmen had an illustrious visitor that evening while they dined at the Piazza. Keen to wish them well, in walked the 68-year-old John Pascoe Fawkner, whose large residence long ago had been the first on the site of what was to become Melbourne. It had then been little more than a cluster of mud huts when it got its name in 1837. Fawkner was a quarrelsome, pious, melodramatic person, 'pint-sized' and asthmatic, inadequately self-educated, and vehemently against the prison system, having been a convict himself as a young man. The distinction he shared with John Batman of having founded Melbourne was naturally a source of great pride for Fawkner, who had built the first pub, developed many business interests, gone bankrupt, bounced back, owned a newspaper, and finished in the Legislative Council when Victoria became an independent colony in 1850. Champion of the 'little' man, he had no time for Catholics, Americans or Chinese immigrants; nor did he like the squatters, with their vast pastoral spreads and their arrogance, strutting along the city streets with their beards and their blue-serge suits, their cabbagetree hats, boots and spurs. But he would have enjoyed meeting the famous English cricketers, who, for their part, had to have it explained to them who the visitor was. They duly expressed their pleasure, and Fawkner told them he hoped they would win the grand opening match, though he hoped it would be a close contest.

Gifts and kind gestures continued to come the cricketers' way, the railway company giving them free passes. But suddenly it was Christmas Day, in a strange land, with no snow to be seen. They dined handsomely at the Café de Paris (which was destroyed by fire ten years later), the toasts being to Messrs

Burrup, Marshall and Mallam, without whose combined efforts they would all have been sitting by the fireside at home in England. And should any Melburnian have offered a 'new chum' a drink, he might have perplexed him with the esoteric local choice, as visualised by *Melbourne Punch*: 'What's your weakness? Nog, Knickerbocker, Sherry Cobbler, Snowstorm, Nightingale, Claret Spider, Jenny Lind, Shandygaff, Brandy Smash, or Sangaree?'

All was bonhomie, causing *Baily's Magazine* to state that 'it is gratifying to find that the letters from The Eleven to home, sent off two days subsequent to their landing at Melbourne, one and all breathe a manly gratitude for their extraordinary, hospitable, and magnificent reception'.

Christmastime or not, much was still happening on the organisational front. Spiers and Pond's agent in Sydney, named Dyne, had sent a telegram to say that he had secured from Messrs Cowper and Robertson of the New South Wales Government a promise to grant facilities for the building of a grandstand on the Domain for the Englishmen's match in Sydney. Since negotiations seemed to have been concluded happily with leading cricket clubs in the goldfields region of Victoria and with the authorities in Tasmania, the tour was taking real shape. It was even hoped to play in South Australia and the new colony (1859) of Queensland, though it transpired that these territories would have to wait for a later English tour before a team from Home would first set foot.

The proud new grandstand at the MCG was finished in time for the Caledonian Games, which drew almost 10,000 celebrants on Boxing Day, the first day of three, and which featured – besides wrestling and cutlass and bayonet displays – the dubious Cœur de Lion Feat, which consisted of cutting a sheep in half at a single blow, on horseback at the gallop. Somehow the cricket ground was restored to perfect condition for the big match. The weather was fine, and everyone looked forward to the ball at Prahran Town Hall on January 3. But for the conscientious English cricketers, Boxing Day was a time for serious practice. (Caffyn's recollection, many years later, that they had practised at a secret location seven miles into the bush – to escape the masses – on Christmas Day seems, like one or two other of his statements, to be a trifle inaccurate. If they did go somewhere secret, on another day, it might well have been to Heidelberg.) They reached Richmond CC's Punt Road ground at 10.30 am and did not leave until after 5 o'clock, and although the venue was not advertised, lots of locals turned up to sate their curiosity. Some went to have a little barrack, but all of those present were amazed at 'Ben' Griffith's power as he heaved one ball way over a distant wagon and into the Royal Hotel, to the even greater astonishment of a man sitting at the bar minding his own business. Thus the Surrey left-hander became known as 'The Lion Hitter'. Then, as if bent on impressing any doubters, Tom Sewell smashed one in the other direction, the ball clearing the trees between the ground and the police barracks. Ned Stephenson also whacked a few over the fence. The touring cricketers were given little room to spread themselves, so great was the crush of spectators, but their fielding drew admiring comments, and the batsmen's defences seemed well intact after nine weeks at sea, even though the ground was very hard and not conducive to batting.

For the captain, the chief distraction was the difficulty in persuading the local match committee that his Eleven should play against 18 rather than 22, and that the selection should be from the Melbourne district rather than just the metropolitan clubs. It was a matter not easily resolved. On December 28, 1861, H.H.Stephenson wrote to M.Hall, secretary, Victoria Committee of Cricketers (a secure independent Victorian cricket administration was still years away from formation, though the NSWCA had already been set up in Sydney in 1859):

Sir, – I understand from Messrs Spiers and Pond that you desire us, the English Eleven, to play twenty-two of Victoria, on the 1st of January, and that it has been brought forward in argument that the Eleven were in the habit of playing twenty-two of Ireland and Scotland. Such, I beg to assure you, is not the case. If we go to Ireland or Scotland, we play (as we did in America) twenty-two of a certain club, residents, and not the strength of the country.

Having shown you in part your error in the matter, I must also assure you that we, as men who are used to a great deal of exercise, having been on board ship a long time, where, of course, we were perfectly idle, are out of condition, and not at all up to the same work that we should be when playing in England, where, even at the beginning of a season, we are in perfect practice. I hope you will, therefore, see the perfect justice of our refusing – which we must do in our present condition – to play more than eighteen of Victoria, or we will play twenty-two resident in the Melbourne district.

Your obedient servant,
H.H.STEPHENSON

The match committee engaged in a vigorous debate. Mr Brodie said that if the local side were to be restricted to Melbourne residents, about eight of the best men in the chosen party would have to be excluded. Another member said 18 should be enough, and if they were afraid, then 'the sooner they took to petticoats, and dressed, as well as behaved, like a number of old women, the better'. Mr Rusden supported this line, saying it would appear cowardly for Victoria to field 22. Even as he spoke, a white feather in an envelope was on its way to the English captain, and the *Sydney Morning Herald* representative was writing that, far from being the frail bunch depicted by their captain, the visitors seemed 'hearty, hale, muscular, well-conditioned men and fine specimens of the English yeoman'.

The committee, after a close vote, stuck to its guns, and while the Englishmen practised this time at St Kilda's ground, some of the Melbourne CC players with them, the contretemps rumbled on. Not content with criticising the Melbourne players for their method of practice (copying the Englishmen on their initial outing by wielding rather idle bats in front of a single stump), the local Press took issue with the committee's stubbornness over the number of players the Victorian team should field.

Still dissatisfied, H.H.Stephenson, keeping wicket, had further cause to lose his equilibrium when he dislocated a finger while taking a fast one from Sewell in the practice match. With everyone having a specified time at the crease, and all the bowlers loosening themselves, 'Farmer' Bennett picked up a slight strain, and Sewell took a ferocious blow on the knee from a shot by Griffith.

Stephenson, upon receiving the match committee's unhelpful letter, wrote again on December 30, from the Café de Paris. It compelled the committee to reconvene on the last day of 1861, on the eve of the match, under the chairmanship of George Coppin at George Marshall's Cricketers' Hotel in Swanston Street.

> *Gentlemen, – I am in receipt of yours of the 28th inst., in which you inform me that you shall play twenty-two against us, and this after settling with me on the previous day that it should only be eighteen. I must again decline to play more than the latter number, for after practising for these last few days, I find the stiffness occasioned thereby has not yet worn off; indeed, some of the men can scarcely walk from this cause.*
> *I trust the brotherly feeling expressed to myself and the Eleven on board the Great Britain will induce you to treat us fairly in the matter.*
> *I am, gentlemen, your obedient servant,*
> *H.H.STEPHENSON*

There was something irresistible in this cleverly-composed communication, the forerunner of all manner of barbed letters and cables which were to be exchanged between English and Australian cricket administrators in the decades to follow, most memorably during the 1932-33 Bodyline Test series.

The secretary of the match committee had gone to see Stephenson the evening the letter arrived, and he now told his committee that the English captain, after some discussion, had agreed to play against 20 rather than 18. Nonetheless, he, the secretary, was convinced that the original English request (for Victoria to field 18) should be met.

Still they were divided. T.F.Wray, a recent Melbourne CC secretary, asserted that if they went in with only 18, not only would there be no interest in the match, but England would get 'almost an unlimited quantity of runs'. Here spoke a man whose name was among those selected to play, although the *Argus*'s pundit had suggested that the committee must have chosen him by mistake, for the balding, 34-year-old, Yorkshire-born Wray was an unreliable fieldsman, a useless bowler, and uncertain as a batsman. Then Mr Kirk, MLA told the meeting that Mr Pond had spoken of 'discourteous' behaviour towards the Englishmen, and referred to their plans to play two elevens later in the tour.

Good old Mr Rusden tried to break the deadlock by proposing that the Victorians played 18 men, in accordance with the English captain's wish. Following a couple of impudent suggested amendments, the vote was taken. Level pegging. But the casting vote of chairman George Coppin saw the proposal through. The match was on.

CHAPTER 6

Advancing Australia

ONLY A few years after this first English team had returned home, Kensington-born author Marcus Clarke, who arrived in Australia in 1863 at the age of seventeen, penned a description of Bourke Street, Melbourne and its surrounding streets and alleyways which fitted the scene when H.H.Stephenson and his cricketers were there. A conspicuous feature was the number of sewing girls and milliners' apprentices haunting the pavements at night. Neatly dressed, they passed back and forth for hours, either for amusement or 'for the purpose of making assignations'. Station-men from the Murray River had brought cattle into town, and tied up their horses before 'goin' on the bust'. Four abreast, they shuffled down the pavement, 'all booted, breeched and smoking violently'. Reeling along behind them might be half-a-dozen sailors from a passenger ship in harbour.

Clarke described a group of 'Celestials' (Chinese), pigtailed, blue-coated, mandarin-capped, 'chattering in their teeth-breaking lingo'. Down in Little Bourke Street was an opium den. On the corner of Bourke and Stephen, a preacher led some hymn-singing, while three boys busily picked pockets. 'Dirty and draggle-tailed women' appeared, while 'popular music-halls have just vomited forth a crew of drunken soldiers, prostitutes and thieves'. Cabmen were often in league with a prostitute who would take up as a passenger after an unsuspecting man had hired the vehicle. Sometimes, Clarke wrote, she succeeded in inveigling the pigeon into her house. Late at night, tobacconists' premises were still ablaze with lamps, and men entered without subsequently emerging, for many of these shops were 'blinds'. The real trade was upstairs.

By 2.30 am only a few wretched creatures wandered disconsolately on the lookout for a stray victim. 'But the policeman reigns supreme. The shutters are up and the lights of the newspaper offices are the only sign of industry. Melbourne is asleep.' It could almost have been London or Liverpool.

Wealthier Australians aimed to replicate English lifestyles, and were heavily dependent on magazines and letters which gave pointers to fashion trends. Most artists were still seeing the bushland through European eyes, and gardens were planted with English roses and wallflowers and lavender – prettier and more delicate than many of the tough indigenous flora – and imported deciduous trees. It was not only people who migrated. So did willow trees and oaks and poplars.

First settled by white men less than three-quarters of a century earlier, Australia in 1862 was a British colony that became a melting-pot of Europeans and Asians. In 1880, Warwickshire-born Sir Henry Parkes, soon to become known as the 'Father of Federation' and Grand Old Man of Australian politics, made his feelings known unequivocally when he declared: 'I object to seven Irishmen coming here to every three Englishmen.' But his dream was unrealistic.

Bourke Street, Melbourne in the early 1860s: a colourful microcosm. The Café de Paris was along on the left.

And as the 21st Century looms, the young nation trembles with anticipation of republican status.

As for the imagined Australian archetypal character/personality, although nationhood was not to be realised until 1901, almost forty years after the Stephenson tour (at which time the future first Prime Minister, Edmund Barton, was only twelve, and the first Attorney General, Alfred Deakin, was five), still there were marked differences between the colonial and his Old World cousin. 'The cultural impetus,' Keith Willey has written, 'came primarily from convict, working-class, Irish and Currency – native-born – sources, superimposed on the original British model.'

Professor Russel Ward takes up the profile description: the typical Australian is taciturn and stoical, a hard case, a great knocker of eminent and pretentious people; he is anti-authoritarian, an improviser ever ready to have a go at anything, but willing to settle for a result that is 'near enough', being too easy-going and sceptical a fellow to insist on perfection. Author Patrick O'Farrell believes that the distinctive Australian identity 'was born in Irishness protesting against the extremes of Englishness'.

'Jack is not only as good as his master, but probably a good deal better.' Such was Thomas Wood's reading of the typical colonial stance. It is supported by Willey's belief that the stereotype was there in convict times and through the gold-rush years and the decades of exploration and nation-building. 'Dinkum Aussie' resurfaced as the 'digger' in both world wars, and there was the 'battler' in the 1930s Depression years. 'Only now, perhaps, is the image fading under the hard glare of consumerism and urbanism and the cultural competition set up by waves of non-British immigrants': this written in 1989.

Yet another view was exercised by Anthony Trollope back in 1873: 'The idea that Englishmen are made of paste, whereas the Australian is steel all through, I found to be universal.' Even then, *Advance Australia Fair* was still some years away from being composed – and then by a Scot.

These were years of economic uncertainty. Blaxland, Wentworth and Lawson had long since cut across the Blue Mountains, but beyond the achievements of Flinders and Mitchell and King and Cunningham and Oxley, of the lost Leichhardt, Evans, the brave Sturt, and Hume and Hovell (who pressed on down to the coast of what was to become Victoria), there was still untold exploration to be done. The seemingly unending wilderness beckoned to be opened up. The wheat, wool and cattle industries were growing fast – as was the union movement, urged on by politically-minded Englishmen. Australia's tradition of bloody-minded strikes took root. Wages fluctuated. The eight-hour working day was established in Australia in 1856 well ahead of many other countries.

In 1861, Britain was responsible for about three-quarters of both Australia's import and export trade, each being calculated at just over £17-million. Although one of the world's most highly urbanised countries (40 percent, rising to 66 percent in the 1890s), Australia in the mid-19th Century imported most of its manufactured goods. Telegraph lines were being opened; newspapers established; Melbourne's Stock Exchange was constituted in 1861 (in which year the first public art gallery was opened in Melbourne), and Sydney's ten years later; monumental general post office buildings were on the drawing-boards in all the major cities; universities had been built; and in December 1861 Sydney had its first horse-drawn tram system (colourful vehicles which ran from Circular Quay to the railway at the other end of town, in Devonshire Street – now known as Central). Sterling was the currency, together with commercial tokens and locally-minted gold sovereigns; British troops were not to be sent home from their garrisons until 1870, the Mother Country having decided it was too costly to maintain the force and demanded in 1862 that it be paid for. Railway services were spreading from the cities (the first fatality came in 1858, at Lidcombe), the mileage of 235 in 1861 expanding to over 12,000 by 1901, the year of nationhood. And a long-range success story was beginning in Adelaide in 1856 with James Holden from Staffordshire setting up a leatherwork and saddle business which projected many years later into Australia's own famous, proudly-owned motor car manufacturers. The first bicycles were to appear on Australian roads in 1876.

Opportunities seemed unlimited as new ideas germinated. In 1861, for instance, Queensland's first sugar-cane crop was harvested. Minerals were discovered at Broken Hill; large copper deposits were found in South Australia (where Germans were establishing a wine industry); tin in Tasmania; pearls in the waters off northern Australia. Most telling by far, however, was the find made by a 6ft 5ins prospector from Gosport, Hampshire in February 1851. Edward Hargraves washed a pan of gold-bearing gravel by the water's edge at Lewis Ponds Creek, near Bathurst, NSW. Another Englishman, Louis Michel, found payable gold a few weeks later at Anderson Creek, in Victoria, and the gold rush exploded.

In the first ten years (to 1861) gold worth over $35-billion (by the values of today) was produced in the Australian fields as men searched and dug and prospered beyond their wildest dreams – or withered from frustration and disillusionment. Hysteria quickly spread. Crews jumped ship, and clerks and labourers abandoned their jobs in Melbourne to head for the allure of the goldfields. 'Men foamed at the mouth and women fainted' lamented one newspaper, and the city fell hushed and rather still as more and more hopefuls saw the world through gold-tinted glasses and gave into their instincts by seeking equipment and heading off to acquire a fortune at the diggings. When nearly half the Melbourne police force joined the rush, citizens were advised to stay at home and lock the doors.

By the end of the 1850s, more than 40,000 Chinese had flooded into Victoria, many having walked 200 miles to Ballarat and Bendigo from Robe, South Australia, a 'port of convenience' where they were able to avoid paying the landing tax of £10 per head. The cities could not cope with the influx of the transient masses. There simply was not enough accommodation. Newcomers had to pitch their tents on the outskirts of Sydney or Melbourne before acquiring gear and provisions and making for what they hoped would be a life-transforming experience. But the goldfields were no place for weaklings.

In June 1861 there had been anti-Chinese riots in the goldfields at Lambing Flat, near Young, NSW, with 1000 mobsters marching to the Orientals' quarter, brandishing 'No Chinese' flags, and hanging some of their quarry from trees by their pigtails. They abused European women who were living with the Chinese, and celebrated the attack with their band striking up *Rule Britannia*. The Government prosecuted three of the ringleaders, but a jury in Goulburn refused to convict them.

Equally well remembered was the Eureka Stockade revolt, near Ballarat, in 1854. A group of 150 angry and hungry gold-diggers, mostly Americans and Irishmen, alcohol prohibited, could stand no more police bullying and corruption, and so dug their defences to await the inevitable violent confrontation. The rebels' leader was Peter Lalor, a graduate of Trinity College, Dublin. Troops and police stormed the stockade just before dawn, and two dozen diggers and six mounted troopers were killed during the conflict. The costly message got through to Victorian Governor Hotham, who relaxed the restraints on the miners. As for the handsome Lalor, who lost an arm in the action, he became Speaker in the State Parliament, ultimately to be mockingly described as a 'smug Tory'.

All this gold served as an extra incentive to the bushrangers who roamed the country. They were not all Robin Hoods, though the customary Australian view is that they were, on the whole, a game and deserving bunch. Whether it was the lucrative and vulnerable armed gold escorts they were targeting on the bush tracks or affluent passengers in the Cobb & Co coaches, which had sprung up in Australia in 1853, these highwaymen were capable of chivalry, humour and, more commonly, a sinister terrorist approach. While the first English cricket tour was in progress, Ned Kelly was still a child of six. But some of the most notorious bushrangers were launching their careers: Frank Gardiner began in 1861, soon followed by Ben Hall. Few of the most famous survived. Brave Hall, like Johnny Gilbert and the gentlemanly 'Thunderbolt' (Fred Ward), was shot dead by a policeman, and the callous 'Black Dan' Morgan was shot by a stockman, while 'Captain Moonlight', son of a Church of England minister, was hanged in 1880, the same year as Kelly. Gardiner was jailed in 1864. The touring cricketers, on their bumpy inland coach journeys, might have reassured themselves that there was safety in numbers.

Public feeling grew strong during the 1850s on the matter of convict transportation. It was time now to stop it, thought the majority, though it was not until 1868 that the last convict ship was to land. Chain gangs were a rarer sight now, and free settlers had far outnumbered convicts for some time. There was a distinct population imbalance between the sexes, and efforts were being made to overcome the shortage of female settlers.

Thanks to the gold rush, Australia's population had doubled in the six years to 1856, reaching a million (excluding Aborigines). Almost half lived in Victoria, which was to boast 2¼-million inhabitants by 1881. When Stephenson's team arrived, Melbourne had a population of 120,000 (of which under 30 percent were Australian-born) – and most of them seem to have turned out to greet the cricketers, either at the waterfront or during the city procession.

Shipwrecks were not uncommon, fifty having occurred around Australia's extensive coastline during the ten years to 1866. *Dunbar*, which crashed into the jagged shore near Sydney's South Head lighthouse in high seas and a gale in 1857, was the most renowned, 121 perishing while one man managed to reach the rocks and survive.

In the arts, names had been made in the goldfields, among them Nicholas Chevalier, William Strutt, Eugene von Guerard, and the whimsical Samuel Thomas Gill, whose honest and animated watercolours – one showing the English cricketers' match in Sydney – provide such an important insight into Australian life as the second half of the 19th Century unfolded. Born in Somerset in 1818, Gill was to become an insatiable drinker, and he died on the steps of Melbourne Post Office in 1880 during an argument over the recent hanging of Ned Kelly. He received a pauper's burial, later made good by a proper memorial.

The next generation of notable artists were mostly still in knickerbockers in 1862: Tom Roberts, Fred McCubbin, Julian Ashton. Among writers, Henry Lawson and Banjo Paterson were yet to be born, but Henry Kendall's bush ballads (*Bell-Birds* being the most famous) were first published in 1862. Born in a bark hut in Ulladulla, Kendall remained impoverished and became completely unhinged, dying of tuberculosis in 1882. Another tragic Australian literary figure, the horseman and poet Adam Lindsay Gordon, had sailed to the colony in 1853, and was soon to give his adopted land the evocative *Sea Spray and Smoke Drift*.

In 1862 came the first attempt at a history of the slowly-flowering new land, Roderick Flanagan's succinctly titled *The History of New South Wales; with an Account of Van Diemen's Land, New Zealand, Port Phillip, Moreton Bay and Other Australian Settlements*. It was published in London.

The most distinguished infant wails while the English Eleven were in Australia emanated from the lungs of Miss Helen Porter Mitchell, the down-to-earth diva who was born in Richmond, Melbourne in May 1861. A long career in opera lay ahead for her as Dame Nellie Melba, one of the crowning moments coming when, many years hence, she was to sing the national anthem at the opening of Parliament House in Canberra in 1927.

On the general sporting front, 1861 saw the running of the first Melbourne Cup, which was won that November in front of 4000 people at Flemington by Archer at 6 to 1, ridden by Johnny Cutts. Legend has it that the horse had been walked 500 miles from Braidwood, NSW in daily stages, but was fresh and willing, and left the favourite behind by six lengths to win the £730 prize. One horse bolted, another refused to start, three fell, and two had to be destroyed. Archer won the Melbourne Cup again in the following year, despite a punishing handicap. Thus, from the beginnings in Hyde Park, Sydney in 1810 and at Raceview, Ipswich, Queensland, where the Champion Race was first held in May 1861, besides the Australasian Stakes, first run in 1859, and the first meeting at Randwick, in 1860, one of Australia's greatest passions was launched. Trotting meetings began in Melbourne in 1860.

The recently-devised Australian Rules football was also making strong headway; bowls was taking on; there had already been great sculling challenges on Sydney Harbour and the Parramatta River; and foot-racing were popular. The glorious beaches, though, were used only by fishermen. Surfing, sunbathing and lifesaving were for the future, though probably the first world's swimming championship had been held in St Kilda in 1858.

The Victoria Yacht Club had been founded in 1856. For those who were unbearably bored in the far outback, there was the hunting of emu and other exotic fauna, and for the evil-minded there was the unspeakable 'sport' of seeking and killing Aboriginals.

Settlers faced conflict not only with the harsh elements but also with hostile local tribes. The worst toll of whites occurred at Cullinlaringo, Queensland on October 17, 1861, when nineteen were slaughtered by the natives, an outrage that was swiftly and resoundingly avenged. Among the dead were close relatives of Tom Wills, the cricketer and co-inventor of Aussie Rules football, who was away when the raid took place. The tragedy caused him to miss playing in the matches against the Englishmen, though interestingly he later devoted much time and affection to coaching the Aboriginal cricketers for their 1868 tour of England.

This was the Australia encountered by H.H.Stephenson and his pioneer batsmen and bowlers as they landed in time for Christmas 1861, their curiosity intense, their legs longing for terra firma.

But Australia had been plunged into deep gloom at this time by the discovery of the remains of the explorers Robert O'Hara Burke and William John Wills, who, with a small party and some horses and camels, had set their hearts on becoming the first Europeans to cross Australia from south to north. Setting out from Melbourne, to a resounding farewell, in August 1860, they were to reach Cooper's Creek, south-west Queensland, where a forward camp was set up. Impulsively, Burke decided to cover the remaining 600 miles with only Wills and two others and supplies for twelve weeks, choosing not to wait for the remainder of the party. Making it not quite to the open sea at the Gulf of Carpentaria, they suffered all manner of cruel privations. There were squabbles, and they warded off starvation only by killing the packhorse. Somehow they made it back to Cooper's Creek, only to find that the base party had left (a mere seven hours previously), having given up on them.

Of the four explorers, Charles Gray had already died on the return journey. The rest now extended their lives with a few edibles given them by the Aboriginals, but their condition worsened. Modern thought has it that they suffered from beriberi. Burke and Wills perished, and when one of the several search parties – which themselves noted and charted much that was new in the dry, dry vastness – found the sole survivor, John King, he was 'wasted to a shadow and barely to be distinguished as a civilised being'. On December 6, 1861, Wills's skeleton was found near a box-tree, Burke's a day later. The impulsive Irishman, Burke, had left a scrawled note, asking to be done justice – for 'we fulfilled our task' – and complaining that the depot party 'abandoned their post'.

What was not as yet known in faraway Australia was that at Windsor, on December 14, the Prince Consort had also recently died (from typhoid), an unbearable loss which caused his beloved, petite Victoria to let out the most desolate cry of despair.

The freshly-arrived English cricketers will have felt and shared the sadness over Burke and Wills. But it was now time for them to fulfil *their* task by playing entertaining cricket and earning their fees as they measured their skills against what they could have been excused for supposing to be nothing but unsophisticated locals.

CHAPTER 7

The Grand Match

NEW Year's Day 1862 marked the birth of a rich and vivid tradition. The unprecedented event, a cricket match between representative English and Australian sides, was the source of a stream that would widen and deepen into a sometimes raging river, coursing out of a period when customs and attitudes were far removed from those of today but when the conflict of affection and misgivings that exists between Englishmen and their Australian cousins was already in place.

After a cool and cloudy dawn, this historic day turned out beautifully, with an azure sky and a cooling breeze from the south. The temperature slowly rose beyond the comfort level as the day progressed, and Caffyn later described how the heat was so intense that it fetched the skin off some of their faces.

From a fairly early hour, people and traffic converged on the ground in Yarra Park, the former Police Paddock, Crown land cleared in 1853 of trees, wattle and wildflowers, a seedbed now for the future gargantuan Melbourne Cricket Ground. Pedestrians, men on horseback, buggies and all other manner of horse-drawn conveyances, and some drawn by bullock, raised clouds of the white dust which was blamed on the recent Caledonian Games. With overflowing trains discharging their eager loads, it was all a sight previously unknown and unimagined in Melbourne. Horse patrols were needed to control the confusion of traffic, and a police constable stood watchfully by every entrance gate. All round the perimeter of the ground were traders and hawkers, boys selling cards (printed locally by Clarson & Shallard) bearing images of the players, with scorecards on the reverse, booths offering refreshment and serving thirst-quenching concoctions as fast as they could pour them. There were fruit stalls and sweet stalls, shooting galleries, Aunt Sallies (customers throwing balls at dummies) and even roulette wheels, while the odd barrel-organ was grinding away. On Jolimont Hill, another moneymaking opportunity had been seized by some men who set up a protective enclosure for private carriages.

An enterprising painter left his brushes and pots at home and hired out his ladder instead: for a shilling he would let you climb up into one of the surrounding gum-trees for a free view of the cricket. And for another shilling he would return later and help you down. Some of those already perched on branches teased the hesitant down below. Only one fellow fell out of the trees all day. He was taken to hospital.

A public holiday had been granted to Government office-workers, bank employees, and the mercantile community, and doubtless hundreds of others gave bogus excuses to miss work. For this was the Great International Challenge, a chance to see cricketers of a higher calibre than had ever been available before in Australia.

The crowd was massive. With no turnstiles in situ, it was left for reporters to guess at the number, but a consensus put it at between 15 and 20 thousand inside the ground and perhaps another 10,000 on the rising ground outside the surrounding picket fence, some of them up in the trees. Almost half those inside had paid half-a-crown (against a shilling ground admission) for accommodation in the enormous new grandstand, which stretched almost a third of the way around the eastern side of the ground and provided space underneath for several publicans, who had stocked up initially with 500 crates of beer. Additionally, champagne was on offer at four shillings a bottle, Scotch at three shillings. And Spiers and Pond added to their astronomical income during the match by setting up their own restaurant under the stand. (The ground had its own water supply for those with less in their pockets.) Amazingly, the promoters had covered all their tour costs by the end of this match, taking £6000 in admission money and subsidiary items, and £1000 from leases which had been auctioned out to refreshment stall-holders.

It was a memorably colourful sight. Women had viewed the day as a challenge, and wore bright, elaborate dresses, and most of the male spectators, while not resembling Regency dandies, had made an effort. There were to be no problems of drunkenness or crowd disorder, the *Argus* finding as the only cause for complaint the smoking in the grandstand, which it regarded as unfair to the ladies.

The ground was a picture, and a credit to Melbourne Cricket Club, which had begun as a village cricket club in 1838 and now had about 100 members. The smooth emerald-green turf, laid over 50 yards square by T.F.Wray in defiance of certain scepticism, had taken well, and the English cricketers were to remark favourably on it. There was simply nothing back home to compare with it. The pitch was flat after much effort with the horse-drawn roller, and the outfield had been manicured. The wooden pavilion, neatly painted and with a twin-gabled roof lending it style, provided a focus from grandstand and outer alike. Built in 1854, it was to survive until it was removed to Richmond CC's ground in 1882 at a cost of £55. It would better have been placed in Melbourne's public museum.

Around the ground were enough advertisement hoardings almost to have satisfied cricket's hungry commercial managers of the late 20th Century. There was a prominent Spiers & Pond board of course, and signs for many hotels, those run by local cricketers George Marshall, Gideon Elliott and Jerry Bryant among those clearly shown in a contemporary engraving, while McGirr's Refreshment Rooms are prominently indicated on the rare original photographs of the opening day. An elegant watercolour by Henry Burn was exhibited in the Collins Street shop window of the engravers Lawson & Pearson a few days after the match, and it was remarked that the painting had 'nearly all the correctness of a photograph, without those sombre shades of colour that distinguish sun pictures'. The point of view was the hill outside the ground, where 'several thousand persons [including the artist, of course] who did not care to pay the entrance fee were located'.

So shaky was local confidence that it was impossible to back the Victorians even at 15 to 1. Nor had the uncertainty over how many locals would be opposing

A delicate watercolour by Henry Burn (1807-84) captures the sense of occasion as Melbourne stages the first cricket match between an English and an Australian 'colonial' team.

the Englishmen encouraged betting. Melbourne CC had staged a trial match on December 21 between a United Victoria XI and Sixteen of the City of Bourke, with Bryant the beneficiary. Dick Wardill, no longer a careless slasher but equipped now with a sound defence, top-scored with 58, and Cosstick, Conway and Stewart showed encouragingly as bowlers. The ground had been dug on three sides of the newly-laid turf only the day before, for water-pipes to be laid, but had recovered quickly. Flags were placed around the chain fence for the first time, and the ground overall 'presented a gay appearance'. 'Tiny' Wells, the 'avant courier' of the All England XI, had umpired, as he was to do in the big match following.

After the trial, 20 players had been selected for the Victorian combination, with a further two to come from the six named in support. From those 26 named in the newspapers, eight were to lose their place in history when a team of 18 (only two of them born in Australia) was agreed at the eleventh hour. The scorer was named as C.Hipwell, and the local umpire was J.A.Smith. Years later, during the thrilling Test match at Melbourne in January 1908, won by England by one wicket, Tom Horan came across Jack Smith in the members' area. Smith, Horan wrote, 'goes back to the real early days of cricket in Victoria'. He had now come in from Mount Blackwood for the Test, and Horan ('Felix') was surprised and pleased to see him looking so well, 'for fully five years back I had heard that he was in poor health'.

The reservations about the local cricketers' ability to compete against the English professionals touched the organisers too, to the extent that they felt obliged to line up some supplementary sporting entertainment in the form of athletics events for prizes. The relief was widespread when the grand cricket match stretched into a fourth day.

There was a buzz from the northern end of the grandstand. The players had arrived. At 11.15, escorted by Christopher Pond, the English cricketers, caps raised and smiling, made their way through the cheering mass. The sight caught the emotions of the *Argus* reporter, who felt that the 'champions of the dear old land' were generating something greater than a welcome: he felt that the demonstration was a sign of 'blood and brotherhood'. He was also concerned for the players' safety as the crowd came close to smothering them as they struggled to reach the room set aside for them under the stand. It was, he declared, a triumph of emotion over good manners. The Victorian players, who had been practising, returned to their tent, and seem to have been less troubled by the fans.

Sir Henry Barkly, Governor of Victoria.

The ground was cleared at 11.45, for the first day's play was due to start at noon. But at that hour there was still no sign of the Governor, Sir Henry Barkly, and his entourage. His Excellency may have been held up in traffic, but all was forgiven when he made his stately entrance into the Vice-Regal box, which was positioned at the centre of the new stand. It was draped in blazing red, with the Royal coat of arms at its head. The national anthem, *God Save the Queen*, was played, the crowd silent throughout, and when the band ceased playing, a tremendous burst of cheering rent the air. Having lost the toss, the Englishmen – Caffyn the first to step into the field, closely followed by Griffith and the rest, with captain Stephenson coming last, considered then to be the position of honour – had already followed umpires Smith and Wells onto the field, where they warmed up pending the arrival of the Governor. Mortlock's catching impressed in particular. H.H.Stephenson now led his men in three hearty cheers for the Governor, who graciously signalled the start of the first-ever Anglo-Australian contest.* It was 12.20 pm on Wednesday, January 1, 1862.

---

* *Pedantically speaking, this might be said to have occurred in Hyde Park, Sydney in February 1830, when 11 soldiers of the 57th (West Middlesex) Regiment, for a £20 wager, played against 11 civilians, eight of whom had been born in Sydney.*

The full England team, with their promoters, who made it all possible: from left –
George Wells, Felix Spiers, George Bennett (seated), William Mortlock, Roger Iddison,
William Caffyn, W.B.Mallam, H.H.Stephenson (seated), Tom Sewell, George Griffith,
William Mudie, Edwin Stephenson (seated), Christopher Pond, Charles Lawrence,
Tom Hearne. Photograph by T.A.Hill of Bourke Street, Melbourne.

The Englishmen, in helmet-type sunhats with identity ribbons of various colours to   match those listed on the scorecards, took up their positions: H.H.Stephenson (orange) as wicketkeeper, Mortlock (pink) long-stop (Hearne long-stopping at the other end to save time), Lawrence (magenta) slip, Sewell (mauve) 'long slip' or short third man, Iddison (brown) point, Bennett (pale blue) cover, Ned Stephenson (white) mid-off, Hearne (black) mid-on, Griffith (pale yellow) long leg, and Mudie (dark green) short leg.

To Billy Caffyn (dark blue ribbon) fell the honour of bowling the first ball. The honour of facing it went to James 'Jerry' Bryant, which was a generous gesture on the part of his captain, George Marshall, his opening partner. Both were English-born, Marshall in Nottingham 32 years previously. He had emigrated in 1854, having earned some money from cricket without making a name for himself at home. Now, however, he was a cricketer of stature, skipper of the colony, regarded as the best wicketkeeper in Australia, and an aggressive, sometimes rash, batsman. According to Fairfax's *Australian Cricketer's Guide* of 1858-59, 'a shooter is a very fatal ball to him'. The ball which hardly left the ground was no uncommon thing in 19th Century cricket, and top batsmen had to know how to handle it.

Marshall, who was to promote the next English tour, in 1863-64, for Melbourne CC, was to be at the centre of a frightening argument in the

intercolonial match in Sydney in 1863, when his appeal for a run-out, which smacked of gamesmanship, was disallowed. In the ensuing uproar, a stone or two was thrown at the players as they left the field, and Marshall, having walked out of the match and persuaded one of his team-mates to do likewise, was threatened physically back at the hotel. Insults in both directions in the press inevitably included Victorian references to Sydney's convict tradition. The sometimes acrimonious interstate rivalry still observed today was establishing firm roots. New South Wales, captained in 1863 by Charles Lawrence, declined to play against their southern rivals for two years.

On New Year's Day 1862, Marshall, Swanston Street hotelier and sports-shop proprietor, organiser of Australia's first professional cricketers' association, who was to die only six years later, was now enjoying his proudest hour, opening the innings against the illustrious English visitors. His partner, Jerry Bryant, came from Surrey farming stock. Now 35, he had played for his native county before coming to Australia, like so many others, with gold fever, only to have been forced to seek a more secure occupation. Bryant's groundsmanship skills stood him in good stead, for he ended up being employed by Melbourne CC, and he was now about to sort out East Melbourne's ground for them, ploughing it up and sowing rye-grass, the only setback being the theft of the 36 trees planted there – and their replacements too.

Bryant was a popular cricketer. He was rather obsessed with the cut shot, but his bowling was based on a 'beautiful, easy delivery' (H.W.Hedley), and he was hard to beat at single-wicket. He became mine host of the Parade Hotel in Richmond Road before moving to Sale and taking another pub. Things then started to go wrong, and he became entangled in legal proceedings. He died in Sale in 1881, aged 55.

Nettleton's precious photograph, showing the extensive new grandstand, and probably shot at the start of play, with All England in the field. The originals of this and the two which follow are in the author's personal collection.

Caffyn's inaugural ball was played defensively by an undoubtedly tense Bryant, and indecision to the second ball almost led to Marshall's run-out. The first over of four balls was a maiden, and the field spread as slow bowler 'Farmer' Bennett began from the end opposite the pavilion. When Marshall drove his second ball towards Ned Stephenson on the off side, the first run for an Australian team against an English was recorded, to cheering which must have echoed that at the launch of SS *Great Britain*.

The series of 'firsts' flowed fast. When Bryant was hit on the body, the English captain cried 'How's that, umpire?', but the appeal was turned down. The batsman was 'caught' at slip off a bump ball, which fooled the crowd. And Mudie failed to get to a lofted drive by Marshall. In the 14th over, with the total 25 and local confidence rising, the first wicket fell, Bryant (11) being lbw. Bennett, the Kentish man who might have come close to transportation in his youth, thus claimed the credit for first blood.

The Ballarat batsman, John Sweeney, came in at No.3, and in the 18th over the first boundary was hit, Marshall driving Bennett to the grandstand. Stephenson now made the first bowling change, relieving Caffyn, whose arm was still paining him after the mosquito attacks. With his third ball 'Ben' Griffith, his replacement, had Marshall caught by Iddison at point for 27 off his lively left-arm roundarm: 42 for 2. In came 'Kit' Mace, a Bedale man, like Iddison, with whom he had once played. He had set out for the Victorian goldfields in the 1850s with three of his brothers, played cricket for the colony, and was to move on soon, part of an extensive family, in search of gold around Otago, New Zealand. There he

Another of Nettleton's photographs, this time with Eighteen of Victoria in the field, and showing the outer ground beyond. Below: Kit Mace.

prospered in business, and found himself playing against another English touring team, George Parr's 1863-64 combination. Mace lived to 76, dying in New Zealand in 1907.

Now, young Mace strove to make an impression, but after driving Griffith for three and then just avoiding a run-out off Mudie's throw, he moved forward to Griffith and was smartly stumped by the English captain for 5: 55 for 3, and the early promise fading. There was a brief stoppage for refreshments before the 23-year-old Jack Huddlestone took strike, a brilliant batsman who had made his name with the huge score of 142 in a match for Richmond in the previous season. If he was somewhat distracted now as he faced the Englishmen, for the roller had passed over his left foot just before the start, he was to be even

further tested a year later when he was out first ball in both innings in the intercolonial match at Sydney. Huddlestone lived till 1904.

He began well, soon driving Griffith to the boundary by the shilling reserve. But an almighty collapse was imminent. Huddlestone on-drove one of Bennett's teasers and was neatly caught by Sewell. Entered Dick Wardill, only 21 and with a dramatic and short life to come (batting triumphs, including the first century in Australian first-class cricket – on this ground, against New South Wales in 1867 – embezzlement, and suicide in the Yarra in 1873). The crowd were disappointed further when Wardill was run out first ball, hitting to Ned Stephenson and having a misunderstanding with his cautious partner Sweeney, who himself was soon out too, leg-before to Griffith for a hard-earned 16: 67 for 6.

Charles Makinson, 'one of our prettiest players', had come in after Wardill, both Lancashire-born, but he too fell without scoring. In the 42nd over, bowled by Bennett, Makinson's 'bails fell' as the *Argus* man delicately put it. Tom Morres, Berkshire-born, had come in to an especially warm reception, and was now joined by Sam Cosstick, yet another immigrant, and equally popular. Cosstick was born in Croydon, and today was his 26th birthday. He was another who had been lured to Australia by gold, but he found a long career in cricket instead, becoming a well-loved professional bowler at £3.10.0d a week with Melbourne CC (who sacked him for drunkenness, later reinstating him), playing in the intercolonials and taking 11 wickets against New South Wales in his debut match in 1861, and 8 for 109 when he first represented New South Wales, against

England batting, left-hander Griffith on strike, the pavilion to the left.

his old colony four years later. He soon returned to the Victorian ranks, and took 6 for 1 against Tasmania when they were bowled out for 18 in 1869, and 8 for 21 against New South Wales, and 9 for 61 (all bowled) against a Combined XIII in 1872, all this before a couple of run-ins with W.G.Grace when the English champion first toured Australia. At Sydney, Cosstick refused to leave after dismissal, causing WG to take his men off, and in an exhibition match he grew frustrated at WG's batting and threw a delivery at him. 'Old Sam' Cosstick was an accomplished drinker, but he knew his cricket inside out, and at the end of Grace's 1873-74 tour he was to utter a fairly accurate prediction: 'Bar WG, we're as good as they are, and some day we'll lick 'em with eleven!' Cosstick had the honour of umpiring the second of all Tests, at the MCG in 1877. 'Old Hoss' died at 60, in 1896, in West Maitland, NSW, where he had been a groundsman.

He avoided inclusion among the numerous ducks gathering at the MCG on his 26th birthday, but not by much. After Bennett had beaten Morres by change of pace, Cosstick too became a victim, spooning the slow bowler to Mudie on the leg side.

Gideon Elliott, in upon Morres's dismissal, hit Bennett wide of Mortlock at deep mid-off for a rare four. Here was another cricketer of great repute. Yet another Surrey-born, and yet another seeker after gold when his ship came in, Elliott was now 33, and as finely bewhiskered as any of his contemporaries. He

was a fast roundarm bowler who struck fear into even the bravest when operating on substandard pitches. A batsman required 'a quick eye to dispose of his shooters and bumpers' (Fairfax). He secured what could be construed to this day as the most wonderful bowling analysis ever in first-class cricket, 9 for 2 off 19 overs. It was for Victoria against Tasmania at Launceston in 1857-58, and on not the finest of surfaces the local team were shot out for 33. Gid Elliott had begun his intercolonial career with figures of 7 for 25 against New South Wales at Melbourne in March 1856. But by now, still mourning for his brother George, who was among those slaughtered by Aborigines at Cullinlaringo 11 weeks earlier, he had already left his best days behind him. He was to die seven years later, at 40. Melbourne CC had tried to help him by appointing him as 'pavilion-keeper'. But he had helped himself rather too much, it seems, when he took over the Royal Hotel in Punt Road, Richmond.

Griffith now bowled him out, and Tom Wray, whose selection had been criticised, joined James Thompson, a Yorkshireman famed for his hitting, one of 11 Melbourne CC players in the side, and the first editor of *Sands & Kenny's Cricketer's Guide*, whose editor was now W.J.Hammersley. (It was Hammersley, in the *Guide* and also as 'Longstop' in his newspaper column, who first coined the expression 'test matches', designating as such the five principal contests during this inaugural English tour. It was to be many years before the term gained universal currency.) By now the 50th over was about to be bowled, and

Thompson – who wrote of himself that he was 'a good bat, but a little too sweet upon his back-play' – marked it with a strong drive off Bennett that eluded Lawrence, and they ran three. The last ball beat Elliott, and another appeal went up, but was not granted. It was half-past-two, and time for lunch. Fifty four-ball overs had been bowled in the 130 minutes, the equivalent of only 33 six-ball overs, though the shorter over meant that more time was lost in changeovers.

It was a long interval, for a banquet had been laid on for the Governor and about 200 guests in a pavilion behind the grandstand. Sir Henry Barkly made it clear in his speech that he wanted the Victorians to do well, and naturally extolled the virtues of cricket, saying that although some had complained that Messrs Spiers and Pond might have made better use of their money by building a reformatory or a railway, cricket contributed much to the education of body and mind. There was, quite properly, no shortage of toasts and speeches, though the masses outside, circling the arena, had finished their eating and drinking long before play resumed at 3.45 pm, a break of 75 minutes. The Queen, the Governor, the English team (responded to succinctly by Stephenson), and Spiers and Pond (response by William Mallam) and the Victorian Eighteen were all toasted, George Marshall causing guffaws when he expressed the hope that his Victorians would put up a better showing than the Americans had made on the cricket field against the English touring team in 1859. Then it was back to business

Ten down at lunch, the Victorians soon lost their remaining seven wickets. Thompson slipped and should have been run out, but bowler Griffith missed the return throw. He caught-and-bowled Wray, though, which brought in the Geelong player Simon Rennie, who made 9 and stayed with Thompson for about 20 minutes before Bennett had him leg-before: 112 for 12.

Next in was John (Jack) Conway, a man whose part in cricket history was to become unusually significant, for not only was he a leading fast bowler and slip fieldsman who would make his first-class debut for Victoria (together with Mace, Thompson and Wardill) at the MCG in a week's time and take a lot of wickets in his first few matches, but his later role was as a leading organiser of tours, acting independently of the resentful Melbourne and Sydney cricket authorities. He was liaison man for the first English Test team to tour Australia (1876-77) and for others to follow, and managed the lengthy, risky and demanding first (white) Australian tour of Britain – and New Zealand and America – in 1877-78, when the team, formed as a private joint-stock company, was away for all of fourteen months. Conway wrote on cricket (as 'Censor') in a strong, lucid style, and the annuals he edited in the late 1870s are today great rarities. Chief among the cricketers he discovered and encouraged was Jack Blackham, the great wicketkeeper. Conway, a brawny footballer too, was born in Victoria – one of only two in this 1862 match to have been true locals – and he died in his native State in 1909, aged 67. His difficult stance in the Australian cricket rumpus during the 1884-85 Test series – about money, of course – left him with few friends. Only seven attended his funeral.

All this lay far ahead as he walked to the middle . . . and was soon walking back again, run out without scoring. Left-hander James Stewart replaced him, and

George Marshall, captain of the Victorians; Tom Morres, allrounder who was among the failures in the Grand Match; and Will Hammersley, player and writer, who coined the expression 'test match'.

Key Melbourne players Gid Elliott, Jerry Bryant and Tom Wray.

J.B.Thompson, editor and cricketer.

Jack Conway, who was to become a major figure in the development of Australian cricket.

was bowled by Griffith for a single, and Sam Hopkinson, born in Yorkshire 36 years before, betraying the nerviness that must have afflicted so many of the players, became the third to be run out for nought, fellow Yorkie Ned Stephenson being the fieldsman. Thompson's bright innings of 17 – second-highest to Marshall's 27 – ended when he hit his wicket, leaving 29-year-old Rochdale-born Ben Butterworth, the renowned long-stop, and his last-wicket partner George Jeremiah Patrick O'Mullane (a rare native-born, only nineteen, who was to keep wicket and score 33 not out at No.11 in his only intercolonial match four years hence; his life ended a year after that). Butterworth, who had made four ducks in his two intercolonial appearances for Victoria, now instigated another pair, skying Griffith, who held the catch to finish with 7 for 30. Bennett had taken 7 for 53 with slows that were 'most annoying and difficult, very dangerous' (*Melbourne Herald*), and the Victorian 18 were all out for 118 in the 75th over. H.H.Stephenson's wicketkeeping had been 'perfect'. It was just before 5 o'clock, and as more cheers resounded, and some spectators rushed towards the players leaving the field, many went home in the belief that that was the end of the entertainment for the day.

Ten minutes later, the Victorians took the field, all in the uniform straw-coloured, red-spotted shirts and round dove-coloured hats trimmed with magenta ribbons. The English openers, Ned Stephenson and George Bennett (who had already bowled 37 overs of guile that afternoon), soon followed. But before play could proceed, the photographer, Mr C.Nettleton, had some business to perform. He set up his tripod and shot the historic scene from several angles, while the players and umpires obediently froze. Nettleton then adjourned to his horse-drawn travelling darkroom, and on the third day, Christopher Pond was able to

show the prints to Sir Redmond Barry, the Irish-born judge and Chancellor of Melbourne University, who 'expressed much satisfaction' with the photographs and was promised a series of views of the All England match to be placed in the Victorian compartment of the Great Exhibition in May. His Honour himself was a generous chap, having launched Melbourne's public library with a gift of many books from his personal collection. In 1841 he had displayed gallantry in a duel with fellow original Melbourne CC member Peter Snodgrass. Sir Redmond, Victoria's first Solicitor-General, and father of four illegitimate offspring, was the judge who, having jailed Ned Kelly's mother in 1878, sentenced her outlaw son to death in 1880 – and died twelve days after him, perhaps the victim of Kelly's curse.

Sir Redmond Barry: followed Ned Kelly to the grave.

The eighteen Victorians spread

themselves over the field, Butterworth at long-stop, the key position he had made his own, while Marshall kept wicket, Makinson stood at point, and the rest were 'judiciously placed'. Conway hurled down the first ball, and Bennett faced it. The over was a maiden. Ned Stephenson then took strike to Cosstick, also fast roundarm, and scored England's first-ever run off Australian bowling by playing the draw shot to the fourth ball for a single. He employed the 'draw' to both sides of the wicket, while Bennett opened his score by what the *Argus* defined as a cut 'sharply to leg'. Tom Huddlestone, substituting for his brother because of the injured foot, fielded well, as did the rest, and with the Englishmen taking no risks, play was quiet in the closing stages. Conway, who had bowled three wides, was replaced by Bryant for the 21st over of the innings, and the last for the day, for 6 o'clock had come. All England were 18 without loss, both batsmen 6.

So obviously successful and lucrative had this opening day of the first Anglo-Australian cricket match been that Spiers and Pond – or so it is believed – were offered the mammoth sum of £15,000 to sell the remainder of the tour. There was no deal. As it was, the hefty first-day takings nearly went up in smoke, for curator Rowland Newbury was so worried about security when he got the money home that he could think of nowhere safer to conceal it than the oven in the kitchen. His daughter was just about to light the oven fire to bake some bread when her frantic Scottish father dashed in and narrowly averted a catastrophe.

The attendance for the second day's play was almost as huge as for the first, and the weather remained beautiful – for those who liked blue sky, high temperature and a touch of southerly breeze. The

Sam Cosstick: full of confidence.

85

players came out a few minutes after noon, to another genuinely enthusiastic greeting, and this time there was no Thompson or Huddlestone, both injured; Blanchard and Ryan substituting. The pitch and surrounds looked good after Sam Cosstick's overnight attentions, but the scorers' tent had been moved a little so that those in the grandstand could see the names on the nearby telegraph board. Yesterday, they had been obliged to use fieldglasses to pick out the score on the distant other scoreboard.

Against the bowling of Cosstick and Bryant, Ned Stephenson and Bennett batted very cautiously, at one point scoring no runs for six overs, apart from a bye when the ball eluded Marshall and hit Butterworth, the long-stop, in the face. A kind of spell was being cast over opponents and onlookers alike, for defensive cricket was almost unheard of in the crude environs of Australian cricket. 'Scientific' was the adjective used by patient and absorbed spectators, who had drawn confidence from the Victorians' total of 118 yesterday, a feeling shared by bookmakers, who put England at 4 to 1. A leg-side boundary to Bennett and a straight-hit four to 'Yorkshire' Stephenson broke the tense silence.

Stewart (fairly fast) and Conway (brisk) took up the attack, with occasional gusts of breeze raising the dust. The much-maligned Wray saved a boundary, but Stephenson struck Stewart into McGirr's tearooms for four shortly before a refreshment break, which dragged on for ten minutes. All England's first wicket fell at last in the 46th over when Bennett was held by Butterworth (fielding so well at long-stop, and inspired, it was suggested, by having the world's best in that position, Mortlock, looking on). Bennett's 11 in an opening stand of 44 had taken an eternity, but the tempo rose with a cut to the pavilion by Mudie and a handsome four to Stephenson, though in which direction it is hard to say, for the *Argus* assured its readers that the Yorkshireman had made a 'beautiful cut to square leg'. Patriotic Victorians were soon uplifted as Conway struck again, bowling Stephenson for 34 to make it 59 for 2.

Mudie was joined by Griffith, and there was a stir of anticipation, with Marshall spreading the field. The chunky left-hander, the 'Lion Hitter', would surely speed up the run rate? He did so, but kept his head down, stabbing twos and threes through the army of fieldsmen, while Mudie played with some elegance, and a straight bat that was seldom seen in the new land. Wardill fielded one ball and had it back sharply to the keeper, suggesting that the Eighteen were far from being all outclassed apprentices. When a disturbance on the hill had troopers advancing into the crowd, few took any notice, such was the attraction of the batsmanship on view, particularly Griffith's. With Makinson fielding well at point, it was high-quality cricket. The occasional ball found the edge of the bat, but the runs accumulated, with every ten on the scoreboard bringing applause. The Victorians had their chance to get rid of the dangerous Griffith when he lofted one between Wray and Stewart. Marshall shouted for Stewart to take the catch, but the fieldsmen ended up leaving it to each other.

All England were 94 for 2 when the dinner bell was rung at 2.20 pm, and it was time again for speechmaking in the marquee. In the chair was the Premier of Victoria, the Hon. W.C.Haines, a trustee of Melbourne CC, resplendent in

The only other known photograph of the match, published in the 1920s, demonstrates how easy it was to get a distant view of proceedings.

mutton-chop whiskers, who sat between the two captains, and after demolishing the cold collation, spoke of having seen most of the Englishmen play in their homeland. Acknowledging that Lockyer and Hayward would have been welcome inclusions, still, he said, England had sent a fine team, and it would surely be some time before Australia could match them 11 a side. He hoped that 1862 would come to be remembered as the year when cricket in Australia made a great advance. He urged the cricketers to speak well of Australia when they returned home. That, he believed, would be better than sending immigration lecturers.

The skippers responded briefly, and Felix Spiers registered a hope that the Englishmen would also speak well of him and his partner when they returned, a plea that must have struck some as gratuitous.

While all this was going on, the rest of the English players had taken the field to practise, surprisingly supported by several slightly bashful policemen, who formed an 'open parallelogram' and tried to be helpful by fielding stray balls. Some saw it as comical, especially when their professional 'imperturbable gravity' was taken into account, and a few mocking remarks floated from the outer. Some boys were then emboldened to go onto the field, so that the English cricketers never had to run after a ball. The breeze abated, the temperature rose further, and fleecy white clouds patterned the blueness above. And the *Argus* man noted that not a Chinaman could be seen anywhere.

A few overs after resumption at 3.35 pm, the hundred having been given an echoing cheer, replacing Bryant, Gid Elliott bowled for the first time, held back by Marshall for some reason, and for the 100th over, Morres came on. Elliott, the man with the reputation, then bowled Mudie off his leg for 22, which brought in

Caffyn, probably the best batsman to date ever to set foot in Australia. It was 4.20 pm, All England, three down, were almost up with the Victorians' total, and almost as if he had learned of Caffyn's arrival, the Governor now entered the ground. The batsman, applauded by the fieldsmen, pretended not to hear the semi-distant national anthem.

'Morres,' the *Argus* reported, 'opened the 107th over with a wide, and thus prevented a maiden.' George Marshall now decided to have a bowl, giving the wicketkeeping gloves to Sweeney, and Griffith and Caffyn moved up a gear. The left-hander powered Elliott to the hill fence, and Caffyn hit a four with his own distinctive touch, the pair, batting 'in true Surrey fashion', seeming impregnable . . . until Cosstick came back and had Griffith caught by long-stop, presumably off a top-edge, after Bryant had first tried for the catch. The left-hander had taken the maiden fifty in Anglo-Australian cricket up to 61, including one mighty leg-side blow off Cosstick over the chain fence between the weatherboard pavilion and McGirr's bar, the ball reaching the gates. Five runs were awarded. 'Ben' Griffith was given a stirring ovation as he left the field.

At 161 for 4 in came Iddison, the roast-beef Yorkshireman, who matched Caffyn confidently stroke for stroke, with the sixteen fielders scattered for Makinson's slow and innocent bowling. All England were 185 for 4 – 67 ahead – when stumps were drawn soon after 6 o'clock, Caffyn 33, Iddison 9, another blissfully happy homeward-wending crowd chattering about the best batting many of them had ever watched, and remembering the best rather than the worst of the Victorian fielding. The sophisticated cricket folk among them will have noted that the Englishmen did not look so underprepared after all following their long sea voyage, while the *Melbourne Herald* observer contented himself with the comment that 'no conception can be formed of the excellence of Caffyn's play until it is seen.'

The expectation was that the match would be over on the third day, though the weather at the start was threatening: heavy cloud, strong wind. The crowd was not so great, though it built up during the afternoon probably to five figures, with the grandstand only just over half-full. The pavements outside the newspaper offices in the city were still home to surging crowds of curious passers-by who searched for the latest score. The *Sydney Mail* confirmed that 'the English news received during the Crimean war was never looked for with more eagerness and interest than was the score of the match between the All England XI and the Eighteen of Melbourne'.

Play was due to begin at noon, but with Caffyn and Iddison already on the field, the Victorians straggled out in twos and threes, attracting shame and causing irritation. It was a major talking point, and among the written complaints was one in the *Argus* from 'TW', who may well have been Tom Wills: ' . . . I believe that they have as much to learn in the command of themselves as in batting and fielding . . . ' He made a telling point when he wrote apropos the long drinks breaks that 'the apology that it was warm weather would seem an insufficient excuse, when it was seen that the visitors from a colder clime were not so much inconvenienced by the heat as to require such frequent libations.'

The Victorian 18 did at least do the Governor proud when he and Lady Barkly arrived soon after the resumption of play, following the example of the two batsmen by raising their caps during the playing of the national anthem. But they continued to annoy during the day by adjourning to the booths for drinks, sometimes leaving the batsmen in the middle for as long as ten minutes. Some of the growling onlookers began to wonder if Marshall was trying to string out time in order to draw the game, for the Victorians were slowly and emphatically being played into a hopeless position, the pitch wearing, bounce becoming unreliable.

Elliott was Marshall's best hope among his bowlers, and he continued his toils, backed by keen fielding by Wardill, Makinson and Butterworth, but when Makinson bowled more of his uncomplicated slow stuff, Caffyn and Iddison feasted themselves, much of it being dispatched through square leg. Relief came through fast bowler Conway, who took over from Elliott and bowled Iddison (31) with a 'ripper'. In came H.H.Stephenson, to special applause, but after tapping a two to square leg and watching Cosstick bowl a couple of maidens to Caffyn, the England captain was bowled by a shooter from Conway, and at 220 for 6 the dominant position was a touch less marked.

But Lawrence, the new batsman, took instant command, while Caffyn remained an elegant fixture. Runs came, four of them when Caffyn cut Conway for what seemed a boundary, though there were enough cries from the crowd to prompt umpire 'Tiny' Wells and scorer Hipwell to go across to examine the spot where Stewart had stopped the ball. The boundary was given. (Today, a video replay would have sorted it out, though perhaps not as animatedly.) Caffyn's next trick was to drive a four and, 'fairly obliged to rest himself', to take to the turf and roll about on it, 'an act of luxurious indulgence which was hugely relished and uproariously laughed at and applauded by general consent of the spectators'.

Stewart for the hapless Makinson, Bryant for Conway, and when the bell rang for lunch just after 2 pm, All England were strongly placed with 270 for 6 off 194 overs, 152 runs ahead.

Melbourne CC president Thomas F.Hamilton, top-scorer with 35 in the first-ever intercolonial, in Launceston in 1851, was in the chair this day, several members of the Legislative Council being among the guests, and he proposed a toast to The Cricketers of Old England. He said he was sure that as long as England brought up her sons to the good old game of cricket she would be able to defy the world. The colony's cricketers would recollect the year 1862 and bless Old England for sending out a team which proved that one must go to England for the best of everything. The president then coupled with his toast the name of William Caffyn, who acknowledged with a few words.

Mr O'Shanassy, MLA then proposed a sympathetic toast to the Victorian cricketers, remarking that if they were to receive a 'sound thrashing' it was at least at parental hands; 'and when the English XI returned home they would be able to say that they had left some promising children behind them'. As far as can be told, no double entendre was intended.

After D.S. (Dalmahoy) Campbell had reminisced about cricket in the colony over the past 22 years, Mr Heales, MLA toasted Spiers and Pond, the latter once more responding, this time emphasising that he had not been actuated by a selfish desire alone when entering upon the present undertaking. He had merely wished to spend, for the benefit of the public, the money he had made from them in business.

The *Argus* was indignant on its readers' behalf at the 'abominable' waste of time created by the almost 1½-hour lunch, the restive crowd being distracted only by the practice conducted by the Englishmen who had not yet batted. Then, just as irritatingly, the English batsmen had to wait in the field until the Victorians belatedly roused themselves to join them. It was 3.40 pm. Lawrence, whose confidence and stylishness were evident even as he played out maiden overs, hit a four to leg, but soon afterwards the prize wicket was captured as Caffyn, on 79, was caught by O'Mullane off James Stewart. That made it 278 for 7, and the Surrey batsman 'cast a lingering look at his destroyer' before heading off for the dressing-room, to wholehearted applause. It was a notable innings, something to natter about as he clipped away at his customers' hair a few years from now.

Tubby Tom Sewell took Caffyn's place, but now Lawrence's contribution ended at 20 – which was to be his highest score of the tour – as Conway caught him at slip off Bryant. Ten quiet overs went by before Sewell (3) was bowled by Stewart, and with last man Hearne joining Mortlock, the crowd were already missing the quality batting of the earlier men. Hearne managed a boundary, and after sloppy work by Bryant to a return by Cosstick had given Mortlock a six with overthrows, the long innings ended when Stewart picked up his third wicket, bowling out England's oldest player, Tom Hearne, in the 220th over. The total, 305, gave them a lead of 187 after virtually two days' batting, and was a bonanza in the context of the runs currency of the era. It would have surprised everybody, nonetheless, that such a score was not to be realised again on the tour.

So keen had the Victorians been to avoid batting that evening that they had followed a refreshment break over in Bryant's pavilion with another not much later in their captain George Marshall's on the other side of the ground. 'It was impossible that they could be thirsty,' protested the *Argus*. But at 5.30 pm England were in the field, and Jack Huddlestone and Kit Mace were kind enough to take their bats out to join them in due course.

They survived until the 6 o'clock cessation, stealing seven runs from Griffith and Lawrence. Bennett was missing, nursing a strain first felt in practice at St Kilda and reactivated by his marathon spell on the opening day, local cricketer-cum-journalist Hammersley taking his place in the field; and when Mudie had two fingers damaged on his right hand while intercepting a powerful hit by Huddlestone, he had to leave the field, the batsman's brother, Tom, substituting.

The fourth day, Saturday, January 4, 1862, saw All England still with two substitutes, Greeves (a 'companion' to the touring Englishmen, who was soon making blunders in the field) taking over from Hammersley, who was not only out of practice but probably had a column to write. Although victory beckoned, the English captain might have been concerned at the growing injury toll.

Lawrence's slow bowling seemed fairly innocuous after Bennett's sinister stranglehold on the first day. But Iddison looked a threat. However, the Victorian

From this animated impression of the first international match, some idea may be gained of the number of booths and advertisements around the ground. On the extreme left can just be seen the steam train.

MELBOURNE CRICKET GROUND, January 1, 2, 3, 4, 1862

Toss won by Victoria   Umpires: J.A.Smith & G.Wells

EIGHTEEN OF VICTORIA

J.M.Bryant	lbw b Bennett	11	[4] b Sewell		0
*G.Marshall	c Iddison b Griffith	27	[5] c Mortlock b Sewell		0
J.Sweeney	lbw b Griffith	16	c Lawrence b Sewell		0
C.Mace	st H.H.Stephenson b Griffith	5	[2] b Sewell		20
J.Huddlestone	c Sewell b Bennett	6	[1] c Iddison b Sewell		18
R.W.Wardill	run out (E.Stephenson)	0	[10] c Lawrence b Griffith		18
C.Makinson	b Bennett	0	[9] run out		0
T.F.Morres	b Bennett	0	[16] run out		0
S.Cosstick	c Mudie b Bennett	8	[12] c Iddison b Griffith		11
J.B.Thompson	hit wkt b Bennett	17	[6] run out		0
G.Elliott	b Griffith	4	[14] c Iddison b Sewell		8
T.F.Wray	c & b Griffith	3	[7] c H.H.Stephenson b Iddison		0
S.S.Rennie	lbw b Bennett	9	[8] c Lawrence b Iddison		0
J.Conway	run out	0	[15] st H.H.Stephenson b Caffyn		1
J.C.Stewart	b Griffith	1	[11] b Iddison		0
S.G.Hopkinson	run out (E.Stephenson)	0	[13] c Bennett b Caffyn		13
B.Butterworth	c & b Griffith	0	[18] c Iddison b Sewell		0
G.J.P.O'Mullane	not out	0	[17] not out		0
Extras	b 7 lb 3 w 1	11	w 2		2
Totals		**118**			**91**

Fall: 1/25 2/42 3/55 4/66 5/66 6/67 7/67 8/71   1/37 2/37 3/37 4/37 5/39 6/39 7/39 8/39
9/75? 10/75? 11/80? 12/112 13/112?   9/48 10/48 11/67 12/81 13/84 14/?
14/113? 15/117 16/117? 17/118   15/? 16/? 17/91

2nd innings: Sweeney given as c Iddison and Cosstick given as c E.Stephenson in some sources

Bowling	Balls	Wides	Runs	Wickets		Balls	Wides	Runs	Wickets
Caffyn	36	0	23	0	Griffith	41	1	9	2
Bennett	148	0	53	7	Lawrence	44	0	31	0
Griffith	116	1	30	7	Sewell	104	1	20	7
Bowling plus extras makes 117					Iddison	88	0	24	3
					Caffyn	28	0	5	2

ALL ENGLAND XI

G.Bennett	c Butterworth b Conway	11	*Bowling*	*Balls*	*Wides*	*Runs*	*Wickets*
E.Stephenson	b Conway	34	Conway	204	5	60	4
W.Mudie	b Elliott	22	Cosstick	124	1	31	1
G.Griffith	c Butterworth b Cosstick	61	Bryant	196	0	33	1
W.Caffyn	c O'Mullane b Stewart	79	Stewart	153	4	50	3
R.Iddison	b Conway	31	Elliott	101	1	48	1
*H.H.Stephenson	b Conway	2	Makinson	60	0	43	0
C.Lawrence	c Conway b Bryant	20	Morres	25	1	9	0
T.Sewell	b Stewart	3	Marshall	16	0	8	0
W.Mortlock	not out	11					
T.Hearne	b Stewart	8					
Extras	b 7 lb 4 w 12	23					
Total		**305**					

Fall: 1/44 2/59 3/110? 4/161 5/218 6/220 7/278 8/280? 9/288 10/305

ALL ENGLAND XI WON BY AN INNINGS & 96 RUNS

openers stood firm until the 25th over, making 37 before Huddlestone (18) steered a catch to Iddison at point off Sewell, the dynamic little fast bowler. Soon, Sweeney went the identical way, and, in the same over, Bryant lost his off stump. Marshall, the skipper, emerged from the tent, to much cheering, but after playing out a maiden, he too fell to Sewell, caught by long-stop Mortlock.

Opener Mace had been watching all this from the other end, and had an escape of his own when Hearne put down a high catch off Iddison's bowling. Thompson was quickly run out as Mace tried for a single, and then Mace himself was bowled for 20 by the lethal Sewell, giving him one of the quickest of 'five-fors'. The demoralised Victorian 18 had lost six wickets for two runs and were in disarray.

Worse followed. Rennie was promoted up the order, but Wray's dismissal, caught behind to give Iddison the first of what were to be over 100 tour wickets, was quickly followed by the run-out of Makinson, sent back by his partner, Stephenson taking off the bails. The local side had now lost eight wickets for two runs.

Wardill brought some relief. Run out first ball in the first innings, he now displayed a certain polish, and was cheered frantically when he took a single, adding confident shots for two threes and a two. But Rennie pushed up a catch to Lawrence at midwicket off Iddison, who then bowled left-hander Stewart. This was the eighth duck among the 10 wickets so far to have fallen, with the total 48.

Cosstick avoided a duck, and some resistance followed, but with Griffith coming on in place of Iddison, the collapse regained its momentum. Wardill, with a worthy 18, was caught at point off Griffith, and after a further 14 runs, Hopkinson cutting a four, Cosstick was caught off Griffith. Caffyn had a bowl, and took the 13th wicket, Hopkinson (13) being caught by the fit-again Bennett. (Poor Greeves, his fumbling substitute, had been hooted by some 'low fellows' as he left the field.) Relief came for the Victorians with the luncheon bell at 2.20 pm. Thirteen wickets were down for 84.

There was the largest roll-up of all the four days in the VIP tent today, Sir Francis Murphy in the chair, flanked by the captains, with toasts offered to Her Majesty, the All England XI (HH acknowledging), the Victorian team (a humorous speech, this one, responded to by Marshall), and the match committee (who must by now have been thinking that it mattered little whether 18 or 22 – or even 30 – of their local cricketers had gone to battle with the hardened, wily Englishmen). R.C.Bagot, who had designed the flourishing Melbourne Cricket Ground, was also honoured, and responded, before the final toast, to Messrs Spiers and Pond, to which both responded.

Conway, the No.15, resumed with Elliott, and should have been run out, but Sewell missed the ball at the stumps. Then, who should arrive but the Governor, compelling another break in play while the anthem was radiated by the brass band. Conway, inspired, darted down the pitch to Caffyn, only to give H.H.Stephenson an easy stumping. Morres was run out for nothing, and Elliott fell to a tumbling catch by Iddison off Sewell, who then closed the match with his seventh wicket of the innings as Butterworth gave Iddison a catch, becoming the tenth duck-maker in a humiliating rout. All out for 91, the Victorians had lost by an innings and 96 runs, with Tom Sewell the proud owner of figures of 7 for 20 off 26 four-ball overs, 17 of which were maidens.

It was seen as ironic or merciful or even ludicrous that just as the final wicket was falling shortly after 4 o'clock, a giant balloon came hovering over the trees behind the pavilion. It was the first to have been manufactured in the colony, 45ft high and 37ft wide, with a cubic content of 25,000ft, and, inflated without expense by the Melbourne Gas Company, it had been approaching the MCG for the best part of two hours. The aeronauts aboard were Messrs Brown, its designer, and Deane, and perched alongside them in the basket was none other than Christopher Pond. On its white silk exterior a portrait of Queen Victoria had been painted on one side, with 'All England Eleven' and the arms of Australia on the other.

Spectators flooded across the field, emotional at the end of the cricket match and thrilled at the sight of the great floating thing now descending into their midst. The Volunteer band struck up with *See the Conquering Hero Comes*, partly in honour of the winning team and partly for the balloon, which had now settled on the ground, rope-anchored in front of the Governor's box, where a photograph was taken.

Soon it was lifting off again, Pond having remained on the ground, his place taken by aeronaut Brown's wife, who was considered very courageous. The balloon circled the arena before heading off towards Fitzroy Square, propelled by the stiff wind on a swirling course in this direction and that as if to presage the pattern of England v Australia Test cricket through the decades that lay ahead. Over the Botanical Gardens it floated, touching a mile-and-a-half in altitude before attempting a descent between Richmond and Hawthorn. The air current was unfavourable there, so onward they travelled, finally touching down, after covering seven or eight unplanned miles, in Albert Street, Fitzroy, the major hazard having been the attacks by a flock of angry swallows.

Meanwhile, all the cricketers had gathered in the Melbourne CC pavilion, where conviviality reigned. As word spread, a few thousand spectators converged on the area, and calls went up for one player after another, so the cricketers came out onto the verandah and bowed their gratitude to the worshippers. 'Speak! Speak!' was the roar in response. 'Three cheers for Griffith!' The allrounder looked very embarrassed. 'Where's Caffyn?' the mob demanded. But he was inside. Heathfield Harman Stephenson tried to pacify them with reference to the English team's next visit here, later in the month, but they wanted Caffyn and Griffith, and there was no escape. So out came Caffyn, the 'Surrey Pet' (who was to receive £10 from the grateful man who won the £100 sweepstake on the match top-scorer), to raise his voice and tell how pleased he and Griffith were to have made the highest scores, and that the team had shown so well; perhaps they might play even better in the coming weeks. His sentiments brought the most tremendous cheers in response. But Griffith was not off the hook. They thundered his name, and the poor chap had to present himself. He mumbled inaudibly and withdrew, prompting calls for the captain. Out came HH, holding hands with

George Marshall. The Englishman then teased the ex-Englishman by showing the match ball, and Marshall, after bowing, niftily snatched it from him, pantomime which the crowd loved. Random cries followed, one bringing out the opposing long-stops, Mortlock and Butterworth, then Jack Conway, and finally two other colts, O'Mullane and Stewart. There seems to have been no demand for the appearance of either 'Farmer' Bennett or Tom Sewell, both takers of seven wickets, which suggests that even then it was essentially a batsman's game.

Around 45,000 had watched the match, excluding those who peered in from outside the enclosure, and if there was disappointment at the performance of the Victorians in almost every aspect of their play and at the laborious run rate (both sides averaged an equivalent of 2.07 runs per six-ball over in modern terms), there could be no doubting that everyone who had attended recognised the significance of what they had witnessed. H.H.Stephenson's opinion about the colonials' bowling – that it was good but contained not enough 'science' or 'twist' and lacked suppleness in the wrist – was soon public knowledge, and no-one reasonably could have taken exception to the verdict.

As for the cricketers of both sides, they went that evening for further celebrations at George Marshall's Cricketer's Hotel in Swanston Street, the Englishmen perhaps thinking ahead already to the long stagecoach ride awaiting them on Monday, the day after tomorrow. The Victorians, for their part, showed how swiftly they had learned from the match by comfortably beating New South Wales at the MCG a week later, Cosstick, Conway, Stewart, Huddlestone, Wardill and Marshall all enjoying success.

And as for the effect the great match had had on unsettled and disaffected English migrants who looked to Stephenson's team as upholders of their own patriotism, Rachel Henning was about to pen a letter (now held by the State Library in Sydney) to her brother-in-law back in England that revealed traces of the heartache and resentment that at some time or other befall most who venture to strange shores:

This ought to take down the Colonial 'bounce' a little. The English players are coming to Sydney next I believe as the Sydneyites wish for a beating also . . . . It was a most audacious thing of the colonials to challenge the first players in the world and to imagine that they could teach the respected grandmother . . . .

CHAPTER 8

Going Bush

C URIOSITY and apprehension competed in the English cricketers' minds as they boarded the stagecoach which would take them to Beechworth, almost 200 miles away and on the eastern fringe of what would later be known as Kelly Country. Beechworth was where Ned Kelly's mother was tried, where Kelly's own preliminary hearing was held, and where Steve Hart, one of his gang, was born in 1860.

Drawn by three horses, with two reserves at the rear, the coach provided as much passenger comfort as the times permitted, though Caffyn, speaking for the entire tossed-about corps, found the journey over the primitive, rutted road 'shaky and fatiguing', and 'glad were we all when it was over'. While bushrangers might have been a source of anxiety, an even greater concern was the well-known fact that Australian coachdrivers relished the steep hill downwards, and had less inclination than their English counterparts to use the brakes. The forward-sloping gallop as the horses were given their heads made for rigid tension among those inside the carriage.

The Ovens region was aptly named, for the temperature during the journey and for the Englishmen's second tour match was around the century mark Fahrenheit. When the first English Test team toured fifteen years later, Jim Southerton, the little Surrey offspinner, was to write in his diary: 'People at home do not know or do not think that it is quite a different thing to play a match at home, fit and well, and to play one out here after the very rough travelling by land and sea one has to go through here, and I defy any team to play anything like up to their form for at least three days after such travelling.'

Hellish journey or not, Stephenson's team quickly regained their poise – aided by an ebullient reception and plenty of refreshment – and demolished the local Twenty-two in two days, either refusing to patronise the substandard rural cricketers or finding that their level of competence was so low that patronisation was in vain. The English captain chose to bat after beating the Ovens 22's skipper, Tuck, at the toss, and by the 6 o'clock close of play on the first evening All England were 210 for 7. About 1500 spectators were present, cheering loudly at the spasmodic fall of an English wicket, the summit of their hopes seemingly being that their humble champions might lose less heavily than the Victorian 18 recently did.

Mortlock (35) and Sewell (41), the openers, and Griffith (46) played well, but 'Tiny' Wells, having umpired at Melbourne, now failed to score in his debut innings. Resuming at 10.30 next morning, the tourists built their total to 264, Iddison making 23 and Bennett, in what was to be a flexible batting order, was left 39 not out. HH failed again with 4, and the 34 extras included a tell-tale 20 wides.

BEECHWORTH, January 9, 10, 1862

Toss won by All England   Umpires: W.H.Gunn(?) & W.Mudie

ALL ENGLAND XI

W.Mortlock	b Weston	35	*Bowling*	*Balls*	*Wides*	*Runs*	*Wickets*
T.Sewell	b Daniel	41	Orr	189,	6	74	4
G.Griffith	run out	46	Daniel	188	1	88	1
G.Wells	c Daniel b Orr	0	Reid	24	1	6	0
W.Caffyn	c Garling b Orr	14	S.U.Brown	8	0	9	0
T.Hearne	b Willett	13	Weston	60	3	29	1
E.Stephenson	b W.J.Brown	12	Willett	52	6	13	2
R.Iddison	c Martin b Orr	23	W.J.Brown	40	3	11	1
G.Bennett	not out	39					
*H.H.Stephenson	c Orr bWillett	4					
C.Lawrence	b Orr	3	*Orr and W.J.Brown each bowled 1 no-ball*				
Extras b 12 w 20 nb 2		34					
Total		**264**					

TWENTY-TWO OF THE OVENS DISTRICT

20 (top score S.U.Brown 4; 12 ducks; Caffyn 84 balls, 1 wide, 9 runs, 9 wickets; Bennett 81 balls, 10 runs, 11 wickets; opening batsman Willett run out) and [following on] **53** (top scores Ward 13, Aitken 8; 9 ducks; Wells 116 balls, 10 runs, 8 wickets; Lawrence 115 balls, 38 runs,11 wickets; 2 run-outs; Ovens captained by Tuck; England used only 2 bowlers in each innings)

ALL ENGLAND XI WON BY AN INNINGS & 191 RUNS

Griffith played against Eleven of the Ovens at single-wicket after the match and beat them, dismissing 10 of them for ducks, with the 11th man run out. The Ovens' only run came from a no-ball. The local XI were: Orr, S.U.Brown, Ward, Dunsford, C.Reid, J.Reid, Hughes, O.Daniel, Weston, W.J.Brown and Baldock.

There was only one word to describe the first innings of the Ovens 22, which began at 12.15 pm and terminated at 3.25. It was an embarrassment from start to finish. In the 166 balls sent down by Caffyn and Bennett, the 21 wickets fell for an all-out total of 20. S.U.Brown was the highest scorer with 4. Caffyn took 9 for 9, Bennett 11 for 10. There were a dozen ducks (in those days more often called 'goose eggs'), which probably mutually alleviated the sense of disgrace – followed by nine more in the second innings. Six batsmen completed pairs, including captain Tuck, as the Ovens players trekked to and fro, managing this time to squeeze out a total of 53. All England's unchanged bowling pair now were Wells (8 for 10) and Lawrence (11 for 38), and only one Ovens man, Ward, reached double figures in the entire match.

It was doleful, pathetic, and almost enough to persuade the Englishmen that they should be moving on, even allowing that they were used to rolling over bucolic local sides across England while refraining from rubbing it in too humiliatingly. Instead, to give the locals their moneysworth, 'Ben' Griffith, with three fielders, took on 11 of the Ovens cricketers at single-wicket. He bowled them out for 1, which was actually a no-ball. Two were lbw, seven bowled, and Mortlock caught one, and the No.11 was run out, the 11 ducks bringing the total registered in the two days at Beechworth to a memorable 32 (plus Wells's for England). Griffith won the match quickly, perforce giving his wicket away soon after passing the tiny target, and afterwards he told Caffyn that he had put him in the shade as a single-wicket player.

The tourists next played six days later, again at the Melbourne Cricket Ground. The stakes were higher now, for a combined team of Melbourne and Sydney players – 22 in the team – had been assembled. This was the first match to be designated in some quarters as a 'test match', though the term was going to have to be bandied about for some years yet before adoption (and subject to the proper quality and quantity of players from both sides). By only a slight stretch of the imagination, this was to be the first England v Australia cricket match.

The Englishmen had reached Spencer Street station 'from the country' at 8 o'clock on the morning of January 14, as the Government were bidding to increase business by offering the public return tickets for the price of singles during the forthcoming match. George Coppin, who was staging *Puss in Boots* at his Cremorne Gardens amusement park on the banks of the Yarra, probably entertained the touring cricketers between matches.

Alas, the first scheduled day of the next match was washed out, but when play got under way on Friday, January 17, 1862, the All Englanders at last felt they were up against serious opposition. And so it should have been, for the Combined 22 consisted of the cream of the talent from the two senior mainland colonies. Nine from Victoria and nine from New South Wales had just played in the intercolonial match, while three others had played against England for the Victorian 18. And at last there is a thread through to the era of Test cricket (Cosstick's umpiring apart), for in the Combined team's ranks was Nat Thomson, a Sydney-born 22-year-old batsman of 'faultless' style who one day would open Australia's first innings with Charlie Bannerman in the inaugural Test, on this ground, fifteen years from now – and become the first-ever batsman dismissed in a Test match.

Midst news items concerning the American Civil War and the financial collapse of the French government, the Australian newspapers devoted lengthy columns to previewing and describing the cricket match, the *Argus* feeling that with a good captain, the 'allies' would make a better fist of things this time against 'the Eleven'. George Marshall did not wish to be captain now, and just before the delayed start, the players elected their leader in the pavilion. Charles Makinson, elder brother of Joseph, the Cambridge Blue and top county amateur allrounder, secured the honour, while George Gilbert, a Cheltenham-born cousin of the Graces who had played for Gentlemen v Players in 1851, 'acted as his colleague' – another way of saying that the former New South Wales captain was now vice-captain.

James Stewart was away and had to miss the match, but Kit Mace postponed his journey to New Zealand in order to play. The only other problem for the Combined team was the sudden withdrawal of Henry Newcombe, who, having just played in the losing Victoria XI in the intercolonial, feared that the onset of wet weather would activate his rheumatism, so he booked a sea passage back to Sydney. His captain had consented to his withdrawal, but the New South Wales players were unhappy, and on their behalf P.C.Curtis (NSW's umpire) sent what Newcombe referred to as an 'offensive' telegram to the NSWCA. The Association rejected the player's complaint.

Admission prices were reduced, and playing hours were to be extended: noon till 7 pm, for the benefit of those who had to work. They at least could watch the final hour or two of play. The first-day washout prompted the committee to schedule an early start (10 am) on the Friday.

Only a few hundred were present then, but the weather had improved greatly, and as the trains unloaded their human cargo, the numbers built up to around 7000. Outside, as ever, were others 'inspecting the game as best they could under the disadvantage of distance', standing on the hill, or in the case of many of the lads, perched in the trees. The booths did good business, though the funfair offerings were not greatly patronised, the boat-swing operator, for one, packing up early. Again, there was to be no crowd disorder throughout the match, and the *Argus* was moved to compliment the oi polloi on its general conduct.

Stephenson won the toss and surprised one and all by asking the Melbourne & New South Wales 22 to bat. Umpires P.C.Curtis and Mudie, his damaged hand still bothering him, took up their positions at half-past-10, and Marshall and Alfred Park opened the innings, Marshall taking strike to Iddison from the upper end and cutting his second ball for three. But Bennett soon bowled him for 5, and after Bryant had hit Bennett to leg for the first four, though hope remained suspended, wickets began to fall, firstly to Iddison and Bennett. Double-figure scores against the English team were almost headline news, and to that eminence now rose Park (18) and Kit Mace (10). (Eight years later, this same Alf Park, NSWCA treasurer 1866-74, came to blows on the pitch with an opponent during a club match, and in 1875 was forced to resign as a trustee of the Domain ground after the revelation that he had tried to influence the margin of victory in an intercolonial match in order to win a bet.)

John Kettle, in at 50 for 5, became top-scorer with 28, starting with a cut four off Iddison, but Huddlestone's wicket had been squandered with a run-out, and when Mace was nicely held by Lawrence at slip it was 58 for 6. Thomson was bowled by a Bennett 'breakback' (not a fast delivery, in the accepted sense of later years), and further wastage occurred with Wardill's run-out. Ned Stephenson took a fine catch to dispose of Gilbert for a duck, and 10 wickets were down by the time the hundred was posted, to relieved cheering. The popular Cosstick made 20, having taken his team past 118, the Victorian total in the opening match. This was seen to have some significance, however slender; but just before lunch Makinson, the captain, disappointingly became the third batsman to be run out.

There was a concerted effort to keep the luncheon speeches short this time and to get back onto the field. The health of the English cricketers was proposed by Captain Edward Ward, Royal Engineers, monocled Master of the Mint, a pioneer of roundarm and currently captain of New South Wales, who had just been bowled by Caffyn for a duck. (Ward's stance was so side-on that he peered over his left shoulder, his backside facing the bowler.)

HH responded, paying fulsome compliments to the colonial players. A few more formalities, then out they went, and Caffyn and Griffith tore the tail off the innings, though not before a meritorious 150 was posted, thanks in the end largely to Hopkinson. The last man, coming in at No.22, was John Kinloch, something of a scholar and an underhand bowler, who had raised a laugh a few days previously by running out Huddlestone in the intercolonial when that Victorian batsman had left his crease prematurely when non-striker, a dismissal (known as a 'Mankad' in modern parlance) which, far from being condemned, caused ribaldry.

The leading wicket-takers in the Combined 22's innings were Caffyn with 6 for 27 and Griffith with 5 for 19. But now Britannia's helmet slipped sideways, for Jack Conway was soon among the wickets, and with two run-outs as well, the All England XI made rather a hash of it. Perhaps they had developed a passing softness during the recent Beechworth fiasco.

At 4.15 pm Conway bowled the first ball to Mortlock. James Moore bowled from the upper end, and Bennett scored the first runs, a two to leg. But he was soon run out, and a rumble of anticipation greeted Griffith, who lost Mortlock in the 11th over, soon followed by his captain, Stephenson failing again with 3. With Caffyn's arrival, a photograph was taken, the long-field men going in a little so as to be included in the camera's range, everyone freezing obediently for a short time. Griffith got back to business with a boundary hit, but was soon deceived by Conway's clever slower ball: 30 for 4. Ned Stephenson (2) played on to Conway, and the other Yorkshireman, Iddison, was quickly dealt with, thrown out by Gilbert. When Lawrence was bowled by Conway, England were in deep trouble at 40 for 7, and the excitement in the field and around the ground was foaming. Maiden overs followed, and some resolute batting by Caffyn and Wells (whose earlier fielding at point had impressed, and who was now greeted as a 'colonial' because he had been in Australia a month longer than the main team) saw the All England XI safely to the 7 o'clock close, the setting sun having shone brightly on the stumps at one end. The score still looked decidedly lop-sided: Victoria & New South Wales 153; All England 73 for 7 from 64 overs. In the words of the English captain, it had become 'an uphill game'.

On the Saturday, a day of cloud and unfriendly wind, before a much larger roll-up, the action was delayed because two of the Victorians were missing. Autre temps, autre moeurs: the 10 o'clock start consequently became a 10.40 start. Marshall handed over the wicketkeeping gauntlets to Thomson, and after a quiet opening, during which local pessimists convinced themselves that the Englishmen would gain the advantage after all, Caffyn, now seen as a prince among batsmen, was caught at slip by Bryant, and Tom Hearne (0) was cleverly caught at the wicket by Nat Thomson. Sewell came in at No.11 and hit his first ball for four, and shortly lofted another which Hopkinson ought to have caught. He misjudged it and sustained a badly cut and swollen hand. England's blushes were spared as the hundred came up, and by the time that 'Tiny' Wells lost his middle stump to Bryant's bowling, he had made a timely 32 (20 singles) and, aided by Sewell's useful 15 not out, had dragged his side up to a final 111, arrears of only 42.

Spiers and Pond, irate at the exploitation of the hill outside the ground, had now partially blocked the view of those on it. Still boys hopped over the fence when the 'Peelers' weren't looking, or outran the authorities and lost themselves in the crowd, the policemen always taking it in good humour.

Kettle's first-innings top-score was rewarded by his promotion to opener in the second innings, which was begun at 12.30. Out he went with Wardill, who quickly fell foul of Bennett's cunning. Bryant was due in next, but was nowhere to be found. Perhaps he was supervising over in his pub's tent. Whatever the case, shouts of 'Time! Time!' rang out, until Gilbert hurried to the middle in his stead.

The next drama was more chilling, for Caffyn let one go at John Kettle which thudded into his body and caused him to lose consciousness. There was great concern among those who tried to revive him, and eventually he had to be carried from the ground. Doctors Campbell and Tracy and others tended to him, and at last he came round, though he never felt well enough to resume his innings. 'Not out (hurt)' was the scorebook entry. Kettle was never to add to his three first-class appearances for New South Wales.

The elusive Bryant replaced him, encouraged as he set out for the wickets by a cry of 'Make a good score, Jerry!' But only a few singles accrued before Caffyn had him caught. It was noticeable how very cautious the Australians now were in their running. Clearly there had been discussion. All around them still were examples of how good cricket should be played. Gilbert drove, only for the ball to be fielded by Iddison and flung back to Stephenson barely as the batsman completed his followthrough. Bennett soon had him, and in came Cosstick to rally the innings a little, only for Thomson to be beautifully caught at point by 'Tiny' Wells just as the luncheon break neared. At 26 for 4, the Combined team had let it slip.

There were eighty for lunch, presided over once more by W.C.Haines, who toasted Captain Ward and the English captain. HH, in reply, took the chance to suggest that the good cricket played by local men vindicated his stand against playing against more than an Eighteen in the opening fixture. And Felix Spiers explained, with regret, that the match must finish this day (no Sunday play would ever have been contemplated in these times): much local finance and effort had been ploughed into the forthcoming match in Geelong, which had been advertised as starting on Monday.

Resumption promptly at 3 pm found Cosstick and Park bulking up the innings with boundaries apiece and singles, the staple diet. They saw the 50 up before Sewell bounded in and had Cosstick (22) taken at cover, Hearne running for a low catch. The Surrey bowler then tore through Mace's defence first ball. Though there was to be no hat-trick, wickets continued to tumble, until a ninth-wicket stand of 37 between Huddlestone and Marshall, one Griffith over producing a sensational 11 runs as Huddlestone hit him to square leg for four and Marshall 'drew' another four. It was time for the skipper himself to have a bowl.

Griffith donned the leg-guards and gloves, and soon H.H.Stephenson was dispensing his medium-pacers, which the *Argus* man saw as 'novel, a sort of curling and dodging'. HH soon held a return catch from Huddlestone, and after Kinloch had run himself out, he had Butterworth caught at slip by Caffyn. Marshall raised the hundred, was dropped at slip by Ned Stephenson, and with a well-earned 25 to his name, he became the first of Griffith's three stumpings, all off Iddison's slows.

MELBOURNE CRICKET GROUND, January 16 *(no play)*, **17, 18, 1862**

Toss won by All England   Umpires: P.C.Curtis & W.Mudie

TWENTY-TWO OF VICTORIA & NEW SOUTH WALES

G.Marshall	b Bennett	5	[10] st Griffith b Iddison		25
A.L.Park	c Mortlock b Iddison	18	[7] b Sewell		15
J.M.Bryant	b Iddison	5	[4] c Iddison b Caffyn		4
J.Moore	st H.H.Stephenson b Iddison	8	[9] c & b Bennett		0
C.Mace	c Lawrence b Iddison	10	[8] b Sewell		0
J.Huddlestone	run out	5	[11] c & b H.H.Stephenson		16
J.L.Kettle	c Lawrence b Sewell	28	[2] retired hurt		0
N.F.D.Thomson	b Bennett	2	[5] c Wells b Caffyn		1
R.W.Wardill	run out	7	[1] b Bennett		1
G.H.B.Gilbert	c E.Stephenson b Griffith	0	[3] c Griffith b Bennett		8
G.T.Curtis	c Iddison b Griffith	5	[16] c Caffyn b H.H.Stephenson		0
S.Cosstick	b Caffyn	20	[6] c Hearne b Sewell		22
E.W.Ward	b Caffyn	0	[20] st Griffith b Iddison		4
*C.Makinson	run out	9	st Griffith b Iddison		7
F.Rowley	c Lawrence b Caffyn	0	[18] lbw b H.H.Stephenson		13
E.Saddler	c Wells b Caffyn	2	[15] c Caffyn b H.H.Stephenson		2
B.Butterworth	b Griffith	7	[13] c Caffyn b H.H.Stephenson		2
S.G.Hopkinson	b Griffith	10	[17] b H.H.Stephenson		6
J.Conway	b Caffyn	0	b Iddison		0
H.Deane	c Lawrence b Griffith	1	[22] not out		1
G.J.P.O'Mullane	b Caffyn	0	lbw b H.H.Stephenson		0
J.Kinloch	not out	3	[12] run out		1
Extras lb 6 w 1 nb 1		8	b 9 lb 5 w 2		16
Totals		**153**			**144**

Fall: 1/5 2/24 3/31? 4/40? 5/50 6/58 7/65 8/89 9/90   1/1 2/10 3/14 4/26 5/55 6/55 7/56 8/56
10/90 11/100 12/101 13/126? 14/126 15/126?   9/93 10/94? 11/100 12/117 13/120 14/120
16/137? 17/137 18/137? 19/148? 20/149? 21/153   15/120 16/131 17/132? 18/140 19/140 20/144
                                                    Kettle retired hurt at 1 for 1

Bowling	Balls	Wides	Runs	Wickets		Balls	Wides	Runs	Wickets
Iddison	128	1	56	4	Caffyn	88	0	26	2
Bennett	64	0	29	2	Bennett	112	0	22	3
Sewell	72	0	14	1	Sewell	68	0	24	3
Griffith	92	0	19	5	Griffith	16	0	14	0
Caffyn	81	0	27	6	H.H.Stephenson	84	2	23	7
					Iddison	62	0	19	4

Iddison bowled 1 no-ball

ALL ENGLAND XI

W.Mortlock	c Curtis b Conway	1		
G.Bennett	run out (Marshall)	5		
G.Griffith	b Conway	16	not out	7
*H.H.Stephenson	c Gilbert b Conway	3		
W.Caffyn	c Bryant b Moore	14		
E.Stephenson	b Conway	2		
R.Iddison	run out (Gilbert)	1		
C.Lawrence	b Conway	2		
G.Wells	b Bryant	32		
T.Hearne	c Thomson b Moore	0		
T.Sewell	not out	15	not out	3
Extras b 6 lb 4 w 10		20		0
Totals		**111**	0 wkt	**10**

Fall: 1/5 2/11 3/21 4/30 5/34 6/36 7/40 8/77 9/78? 10/111

Bowling	Balls	Wides	Runs	Wickets		Balls	Runs	Wickets
Conway	132	8	25	5	Conway	20	2	0
Moore	138	0	36	2	Kinloch	20	8	0
Gilbert	28	0	7	0				
Bryant	42	1	9	1				
Cosstick	28	0	11	0				
Ward	24	1	3	0				

MATCH UNFINISHED (Drawn)

English cricketers aboard Cabbage Tree Ned's coach, with the dozen greys up front, about to leave the Cobb & Co office in Geelong.

HH struck again with his 'twisters', but Ned Stephenson missed two more catches, and Conway, never one to listen to authority, ignored the plea of his captain to hold on, had a swish at Iddison's first ball to him, and was bowled, retiring 'in disgust'. Hopkinson hung on, despite his painful hand injury, and the errors from both sides piled up, Iddison missing a catch at square leg from Rowley. The English skipper won a couple of leg-before shouts, and at 6.20 pm, with Kettle unable to bat, 20 out was all out; total 144, HH with the bowling honours for his 7 for 23, and the United Elevens' overall lead 186, with only half-an-hour left in the match.

Griffith and Sewell batted through the 10 overs remaining, and took 10 runs off the contrasting bowling of Conway (fast) and Kinlock ('swift' underhand), with two substitutes among the army of fieldsmen, Hopkinson and poor Kettle not being up to it. Stumps were drawn at 7 o'clock, and the crowd, which had stayed resolutely to the close, rapidly vanished, leaving an empty field but some little activity in the booths. In the outside world, there was a state of alarm for those who wanted it: 'in the event of a war breaking out between England and America, several citizens of the Northern States resident in Ballarat are prepared to become naturalized British subjects.'

After a free Sunday, the All England XI set out on Monday, January 20, for Geelong, forty miles away to the south-west. This time they travelled in the comparative comfort of a railway carriage, in the first train of the day; but upon arrival in the town at 10 o'clock they were ushered into another coach, though no ordinary coach and with no ordinary driver, for this was the famous 'Cabbage Tree Ned', Edward Devine, the colony's champion whip, and the vehicle was his 'Leviathan', Cobb & Co's pride, which could hold as many as 89 passengers. On its roof, a brass band merrily played, while attached all around the vehicle were flags, a 'curious medley of stars, stripes, and union jacks'. As the cricketers appeared, the band struck up with *Auld Lang Syne*, before 'Cabbage Tree Ned' took off a touch impatiently. Devine was a renowned practical joker, but on this great day he concentrated on conveying his illustrious passengers swiftly and safely to Geelong's cricket ground, through the usual swarms of welcoming citizens, his mighty carriage pulled by a dozen greys ('twelve spanking great tits' according to *Baily's Magazine*). Round by the Western he thundered, returning down Mercer Street to Gosling's British Hotel in Corio Street (a shopping complex now stands on the site), bunting hanging from almost every corner. There the travellers had an hour to settle into their rooms and refresh before hopping back into the giant coach for the short journey to the ground, a new venue which was situated between the eastern side of the Botanical Gardens and the Rifle Butts.

The Government had been persuaded to grant twelve acres of common land, and the costs of fencing it in, erecting a modest pavilion and preparing the ground were estimated at £350, which was largely met by public subscription. The disappointingly low attendances during the three days of play were to leave the match committee with a deficit of about £60, but Corio Cricket Club eventually paid this off in exchange for rights to further use of the ground. By 1864, George Parr and his players thought it as good as anything outside England.

Now, after much effort, the ground looked good. Although the outfield was quite rough, Sam Cosstick had prepared a smooth square, having borrowed a five-ton roller, Strachan & Co making their fire engine available for watering the dry ground. A modest stream of people began entering through the gate on the western side.

After earlier and short-lived suggestions that the local organisers planned to field a team of 44, the Twenty-two of Geelong & the Western District were bolstered by the inclusion of 'metropolitan cracks' George Marshall, Jerry Bryant, George Cosstick, Tom Morres and Tom Wray. Local player Simon Rennie, a customs officer, who had played in the opening tour match at the MCG, was readily elected as captain, and boldly took first innings when he won the toss.

The poor attendance, even though public holidays had been granted, was blamed on the high admission price of half-a-crown and the free view of the low-lying ground which could be had from the heights of the Botanical Gardens. Once in Corio Oval, only a handful paid an extra half-crown to occupy the stand, and the overall shortage of spectators, together with their reluctance to spend at the booths and sideshows, meant poor takings all round. Spiers and Pond had pocketed £179 from their auction for the rights to nine refreshment booths, but few of the holders recovered costs. Upston, Bedford, Hoffman & Fordham took space in the *Geelong Advertiser*, offering a 'sumptuous lunch, comprising all foods in season, with wines, spirits etc', for ten shillings on the first day, 7/6d on the second, and five shillings on the third.

The performance of the local team, with its guest players, was heartening. Anticipating some kind of humiliation, the fans were delighted with a total of 111, which, after all, matched the score achieved by All England themselves in the previous game. Only three batsmen made it into double figures, and they were all locals: Rennie himself and Timms (both 17), and Smith an astonishingly patient 15 in almost three hours.

This was rabbit country. A landholder named Austin had imported some of the cute little long-ears in 1859 and released two dozen of them as game. They bred as only rabbits do, and a nationwide infestation raged until almost a century later. The plague had begun here in Geelong, but although the 'big names' from Melbourne contributed little to the score in the grand cricket match against All England, the town's cricketers, in the first innings at least, proved not to be complete rabbits

While H.H.Stephenson's wicketkeeping was admired, and the performances of Hearne at long-stop (it was Mortlock's turn to umpire), Wells at point, and Sewell at slip had drawn glowing comment, the fielding of some of the Englishmen was perceived as careless, and the deduction was made that they knew they would win, so why overdo it? Still, the Geelong 22 were 10 down for 73 when the luncheon bell rang at 2.30.

At 12.15, Marshall and Wray had started the match to Caffyn's 'shooters' and 'lengths' and Iddison's 'twisters', and if Wray was encouraged by calls of 'Go it, Tommy!' he and his partner were soon gone, and four others besides. At 19 for 6 it looked extremely ominous, but Rennie, Timms the colt, and Smith, with helpful little contributions from the rest (there were only three ducks in the innings), took the total to a respectable 111, Billy Caffyn taking the bowling honours with a juicy 10 for 37.

Less than an hour had been taken up by luncheon, with chairman George Stavely, Irish-born and a self-confessed ignoramus about cricket, welcoming the men who had come so many thousands of miles to 'teach us cricket'. H.H.Stephenson assured the company that win or lose his players would act like men. Felix Spiers, in his brief speech, complimented Rennie on his batting, to which the local captain made a modest and articulate reply.

Many now-long-dead but picturesque expressions were embodied in the newspaper report of play: batsman Bryant 'got one for a poke'; 'McPherson's middle stump was sent agee'; several others 'got a lift at a ball' [lofted it]; and Iddison 'cut to between corner point and long slip'. And one term – 'sundries' – here found an early use that was to establish itself as one of so many adamantly alternative words that distinguish Australian cricket parlance from the rest.

There was time that first evening not only for the English XI to face 14 overs in which Iddison and Lawrence made 21 before the 6 o'clock finish, but for the country-cousin cricketers to demonstrate their shortage of skill in the field, for one ball from Tait's first over 'enabled Lawrence to slip for three, the ball having passed through three pair of hands before it was stopped'.

The second day brought uncomfortable hot winds and an even smaller attendance, with the grandstand all but deserted. Iddison (28) and Lawrence (18) took their opening stand to 55, but only two more double-figure scores followed – Caffyn's 12 and Ned Stephenson's face-saving 26 not out, which included an all-run five, followed by a skyer that saw fieldsmen Cox and Frazer colliding while the ball fell between them – as All England slid to an all-out 128, a lead of merely 17. Morres took four good wickets for 11. The captain failed again, bowled off bat and pad by Timms without scoring. Twelve wides and nine byes helped the cause, and it was proudly remarked by some of the locals that when only runs off the bat were considered, the Geelong side actually had a 107-106 advantage.

Joseph Martyr had taken the chair at lunch on the second day, and during his response, H.H.Stephenson admitted again that his were not the best eleven cricketers in England, though they were the best cricketers to work together. Caffyn toasted the Victorian cricketers, and Marshall responded.

It was anything but a smooth afternoon's cricket. At 2.40 pm such a storm blew in that the players had to lie flat on the turf for a time, while spectators rushed to the booths for shelter. The wind and dust were fearful, and soon the board-and-canvas back wall of the grandstand was torn down, followed by the awning roof. Rain came cascading down, at least making conditions much cooler. Then, all of a sudden, it had passed. No more than half-an-hour was lost.

The Englishmen, Tom Sewell in particular, now got serious. Having taken two wickets on that second evening, on the third day, play starting at 11.10 am, they blew the Geelong 22 away for 80, fast bowler Sewell taking 15 for 27 off 45 overs, bowling 10 of his victims, including Marshall (a fast one 'shivering his timbers') for 12. Bryant topped the innings with 16, including a four off Sewell into the scorers' tent. Cosstick made 11. Roger Iddison picked up the scraps with figures of 6 for 32.

At the start, a southerly was blowing at near to gale-force, often lifting off the bails, and some of the Englishmen took the field in their flannel jackets. There were three rain hold-ups before lunch, and much sawdust was needed. Sewell relished the conditions.

Tension intruded while Marshall and Rennie were together, when umpire Mortlock challenged his colleague Birdsey's signal for a four. Mortlock believed that there had been no agreement to grant a boundary for hits to the end fences. 'After a little "barney",' said the *Advertiser*, 'it was settled at two.'

Lunch had been delayed with 19 wickets down, but was taken with the score at 80 for 20 wickets, a flattering gesture, perhaps, to the last batsman Armytage, though Sewell disposed of him afterwards to clinch his 15th wicket of the innings. Sixty sat for the official lunch, to the embarrassment of the caterers, who had no option but to serve meagre plates. There were more speeches.

The pitch well rolled and the bowling carnage complete, All England needed 64 for victory, and got them with ease. The two Stephensons opened, and while the bails continued to be blown off, and the stumps were changed, only 'the Sheffield blade's' (Ned's) wicket was lost, after he had hit a five to leg. Mudie made an unbeaten 27, and the captain was glad to be in at the finish, into double figures at last with 16 not out. It pleased everyone that the young native-born Timms was awarded the prize bat by Spiers and Pond's agent Mallam.

A farewell banquet was staged that evening at Mack's Hotel (since demolished), in Brougham Street. Mr Bonsey, who said he had played at Lord's, was in the chair for a delightful occasion. The band played, there were toasts

CORIO OVAL, GEELONG, January 20, 21, 22, 1862

Toss won by Geelong   Umpires: Mr Birdsey & W.Mortlock

TWENTY-TWO OF GEELONG & THE WESTERN DISTRICT

111 (S.S.Rennie 17, W.Timms 17, H.Smith 15; 3 ducks only; Caffyn 168 balls, 37 runs, 10 wickets; Iddison 108 balls, 37 runs, 5 wickets; Griffith 72 balls, 17 runs, 4 wickets; Sewell 103 balls, 7 runs, 2 wickets; Bennett 20 balls, 9 runs, 0 wickets) and **80** (J.M.Bryant 16, G.Marshall 12, S.Cosstick 11, G.Rippon 11, extras 10, including 8 byes; 10 ducks; Sewell 180 balls, 27 runs, 15 wickets; Bennett 20 balls, 11 runs, 0 wickets; Iddison 156 balls, 32 runs, 6 wickets)

ALL ENGLAND XI

R.Iddison	c Marshall b G.Tait	28			
C.Lawrence	c H.Timms b Marshall	18			
G.Griffith	c Bryant b Marshall	5			
T.Hearne	c W.Tait b Morres	5			
W.Caffyn	b Bonsey	12			
E.Stephenson	not out	26	[1] b Morres		8
T.Sewell	c Cox b Bonsey	1			
*H.H.Stephenson	b W.Timms	0	[2] not out		16
G.Bennett	c Bryant b Morres	7			
G.Wells	b Morres	4			
W.Mudie	c Fraser b Morres	0	[3] not out		27
Extras	b 9 lb 1 w 12	22	b 7 w 6		13
Totals		**128**	1 wkt		**64**

Fall: 1/55 2/60 3/62? 4/81 5/81 6/90 7/92 8/121 9/128 10/128   1/10

Bowling	Balls	Wides	Runs	Wickets		Balls	Wides	Runs	Wickets
J.M.Bryant	80	1	19	0	J.M.Bryant	68		13	0
W.Timms	16	0	3	1	G.Tait	12		3	0
G.Tait	120	5	21	1	G.Marshall	8		4	0
G.Rippon	12	1	6	0	W.Bonsey	20		8	0
A.McPherson	20	0	10	0	T.F.Morres	36		20	1
G.Marshall	44	1	21	2	H.Smith	8		1	0
W.Bonsey	44	0	15	2	*Bowling plus extras makes 62*				
T.F.Morres	32	1	11	4					

3 wides unattributed

ALL ENGLAND XI WON BY 9 WICKETS

aplenty – to the Queen and Royal Family, the Army and Navy, coupled with the Victorian Volunteers, the All England XI – with overwhelming applause greeting the last. HH spoke of his gratification at the cordiality all around him and his players. Then came a song, *My Ancestors Were Englishmen*, followed by another, *There's a Good Time Coming*. A proud speech by Mr Curle proclaimed that the district produced wheat, wool, wine and gold, and was proud of its rising generation. Then the band struck up again: *Come Let Us Be Happy Together*, before Simon Rennie spoke of his enjoyment of the match and his pride in his Geelong & Western District team, many of whom had been strangers to each other before this match. Soon it was William Mallam's turn, and after expressing regret that neither Mr Spiers nor Mr Pond was here today, he told of how he and

H.H.Stephenson had picked the touring party 'after the first six had offered'. Not another Eleven in England could beat them, he insisted, a claim he was willing to back with 'a very large sum of money'.

Before the gathering reluctantly dispersed, there were more toasts – to the Ladies, the Press, and the Chairman himself – and more songs. Then it all subsided into history. There would be squabbles between the local cricketers and the Town Council over the claims to Corio Oval, but the new ground was to flourish for years yet. Jack Hobbs made a century on it during England's 1920-21 tour, and in 1931 the precocious little 17-year-old Lindsay Hassett, a product of Geelong College (founded 1861) and future Australian Test captain, scored 147 against the touring West Indians. But by 1976, having been a military training ground during the Second World War and later a centre for trotting and greyhound racing, it had become derelict, and the stand and other old buildings were demolished. Kardinia Park had long since become the supreme cricket venue in the vicinity. On January 29, 1987, 125 years on, a commemorative plaque prepared by the Geelong Cricket Association was unveiled at the site in the presence of the manager of the current England touring team.

CHAPTER 9

Scenic Sydney

THE ENGLISH cricketers must have heard a lot already about Sydney, and must have felt a peculiar anticipation about venturing north-east to the harbourside city widely regarded as a place of excitement and extraordinary natural beauty, though Victorians never tired of referring to it as a penal settlement.

They sailed in *City of Sydney* on the Friday and reached Sydney early on the morning of Monday, January 27, 1862, passing into Port Jackson before most Sydneysiders had vacated their beds. The cricket fraternity had been up for some time, especially those important enough – including a large cluster of politicians – to have secured a place on the steamer *Kembla,* which had 150 selected people aboard as she departed Phoenix Wharf and made up the harbour to greet the incoming vessel.

Kembla had reached the inner South Head as *City of Sydney* came into view, and three cheers immediately went up from the smaller vessel, while the band started up. On the poop of the ship, the All England cricketers, many of them still unsteady from seasickness, stood waving their hats. Down the harbour they chugged, past inlets and coves where the land was as yet sparsely built upon and lines of people perched, waving frantically, and past Fort Denison ('Pinchgut'), towards Sydney Cove (Circular Quay), beyond which lay a city sprawl with no colossal buildings as yet (the majestic town hall was not built until 1879) and certainly no bridge to span the deep and beautiful waters.

Thousands stood waiting around the Quay as *City of Sydney* cruised into view around Bennelong Point (from which the weird outlines of the Opera House were to rise 100 years later). But the onlookers were now distraught to see the craft sail on across the mouth of Sydney Cove, past Dawes Point, and out of view. The plan had gone awry. But it was soon put right. The cricketers were rowed to the smaller vessel and somehow squeezed aboard and brought to the Quay, to an astonishingly enthusiastic reception. A band played and church bells beyond were ringing and flags fluttered from most of the sandstone buildings as the idolised cricketers stepped ashore and managed to clamber into horse-drawn tramcars named 'Old England' and 'Young Australia'. Through the throng the horses worked their way, and up Pitt Street to Tattersall's Hotel – the sporting centre of Sydney, where the Hilton now stands. Here the players had to negotiate another animated cluster of fans as they pushed through to their sanctuary. The crowd called their names, and HH, Caffyn, Mortlock and others satisfied them by appearing at the upstairs windows before sitting down with the 150 cricketing, business and political guests to the lavish champagne breakfast laid on by host William J. O'Brien.

Tattersall's Hotel, Pitt Street, Sydney, the English cricketers' next temporary home.

The Hon. W.M.Arnold proposed the toast to Our Visitors, the Eleven of All England, remarking on the points of similarity between the two countries – 'except that here we have a blue sky instead of one there that I will not stop to describe'. To anyone who trivialised cricket (and the magnitude of the crowd that morning suggested that few in Sydney fitted this description) he said that it was natural to admire superior skills in any walk of life. A failed cricketer himself, the honourable gentleman had entered a life in which it was even more difficult to keep up your wicket. He complimented Messrs Spiers and Pond on their enterprise, but hoped they would not next bring out an English cabinet. 'I am afraid that my friend Mr Robertson would feel rather uneasy if he saw landed and travelling on our cars in Pitt Street Lord Palmerston and Mr Gladstone, sent to have a shy at our wickets!'

The Robertson to whom he referred had been the key figure in allowing the match to be staged on the Outer Domain. This wide open space, which stretched below the Botanical Gardens, from Macquarie Street with its old hospital and Parliament buildings at the western end and Woolloomooloo to the east, was public land, and no enclosure could be erected on it or admission fees charged. As Hyde Park had become overcrowded and unsuitable for cricket matches, Governor Denison in 1856 had granted permission for matches to be played on the Domain. Club matches there were soon followed by Sydney's first intercolonial match, against Victoria in January 1857, Richard Driver, MLA, William Tunks and Captain Ward supervising the ground preparations. But the ban on fees and enclosures remained strictly in force.

The All England match had been in jeopardy, there being no alternative ground. What was to become the Sydney Cricket Ground in all its glory was still a primitive playing area, used by the militia and some clubs. It was known as the Garrison Ground, and was too far out of town for comfort. The Albert ground in Redfern had not yet been built. Randwick racecourse was a possibility, though much would have had to be spent to convert it. A block of land in Haymarket, in the south of the city, was briefly considered, but it was now about to be built on. Spiers and Pond had days of anxiety, though they would have been lifted by one politician's assertion as the matter raged in the NSW Legislative Assembly: 'There would not be a working man or labourer in Sydney,' said Mr Hoskins, 'even if he was earning thirty shillings a week, who would be mean enough to insist on going into the Domain for nothing knowing the cost to the promoters.'

The man who finally ripped through the red tape was Lands Minister John Robertson, a scheming bully who was to be New South Wales Premier five times, and had 'a natural gift for profanity and an uncompromising directness of speech'. He was prepared to turn a blind eye by sanctioning the ground's enclosure and letting Spiers and Pond charge an entry fee. But there was uproar from the Opposition benches. Mr Dalgleish, member for Sydney West, led an Anti-Domain Closing Movement, and presented to the Assembly a motion demanding continued free public access.

Robertson branded him a 'popularity hunter', and referred to the forthcoming cricket match as 'an exceptional matter' and the English visit as 'an unusual thing' – adding somewhat pessimistically that it was 'something not likely to happen again'. He filibustered the objection clean off the political agenda.

If 'The Great John' had become something of a public hero over the issue, Robertson was now transformed into a villain. Without consulting Spiers and Pond, he arranged for a 1500-seater stand to be erected for the match to the exclusive advantage of himself, his colleagues in both Houses, and all their families, friends and hangers-on – and free of charge. The *Sydney Morning Herald* suggested – in vain, of course – that the hat should be passed round in Robertson's stand each day not only to alleviate the expenses of the fixture but to disguise from English eyes the mean character of Government members.

Those English eyes were rather bleary towards the end of their first day in Sydney, for the entertainment had been formidable. Following the champagne breakfast, lunch had been taken on the flagship out on the harbour midst the Anniversary Regatta (Australia had been settled by the British 74 years ago that weekend), and in the evening they attended a gala dinner in their honour at the Victoria Club, where many of the same local faces were present. So many toasts, so many sips and gulps: it was no surprise when, upon the request of the English camp, the committee announced that the start of the match would be postponed until Wednesday, the day after next. The official reason: the visitors were exhausted and seasick.

The cricketers recovered their strength on the free day, though the invitations continued to pour in. Nine of the players, with friends, were driven in horse-drawn carriages out to South Head, admiring the scenery all the way. After a short stop at Mr Billings' hotel at Watson's Bay, during which he 'exhibited his feats with the lions', they went on a short boating and fishing excursion to Camp Cove, returning to Tattersall's at 7 pm, relaxed and ready for the big match tomorrow.

Wednesday, January 29, 1862, and business in Sydney was at a standstill. Even retail stores, including David Jones and Farmer's, were closed for the duration of the match. Thousands flocked to the Domain for the town's first-ever cricket encounter between the local champions, 22 of them, and the artists from Old England. It was a beautiful day, with a cloudless sky and a gentle nor'easterly breeze, and the people responded to it, for they dressed up in the best fashion and their manner was communally cheery. They converged on an area they could now scarcely have recognised, for the Government stand was imposing in itself, but yet was dwarfed by Spiers and Pond's 4000-seater. Opposite the row of ten flag-bedecked refreshment booths, which sold fruit and cakes and drinks, was the line of shrubbery and fine trees. The music of the bands competed with the general hum of conversation – some of it by way of complaint from those who took early lunches, for the half-cooked wing of a chicken was costing 7/6d, well above the usual tariff. Scorecard vendors, the legendary, craggy-faced 'Garden Honey' surely among them, threaded through the dense crowd. And there was a small tent to accommodate the Press.

The promoters had instructed the gatekeepers to let in anyone who was unable, or even unwilling, to pay the shilling admission, and at its peak the attendance was estimated at around 23,000. Somehow Fat Boy, one of the entertainers, squeezed his way in, but no vehicles were permitted. Most of those present were aware of the political wrangle over use of the ground, and some expressed themselves with hisses and catcalls as they passed the 'selfishly prodigal' politicians' stand, John Robertson taking as much abuse as anybody. The ministers were to boycott the banquet at the conclusion of the match when they discovered they were not to feature among the official toasts. Cricket, for once, had outmanoeuvred the politicians.

Above the irritations, it was a picture of paradise. Beyond the eager, colourful crowds encircling the field, from the higher ground were visible the rich foliage of the Botanical Gardens and the blue waters of the harbour, with the distant cliffs and the lighthouse at the Heads, aspects which generations of new buildings have long since rendered impossible.

Before its detailed description of play, which dealt with almost every ball, the *Sydney Mail* mused on the development of cricket in the colony, stating that 'bowling has gone ahead at a fearful pace, and it is at the head it goes as often as not' – which suggests that there were Lillees around in those days; and the paper remarked with satisfaction on the close relations between old country and new.

The Governor, Sir John Young (later Lord Lisgar), and his wife arrived just before the 12 o'clock start, the band playing the national anthem as they took their positions in the Vice-Regal box between the two large stands, and soon the players ended their warm-up, removing the single stumps, and the captains shook hands and tossed.

H.H.Stephenson won the choice from the New South Wales captain, George Gilbert, and signalled that All England would be batting. Tom Hearne, umpire for

A graphic illustration of the big match in Sydney, with spectators of all ages and both sexes.

this match, walked to the middle with local official P.C.Curtis, and soon, to everyone's relief, the grand contest was under way, the legion of NSW fieldsmen, in their white flannel shirts, having spread themselves around the Domain.

Will Mudie and 'Ben' Griffith opened, and when the word was given, James Moore bowled from the northern end to Mudie, who took two to leg off the second ball. The slim, erect Captain Ward bowled from the southern end, advancing with a little hop; but first blood went to Moore, who had Mudie caught at mid-on in his third over with the total 8. Mortlock came in, and with the bowling tight and the fielding good, it was serious cricket . . . until some dogs ran onto the ground, sparking laughter in some quarters, impatience in others.

Gilbert put down a one-handed chance from Griffith, and Ward, as so often with frustrated bowlers, went for four next ball when Mortlock lifted him to the fence. Soon Nat Thomson, the future Test player, was appealing unsuccessfully for a catch behind off Mortlock. Maiden overs were fairly common, and the fielding continued to impress, but when Gilbert gave himself a bowl, both batsmen advanced to his slows and took runs, the fifty coming up just before Moore hit Mortlock in the body, causing him to take a breather.

Then Griffith (20 in two hours) was caught off Gilbert out at long-off by Gregory – 54 for 2 – and Billy Caffyn entered, to the kind of expectant buzz that has greeted the WGs, the Bradmans and the Bothams over the years. Gregory

(probably one of the great cricket family: almost certainly Ned, a conspicuously fine fieldsman then aged 22, or perhaps Walter, or even 16-year-old Dave) put Mortlock down at slip, and Caffyn, beginning quietly, had his piece of luck when Moore failed to hold him at mid-on. All England were lucky to be only two down for 60 at lunch, which was taken at 2.30 pm and lasted an hour. Poehlman's hostelry provided refreshment, including the luxury of ice, for the players. It was at Poehlman's establishment in the city, the Central House Café in George Street, that local cricketers often gathered, and there the NSWCA committee had selected their team for this match, from forty candidates.

Caffyn, although his style, timing and placement skill won praise wherever he played, was lucky again when Kettle floored a high catch off Gilbert's bowling, and Mortlock should have been caught-and-bowled by Moore. Into the nineties went England, runs never easy through the thick tussocky grass, with all those fieldsmen lurking. Thomson had a bowl, Brown taking the gloves behind the stumps. Mortlock drove Moore to the northern fence for four; and yet again Caffyn was reprieved as Ward at mid-on missed him off Thomson. Soon after the hundred had been posted Mortlock lofted Ward only for Deane to leave the catch to a non-existent somebody else, and then hit another to Fowler at long-on off Readett which was also missed. New South Wales were doing themselves no favours, and the Surrey men must have felt free to hit in the air with impunity.

Fast bowler Ward now came in for some punishment. Caffyn wafted him consecutively to the western fence, and Mortlock drove him to the northern fence. And when Ward's captain took over, Coulter dropped Caffyn at mid-off. Relief came only with Billy Mortlock's dismissal at last, Gregory managing to secure the catch at long-on off the bowling of his long-suffering skipper Gilbert.

All England, in uniform, freeze in the field at Sydney's Domain while the photographer does his stuff for posterity.

Mortlock's 76 had taken 3½ hours, and earned him a ground collection, a substantial £20.

At 137 for 3, and with little time remaining, Charlie Lawrence entered – only to exit quickly, run out for 2 after Caffyn called him for an overthrow. When stumps were drawn at 6 pm, All England were a hard-earned 145 for 4 off 122 four-ball overs on a ground where the thickly-grassed outfield meant that 20 runs here were said to be worth 30 to 35 on the MCG. Caffyn was unbeaten with a fortunate 34, Bennett 2.

The crowd was just about as immense on the second day, and the Sydney weather remained almost as good. And Caffyn continued to give catches that were declined: this time Taylor downed him at long-off off Gilbert. But there was a new factor this day. George Moore, perhaps having had a word overnight, was at last given a bowl. Elder brother of James, like him he had been born in Ampthill, Bedfordshire, and emigrated in 1852. George, now 41 years old, was a confectioner in remote West Maitland, and bowled a cunning slow roundarm. Far from being at the tailend of his career, he was to make his debut in intercolonial cricket nine years hence, a month short of his 50th birthday. Moore's greatest legacy, however, came not from anything he did on the cricket field but in the fact that his daughter became the mother of one of the most aggressive batting geniuses the world has seen, Charlie Macartney, whose audacious deeds included a century before lunch in a Leeds Test match in 1926, and 345 in a day against Notts. One of the earliest memories recorded in Macartney's 1930 autobiography is of his grandfather, George Moore, lobbing green apples to him when he was five, with young Charlie wielding a cedarwood bat carved for him by Gran'dad, who was to reach the age of 96. In more senses than one, truly were the seeds of greatness being sown in this 1862 match on the Sydney Domain.

Moore senior winkled out the overnight batsmen Caffyn and Bennett, and also the only batsman to reach double figures after them, Ned Stephenson, to finish with 3 for 10. Caffyn went to a close-in catch, and Bennett, having escaped a sharp miss to Thomson behind the stumps, fell the same way, Deane falling forward to clutch the ball. Poor Gilbert, probably having lost count of the misses off his slow bowling, now passed Sewell only for Thomson to muff the stumping. George Moore then lured Iddison into giving a catch to Taylor, which was also spilt, though he survived little longer, being run out by Coulter attempting an overthrow second. Sewell survived another chance off Gilbert before holing out to Taylor, whose captain must have been tempted to kiss him. Ned Stephenson hit strongly for 17 in little more than ten minutes before old Moore had him caught, and at the modest position of No.11 in came the captain himself, only to run out little Wells straightaway. All England all out 175, a total that might have been halved had a few more catches been held.

In the 45 minutes before lunch, the New South Wales 22 lost two wickets for 24, Caffyn (northern end) and Sewell opening to Clarke and Brown. Mortlock shocked everyone by allowing a four through, but overall the English fielding was many classes above that of the locals. Brown was soon run out by Lawrence's throw to HH, and Sewell bowled Clarke. George Moore went in at No.4 just before the interval.

George Moore, canny cricketer, grandfather of the legendary Macartney – photographed when 55, fourteen years after his exploits against the 1862 All England XI.

After the break, old Moore found Sewell's pace too much for him, as did Gregory first ball. Iddison came on and had Thomson neatly caught by Mudie at slip, and bowled Myrtle soon afterwards. Deane was run out on Sewell's throw, and in came the captain, George Gilbert, an exuberant man whose batting was to be described as 'a little too much harlequinade' as he played to the gallery. He contributed a valuable 10. Griffith and Wells bowled, and when Iddison came back with his teasing slows, Gilbert was caught.

All this time John Kettle, who had top-scored for the Combined team at Melbourne and been knocked out by Caffyn in the second innings, was batting watchfully and skilfully for 39, playing determinedly forward to almost every ball. Griffith now had him caught at point, but his score was incredibly the highest yet made on the tour against the Englishmen, who, taking into account also the farcical days at Beechworth, had seen 179 batsmen come to the wicket before this match. Stephenson and his team generously joined in the applause as Kettle left the field. Soon stumps were drawn, with New South Wales 93 for 10 wickets, still 82 behind.

The third day attracted a crowd at least as big as on the opening day, a high proportion of it being women and children, though many spectators insisted on entering the Domain without paying, having noted the privilege extended to 'a few indigent persons and youngsters'. Those who paid the shilling and those who didn't all saw several hours of breathtaking cricket.

Play began at 11.30, and after Sewell had bowled Curran, the rheumatic Newcombe brought up the hundred. But inside two hours the NSW 22 had been disposed of, the last 10 wickets going in a hurry. HH made three stumpings, the one to dismiss James Moore being particularly smart. Tom Sewell again had spectacular figures, 9 for 28 off 34 overs, while Iddison took five and Griffith four. Ward, his bowling having disappointed, made 18, a run, like a shilling, being worth a lot in those times.

With a lead of 48, All England returned to the crease, only to suffer their greatest reversal to date. They were bowled out for a pitiful 66 in a mere 41 overs by the only two bowlers used, George Gilbert and George Moore, leaving the New South Wales 22 a target of 115, a dozen fewer than they had made in their first innings. All of Sydney was a'chatter.

The flexible batting order had continued, with 'Tiny' Wells and H.H.Stephenson, who had been last in together in the first innings, now opening the second, Gilbert bowling from the northern end, Moore from the southern, slow men both. And in the period left before lunch, Wells was caught, Ned Stephenson stumped, Griffith run out (and showing his disapproval at the verdict). At 15 for 3, the Englishmen had a reflective interval.

Captain Stephenson was caught off a casual cut without addition, and when Mortlock was well caught at long-off for 10, having hit one of the only two fours of the innings (Iddison was about to hit the other), England were half out for 24.

Both Caffyn and Lawrence were caught on the drive, making it 28 for 7, at which point Iddison and Mudie steadied the ship, almost doubling the score before Mudie (12) became another victim of an airy drive: 54 for 8. Bennett was run out before he had scored, and Iddison was the last to go, caught at long-on one-handed by Readett. A catch in the deep seemed the fashionable way to get out, and what a difference it made to the cricket of the locals that catches were now being held. Gilbert's figures were 4 for 46, George Moore's 4 for 20.

*S.T.Gill's watercolour of the first big Sydney match conveys the crush of the
crowd and the excitement of the occasion.*

There was little time left that day, but between 5.30 and the close All
England set the colonials back on their heels. New South Wales needed 115, but
lost three wickets for 8, Clark and Lewis being bowled by Griffith from the
northern end, the bowler probably still fuming over his run-out, and Sewell
having Brown caught by Iddison at point. The afternoon's dramatic events had
seemingly been too good to be true.

In the evening both teams went to the Victoria Theatre, where *Shandy
Maguire* was being performed, and all the players mounted the stage at the end,
together with a bunch of NSWCA officials, one of whom presented a prize bat to
Mortlock for top-scoring. The Surrey player bowed and his captain expressed
thanks on his behalf. John Kettle then received his bat for top-scoring for New
South Wales, Gilbert making the response. Christopher Pond stepped forward as
the curtain fell, the audience having shouted for him and his partner, and further
joyous remarks were made before the evening's entertainment continued with a
burlesque of *Aladdin.*

For the fourth day, a Saturday, just as many people turned up at the Outer
Domain, pouring through the gates from 10 o'clock, many up from the country,
others taking advantage of the half-day holiday. Their reputations in peril,
England bowled and fielded with urgency today. Two more wickets fell quickly,
followed by the key dismissals of Thomson, who ran himself out to make it 12
for 6, and Kettle, lbw to Sewell for 1: 16 for 7. The 10th wicket fell at 22, the 15th
at 47, when Curran, the only scorer of double figures in the entire innings, was
out. And when Mudie, having put two chances down, held his fifth catch of the
innings, New South Wales were all out for 65, to lose by 49 runs, and 'Ben'

OUTER DOMAIN, SYDNEY, January 29, 30, 31, February 1, 1862

Toss won by All England   Umpires: P.C.Curtis & T.Hearne

ALL ENGLAND XI

W.Mudie	c Curtis b J.Moore	6	[9] c Curran b G.Moore		12
G.Griffith	c Gregory b Gilbert	20	[4] run out (Gilbert/Thomson)		1
W.Mortlock	c Gregory b Gilbert	76	[5] c Brown b G.Moore		10
W.Caffyn	c Deane b G.Moore	38	[6] c Gilbert b G.Moore		5
C.Lawrence	run out (Fowler/Brown)	2	[8] c Gregory b Gilbert		0
G.Bennett	c Deane b G.Moore	3	[10] run out (Brown)		0
T.Sewell	c Taylor b Gilbert	5	[11] not out		3
R.Iddison	run out (Coulter/Gilbert)	2	[7] c Readett b Gilbert		24
E.Stephenson	c Kinloch b G.Moore	17	[3] st Thomson b Gilbert		2
G.Wells	run out (Newcombe/Thomson)	1	[1] c Gregory b Gilbert		1
*H.H.Stephenson	not out	0	[2] c Curtis b G.Moore		8
Extras b 2 w 3		5			0
Totals		**175**			**66**

Fall: 1/8 2/54 3/137 4/139 5/149 6/152 7/155 8/157   1/4 2/6 3/8 4/15 5/24 6/28 7/28
       9/174 10/175   8/54 9/56 10/66

Bowling	Balls	Wides	Runs	Wickets		Balls	Wides	Runs	Wickets
J.Moore	148	1	25	1	Gilbert	84	0	46	4
Ward	96	0	34	0	G.Moore	80	0	20	4
Kinloch	68	0	12	0					
Brown	16	0	8	0					
Fowler	8	1	4	0					
Gilbert	115	0	50	3					
Thomson	16	1	5	0					
Readett	44	0	15	0					
Coulter	24	0	7	0					
G.Moore	48	0	10	3					

TWENTY-TWO OF NEW SOUTH WALES

J.Clarke	b Sewell	9	b Griffith		0
E.Brown	run out (Lawrence/H.H.Step'n)	7	c Iddison b Sewell		4
G.T.Curtis	c E.Stephenson b Sewell	8	[6] c Iddison b Sewell		8
G.Moore	b Sewell	2	[14] c Mudie b Griffith		0
J.L.Kettle	c Wells b Griffith	39	[8] lbw b Sewell		1
- Gregory	b Sewell	0	[12] b Griffith		4
N.F.D.Thomson	c Mudie b Iddison	7	run out (Wells/H.H.Stephenson)		2
- Myrtle	b Iddison	3	[19] c Mudie b Iddison		0
H.Deane	run out (Sewell/H.H.Steph'son)	2	[17] c Iddison b Griffith		1
*G.H.B.Gilbert	c Wells b Iddison	10	c Mudie b Griffith		1
- Curran	b Sewell	4	[15] c & b Iddison		15
H.C.E.Newcombe	b Sewell	11	[9] b Griffith		0
O.H.Lewis	c Mortlock b Griffith	0	[3] b Griffith		1
E.W.Ward	st H.H.Stephenson b Iddison	18	[11] b Sewell		2
- Taylor	b Sewell	0	[18] st H.H.Stephenson b Iddison		2
T.H.Lewis	c & b Sewell	1	[5] c Mudie b Griffith		1
J.Moore	st H.H.Stephenson b Sewell	0	[16] c Lawrence b Griffith		2
J.Kinloch	b Griffith	0	[20] b Griffith		5
- Cleeve	b Griffith	0	[4] b Sewell		0
- Fowler	run out (Iddison)	0	[22] not out		6
- Coulter	not out	2	[13] run out (E.Stephenson)		2
- Readett	st H.H.Stephenson b Iddison	0	[21] c Mudie b Griffith		2
Extras lb 4		4	b 1 lb 3 w 2		6
Totals		**127**			**65**

Fall: 1/9 2/24 3/27 4/34 5/34 6/47 7/68 8/70 9/89   1/3 2/7 3/7 4/9 5/9 6/12 7/16 8/21 9/21
      10/90 11/99 12/104 13/108 14/108 15/116   10/22 11/28 12/31 13/31 14/33 15/47
      16/116 17/125 18/125 19/125 20/126 21/127   16/49 17/51 18/51 19/51 20/58 21/65

Bowling	Balls	Runs	Wickets		Balls	Wides	Runs	Wickets
Caffyn	28	13	0	Griffith	181	2	22	11
Sewell	136	28	9	Sewell	116	0	30	5
Mudie	32	22	0	Iddison	64	0	7	3
Iddison	108	28	5					
Bennett	48	8	0					
Wells	24	3	0					
Griffith	80	21	4					

ALL ENGLAND XI WON BY 49 RUNS

*A primitif picture shows the New South Wales 22 in the field against England, and the
undeveloped landscape beyond the bounds of the Domain.*

Griffith was feeling better with figures of 11 for 22 off 45.1 overs. Sewell had 5 for 30, Iddison 3 for 7, and the Englishmen were looking unbeatable once more. And no-one seems to have complained at the run rate: 433 runs over four days.

The New South Wales men did have something to be proud of: for a start, the margin of defeat was much lighter than that suffered by the Victorian 18 in the first tour match. Nor had New South Wales allowed England anywhere nearly as many runs. These precious facts came in useful when the inevitable old arguments between intercolonial rivals were rekindled.

Great was the admiration for the English cricketers. They bowled over 800 balls, of which it was estimated that 665 were either not scored from or even intercepted by the bat; and yet only one bye resulted, a tribute to the combination of wicketkeeper H.H.Stephenson and his long-stop Mortlock. Added to all their individual skills with bat and ball, they showed well as ambassadors – Griffith's show of dissent apart – giving friendly advice to their opponents and being generous with applause.

So feverish had been interest in the game that the *Sydney Mail* saw fit to reprint its main edition. Freeman Brothers, of George Street, had immortalised the event with a panoramic photograph, and as excitement continued to spread, the

Clarence River cricket authorities conveyed a request to Spiers and Pond to bring the team to northern New South Wales. Unluckily for them, the calendar was now pretty full.

The Englishmen had to brace themselves for another banquet, this one at the Hall of Exchange, with 150 people present, including both teams, but without any Government ministers. The tourists found their names on individual shields that were suspended from the pillars in the hall, laurel wreaths around them. How susceptible to swelled heads some of the cricketers must have been.

The Hon. J.B.Darvall, president of the NSWCA, lawyer and politician, presided over the occasion, in the presence of the Governor and three MPs who tonight had put cricket before politics, and after the anthem the speeches flowed, the most remarkable being a toast to the Prince Consort. Communications being so limited, nobody in Australia yet knew that Albert had been dead for a month.

The toast to the Governor, Sir John Young, who had evidently been a cricketer in his youth, was duly cordial and flattering, the band following with a rendition of *Fine Old English Gentleman,* His Excellency's response a masterpiece. He spoke of the natural beauty of the Outer Domain and said that the ancient Greeks would surely have chosen such a site for their own athletic pursuits. He thought back to the huge attendances on Epsom Downs on Derby Day, but declared he would sooner be at a cricket match. Cricket 'brings together men of all classes and all grades in society upon a perfectly equal footing,' he said, perhaps then overstriding in terms of optimism by suggesting that the 'admirable system of umpires' ensured that there would never be disputes. He also believed that cricket demanded 'studied and continued temperance', even more so here than in England, the weather being so enervating. The English cricketers doubtless went on sipping. The Governor was sure that they would have many good memories to enjoy in later years as they sat by their firesides, reflecting on how their voyage to Australia had taken only a quarter of the time taken by ships fifty years earlier. His eulogy went on, to be met at the end by a standing ovation.

Mr Darvall spoke again, in extraordinarily warm terms: 'In New South Wales we could not grow hops, cherries, and cricketers as they do in Kent or Surrey, but there are three sentiments which have taken deep root in this colony; they are – love of sport, love of fair play, and love of Old England' [vociferous cheering]. By the time he had finished, it was no easy matter for H.H.Stephenson to compose a response. The hospitality and kindness had been overwhelming, even displayed by 'the poor boys without shoes or stockings'. But by way of a

George Gilbert, captain of NSW, and cousin of the Graces of Gloucestershire.

minor grumble: 'No doubt these poor fellows meant their attentions as a kindness, but they were a great bore' [laughter].

The vice-chairman became more high-flown than his predecessors, saying that the English cricketers were 'of the same mettle as the soldiers of the British Army; they were brothers of those who did the daring deeds of Alma, who made the splendid chivalrous charge at Balaklava, and made so splendid a stand at Inkerman'. Should Britain go to war again, they were assured that the Volunteers of New South Wales would offer full support.

Service chiefs responded, and then HH stood again and toasted the Twenty-two of New South Wales – 'jolly good fellows', brethren rather than opponents – revealing that Gilbert, the locals' captain, had let him bat on yesterday when he ought to have been out. Was this a bat-pad dispute, or perhaps a bump ball that wasn't? Was HH's integrity thus placed in question? George Gilbert in turn praised the visitors, who had taught so much already by example. He admitted that his own men had much to do about their fielding and catching. (Gilbert, who had played for Middlesex before emigrating in 1852, was once a tobacconist, a 'muscular Christian', selector as well as captain, with a growing family. In England in 1886 his half-brother, caught stealing in the pavilion, was given 28 days' hard labour and banished to Canada. George himself fell on bad times, once abandoning his wife and tramping around New Zealand. They both begged for assistance from the NSWCA in those hard years. Gilbert died poor in 1906, aged 76.)

Vice-chairman Isaacs toasted Spiers and Pond for their spirit and enterprise, and the former – with Pond, through 'indisposition', unable to attend – was duly appreciative, and affirmed that Mallam had been told to spare no expense in gathering the best cricketers available for the tour. Mallam in turn spoke of his mission, saying that if this tour had not come off, it would probably have been many years before one did. He referred to the ignorance of Australia which prevailed in England – one phenomenon which remains unchanged across the years – and said that this tour would result in the cricketers returning home to paint a more realistic and encouraging picture of the colony.

The ladies, the Governor's wife in particular, were toasted as the band played *Here's a Health to All Good Lasses*, and, it being a 'stag' dinner, Sir John Young rose to respond, pointing out proudly that Lady Young had heartily bestowed her applause on local and visiting players alike. He finished with the remark that not only had there been a 'fine display of health and beauty amongst the spectators, but also the display of good feeling and good order'. Clearly an early Euro-sceptic, he suggested that this was a spectacle that not many of the capital cities of Europe could rival.

Several further toasts were taken up, much of the content phatic, apart from Mr Darvall's strong plea for a major cricket ground to be established in Sydney; and then, at 11 o'clock, all was finally done with, the company cheering the Governor loudly as he left the room and headed off to his waiting carriage.

On the Monday, the team were treated to a benefit picnic cruise. The steamer *City of Newcastle*, with 150 on board, left Circular Quay and headed up-river as far as Hunter's Hill, showing the Englishmen 'the romantic scenery of the harbour' and 'the many picturesque villas which adorn its slopes'. After returning briefly to the Cove, they chugged along the southern bays before crossing from Watson's Bay to Middle Harbour, where some went fishing, and after lunch the German band struck up on the poop deck, and the dancing began. Someone suggested moving on to Manly, which was then a natural wonderland, home to rosellas and whipbirds, bottlebrush trees and wildflowers, though no Norfolk Island pines were yet noticeable. So Captain Harding upped anchor and off they went, for more fun at 'Mr Chalk's new room at the Steyne Hotel'. As the *Sydney Mail* delicately put it, 'at about 6 o'clock the stragglers in the bush were summoned by the repeated firing of the steamer's gun'. The skipper then took them round North Head back to the beach they had recently inhabited, and as they plied back into the Harbour the merry passengers danced the polka and waltzed until the sea spray became too much. Believing that those who had stayed behind on the small fishing boats had made their way back to Sydney independently, the skipper had almost reached the Quay when prevailed upon to turn round and have one final search for the boats. It was as well that he did. There they still were, 'having experienced no small amount of surprise and vexation at seeing the steamer pass without waiting for them'. Darkness was falling and the waters were getting choppy. But all ended well, and the English cricketers thanked their hosts profusely for a memorable outing.

As they moved on, the tourists will have known well enough that their visit had altered perceptions. Not everyone had been in awe when they arrived. But Sydney cricket knew where it stood as they departed. The influential Richard Driver had been so excited by rising standards in intercolonial cricket that he had told Will Hammersley, the one-time Victoria captain, that 'eleven natives could play any eleven in the world'. Hammersley, a Cambridge Blue and former Surrey player, knew better: 'Pardon me, Mr Driver, but you don't know yet what cricket really is.'

Despite having dubbed this recent match as the second 'test match', Hammersley regarded Australian cricket as still crude and unscientific. Now, after the All England victory at the Domain, Driver amended his opinion, though he added prophetically: 'But mark me, some of our natives will astonish the world yet.' Both lived to hear of Australia's victory in the first of all Test matches, in 1877, and of the shock defeat in one day of MCC – WG and all – at Lord's in 1878 by Dave Gregory's pioneers.

As H.H.Stephenson and his band boarded the coach to cross the Blue Mountains to Bathurst for the next engagement, Charlie Lawrence was aglow with the knowledge that the Albert club, having considered the 'propriety' of engaging him as professional coach, had decided that terms might be mutually agreed.

For the tour itinerary, the news about to be conveyed was not so good, for only six people, including the Press, bothered to turn up on February 6 at the Commercial Hotel in Goulburn for a meeting aimed at finalising arrangements for the visit of the Englishmen. Plans for a match in Goulburn were therefore scratched. Spiers and Pond had reduced their terms from £750 plus expenses to £600. In mid-January, they had started negotiations with Bathurst, to the west and about the same distance from Sydney, a town near which Hargraves had found his fateful gold eleven years ago. Spiers and Pond's asking price here was also shaved down from an opening £750 to £600, and after a meeting of the town elders an offer of £500 was telegraphed to the sponsors, who accepted it. Then began the work of collecting local pledges to meet the financial commitment.

There was the odd protest at the fact that the visit of the English cricketers would interfere with the town's race meeting, but on January 18 the *Bathurst Free Press* fired a swift retort to that: 'Every spirited Briton in the district would surely prefer to witness a display of the cricket science and agility of eleven men, the pick of millions, to the confusion, gambling and cruelty of horse racing'. Advertisements appeared in the paper: local players would practise every day from 5.30 to 7.30 in the morning and between 4 pm and sunset; publicans wanting booths at the match should apply to the Guarantee Committee; any match surplus would be given to charitable institutions in the district. Tickets for the grandstand were available for a shilling from Mr Turner at Rogers' Hotel. He was the uncle of the about-to-be-conceived Charles Thomas Biass Turner, who, 33 years later almost to the day, became the first Australian to take 100 Test wickets. Meanwhile, Charles, CTB's father-to-be, played host to the local cricketers, who were to meet at his inn in Durham Street.

Cricket fever swept the region. News of the earlier matches had been avidly devoured from the newspapers, and now Bathurst's turn had come. The townsfolk knew their best cricketers could not hope to match the Englishmen's play, but that did not diminish their pride and excitement. The local paper believed that the visit ensured that Bathurst henceforth would play second fiddle to no other inland town in the colony. Just as determinedly, the gathering at Charles Turner's had vowed that they would meet the incoming cricketers on the Sydney Road, and that it would be a 'truly English shake-hand meeting accompanied with a hip-hip-hip worthy of a hearty Australian welcome'.

And so it was. Those in the crush who had emigrated, recently or long ago, were stirred by deep emotion. 'In meeting with these eleven Englishmen,' as an editorial put it, 'a sight of very England itself' was obtained. The planned orderly procession stood no chance. People rushed out along the Sydney Road that afternoon on foot and on horseback, carriages rumbling along through the mass, one vehicle holding the Buckingham band, another most of the Bathurst 22.

Hoisting their banner newly arrived from England, members of the Kincora Lodge joined the throng. About four miles out of town, William H.Oakes, honorary treasurer of the match committee, brought some order by halting and lining up the carriages so that the incoming coach could drive through. From this position a broad view across the plain could be had.

Around 5 o'clock, a rising cloud of dust could just be picked out on the horizon, and up went a cry of 'They come!' Fifteen minutes later, drawn by six grey horses and crammed with English cricketers, Gaynor's American coach was with them, and after all the great anticipation many of the citizens were struck dumb with wonder. But cheers rang, and the band struck up, and with the Englishmen quietly raising their caps in acknowledgement, the cavalcade of a thousand souls headed towards Bathurst midst a certain chaos.

In the town, the bells of All Saints rang loudly, and a further thousand people were noisy in their welcome as the weary travellers disembarked and entered their new home, the Club House Hotel. In sad reality, for the Bathurst community the best was already past.

For a start, there was no Press tent at the ground, so the local reporter had to sit on the grass in the full glare of the sun next morning. Then, after the threat of rain receded, spectators were coming through the ground entrance on the Denison Bridge side for two hours before the start of play at 1 o'clock, 'the youth and beauty of the district' filling the grandstand. Perhaps the six-year-old George Bonnor, an Australian batting giant of the future, was there with his Herefordshire-born father. Besides the fifteen refreshment booths there were numerous fruit stalls, and with 3000 in the ground later, the town was shorn of a large chunk of its population.

But there were major problems, for the pitch was too dry, and the ball flew dangerously, and on such a vast field everything seemed distant, and the local opposition proved feeble, and, worst of all, the weather was to turn vicious.

Bathurst having decided to field and giving three cheers to England's openers, a nervous 18-year-old named Tress began the bowling to George Bennett, who opened with Ned Stephenson, and it was not long before the local reporter was worriedly noting that the Englishmen looked even better players than had been expected: 'the ease and grace with which everything was done was truly admirable'. The disparity was emphasised by the poor fielding and catching by the locals, and the reporter hinted that any inflated opinion they might have had of themselves would now need revision.

By the first evening All England had made around 200 runs for the loss of nine wickets, H.H.Stephenson having put himself in at No.11. Tress had become the local hero with eight wickets for 70 off 43.3 overs by the time the innings closed next morning for 211, three of his victims being caught-and-bowled. Bennett scored 38, Griffith 35, Sewell 21, Wells 18 not out, Hearne 17, Caffyn 16, and Ned Stephenson 12, but the captain failed again with 7. Thirteen wides and 22 byes helped the cause. Iddison and Lawrence were both bowled for ducks by Tress, and while Lawrence had compensation later with a bucketful of wickets, the Yorkshireman was left to reflect, as cricketers often do, that it was a long way

BATHURST, February 6, 7, 1862
Toss won by Bathurst   Umpires: W.Mortlock & unknown

ALL ENGLAND XI

G.Bennett	c Perry b Tress	38	*Bowling*	*Balls*	*Wides*	*Runs*	*Wickets*
E.Stephenson	c & b Tress	12	Tress	175	4	70	8
R.Iddison	b Tress	0	G.Richardson	140	9	85	0
G.Griffith	c Dargin b Cassidy	35	Cassidy	32	0	30	1
C.Lawrence	b Tress	0					
W.Caffyn	c & b Tress	16					
W.Mudie	run out	2					
T.Hearne	c & b Tress	17					
T.Sewell	b Tress	21					
G.Wells	not out	18					
*H.H.Stephenson	c Grut b Tress	7					
Extras b 22 lb 10 w 13		45					
Total		**211**					

TWENTY-TWO OF BATHURST

49 (top score Hooper 9; 10 ducks; captain: J.Cassidy; bowling: Lawrence 102 balls, 24 runs, 11 wickets; Bennett 100 balls, 19 runs, 7 wickets) and **25 for 6** (Iddison took at least 3 wickets, Lawrence at least 1; 1 of the Bathurst batsmen was run out)

MATCH UNFINISHED (Abandoned: rain)

to travel – in his case across the Blue Mountains and back – to make nothing.

There was no danger that the visitors would be pressed in this match. By lunch on this second day they had removed 18 of the Bathurst 22 for 42 runs, and with Lawrence and Bennett bowling through the innings, they had the locals all out for a derisory 49, which included 10 ducks. Lawrence took 11 for 24, Bennett 7 for 19.

Bathurst followed on and were 25 for 6 when, around half-past-five, a truly terrible storm broke over the ground. Rain washed down and lightning flashed. People huddled in whatever shelter they could find, and some of the tents and booths were torn from their moorings. Not the least worry was the horses. But there were no reports of injury to human or animal, though several bridges were washed away and fences came down. The cricket ground was flooded. So wet was it that there could be no play on the final day, and there was only the gloomy sight of the booths and stalls being taken down.

Of course, there was a gala dinner. H.H.Stephenson and the local captain, Cassidy, sat one side of the chairman, W.H.Oliver, with Christopher Pond on the other. The tables were heavily laden with good food and wine at Mr Chapman's Club House Hotel, and when all had had their fill, the toasts and speeches began. This time, after Her Majesty had been toasted, a great deal was made of the toast to Prince Albert, her eldest son, who was a bit of a cricketer, among other things, and would one day become King Edward VII. His name had been coupled with those of his father, the Prince Consort, and the rest of the Royal family. Australia still had no way of knowing that the Queen's beloved husband had died eight weeks earlier.

Next, the Governor was remembered, then the Army and Navy, then the All England XI, to which HH responded with something brief and appreciative, touching on the warnings he had been given about the journey across the mountains to reach Bathurst: it would be a rough one, they were told, with breakdowns and upsets and hair-breadth escapes. But they had undertaken it, and while there were many ups and downs along the tracks, the warm and hearty manner in which they had been received had amply repaid them. Looking at the numbers that came to greet them, they had scanned the crowd and were glad to see so many 'right English faces' among them.

In responding to the Spiers and Pond toast, Pond reiterated that financial benefit had not been their sole motive in creating the tour, and they would like to repeat it every two years. As for a deeper purpose, he hoped that the colonies would benefit from the tour by way of impetus to emigration of the kind of people Australia needed, namely 'men of small capital and large families'. Nor had they been easily frightened when told of the hazards of travelling across the Blue Mountains. H.H.Stephenson, he said, was planning to write a book on the tour, and would write favourably about their hosts. (No such book was ever published.)

HH addressed the gathering, wishing the local cricketers well, complimenting one in particular (undoubtedly Tress, for his 8 for 70) and lamenting the fact that they were so obviously nervous as the match started. Cassidy, their captain, replied, saying that they had proved wrong those people who predicted they would not bowl England out in a week. And when they batted, they gradually learned to relax as it became clear that the Englishmen were not bowling at their legs, arms and bodies, but at the stumps (seven of Lawrence's 11 wickets were bowled).

Mr Oakes announced that a surplus of between £100 and £160 had resulted, and would go to the charitable institutions. He then adjourned the dinner, it being 10 pm, so that they could all go to the theatre, where the presentation of prize bats would take place. There, the curtain went up, with the cricketers on stage, the auditorium 'tolerably well filled', and Cassidy presented the bats to Bennett for top-scoring with 38, and Hooper, a player from Sofala, whose modest offering of 9 was top score in Bathurst's innings of 49. Pond then gave a bat to the bowling hero, Tress.

Back in the hotel, HH was presented with a chain made of 'colonial gold', and understandably found it hard to express his gratitude adequately. Mr Chapman, their host, had given each of the team a specimen of gold-bearing quartz, while some had received pieces of stalactite from the Fish River Caves.

More toasts, more songs, more music from the Buckingham band, until at midnight it was thought time to end it. The team left Bathurst at six in the morning on the Sunday, unable to stay longer because of the important match coming up in Sydney, the irony being that the Victorians were going to be late in arriving, causing the match to be postponed 24 hours.

The return coach trip behind them, the Englishmen settled into their Sydney lodgings again and prepared for the match against Twenty-two of New South Wales & Victoria. But of the Sydney-bound *Rangatira*, bearing the Victorian contingent, there was no sign. Alarm intensified. Feeling uneasy, Spiers and Pond tried to commission a search vessel but none was available. Then, out of the night, *Rangatira* entered Sydney Harbour, battered from an inordinately rough 4½-day passage, and the cricketers finally disembarked a little unsteadily, to be taken to their Pitt Street hotel. They gamely agreed to start the match at noon next day.

In the absence of the overdue Victorians, the Englishmen and their New South Wales opponents had got up a scratch match between 1 pm and 6.30, by way of entertainment for the couple of thousand disappointed onlookers. Five New South Welshmen joined six Englishmen in each team, the Stephensons being the captains, and success came the way of Kettle (24), Griffith (36), and Mortlock (33), with HH (38) relieved to feel some runs coming from his bat at last. Hearne scored 23 later, and although the other innings was truncated, it had been a helpful workout.

The roll-up for the big match next day was not at first quite as impressive as for the earlier one on the Domain, morning showers having deterred many. But as word spread that the United Elevens' team was complete with the late arrival of the feared-for Victorians, the crowd swelled to around 10,000 – including the Governor – with many stalls and sideshows, one featuring the 'Female Prodigy', and another 'the oleaginous Australian Youth' who 'announced his levees'.

OUTER DOMAIN, SYDNEY, February 12, 1862
Scratch match

H.H.STEPHENSON'S XI

R.Iddison	c Gregory b Sewell	6
J.L.Kettle	c Hearne b Bennett	24
G.T.Curtis	c Cleeve b Caffyn	8
G.Griffith	b Wells	36
F Rowley	lbw b Bennett	2
W.Mortlock	c Cleeve b Bennett	33
J.Moore	c Gregory b Bennett	2
C.Lawrence	c Gregory b Bennett	3
- Curran	b Bennett	0
*H.H.Stephenson	b Wells	38
W.Mudie	not out	17
Extras b 6 lb 1		7
Total		**176**

E.STEPHENSON'S XI

N.F.D.Thomson	b Iddison	5
T.Hearne	c Rowley b Lawrence	23
G.Wells	b Lawrence	17
A.L.Park	not out	2
W.Caffyn	not out	7
		0
3 wkts		**54**

Did not bat: Gregory, *E.Stephenson, T.Sewell, G.Bennett, Cleeve, Muddle

128

Nat Thomson in later years. He became a Test cricketer in 1877.

Elsewhere, in a sombre tent, an enterprising 'mechanician' presented a 'living phenomenon of the players and everything moving', which presumably was a magic projection thing all done by mirrors. Bands played and drums banged and scorecard vendors shouted.

There was a sense of occasion as 'the test match of the tour' commenced just after 12.30 with the entry of the umpires, Mudie and Curtis. Bennett took strike for All England, facing George Gilbert, with George Moore bowling from the other end. All went according to expectation, with Bennett and Iddison both missed in the deep, before the first wicket went down at 21. From that point on, thrills rippled round the ground as England lost all 10 wickets for a further 39 runs. A sensation was unfolding.

Thomson stumped Iddison (14) to start the collapse. Cosstick then ran out Bennett, before further catches were spilt, one even by the superb Gregory.

Griffith and Caffyn tried to rally England, but the left-hander holed out for 11, the only other double-figure score of the innings, which made it 42 for 4. Without addition, Caffyn (6) was run out, a blow that had real significance (and possibly caused him to reveal his temper, as *Cricket* once described: he would fling his bat into the tent from ten or fifteen yards away, then one glove, then the other, then Billy himself, 'stamping his feet and telling us he ought to be horsewhipped for getting out').

Ned Stephenson was stumped without scoring, and a one-handed running catch by George Moore put paid to Wells. With Sewell's departure to a fine catch by Gregory at straight-hit, H.H.Stephenson's demise at long-off, and Hearne's dismissal at point, All England were suddenly all out and done for a pitiful 60 in 41.3 overs, the bowling having been carried exclusively by Moore and Gilbert, the slow bowlers, who took four wickets each.

At 4 o'clock, the Englishmen took the field with their reputations on the line, and knowing there was much work to be done. This was the strongest combination they would face on the tour, the cream of the two colonies. Park and Brodie opened quite confidently to the bowling of Sewell from the northern end, Griffith from the other, scoring 13 before Brodie was out. Four were gone by the time the fifty appeared, Caffyn having missed a catch at long-on. He made amends by bowling the talented Kettle, but Nat Thomson was soon hitting a four that brought the scores level, then pushed Lawrence for a single that gave the United 22 a prestigious first-innings lead to twin with the one they secured at Melbourne. Thomson fell to a hot caught-and-bowled to Caffyn, who was then hit to the Parliamentary tent by Cosstick to raise the 70. Park, the top scorer, was next run out for 20, and Cosstick, the last of the four batsmen to reach the distinction of double figures, was held by Iddison in the long-field. When stumps were drawn at 6.30, the Twenty-two of New South Wales & Victoria were 81 for 12 wickets, 21 ahead with nine to fall.

Resuming at 11.15 next morning, the United side lost two more wickets before a run was scored, but the remaining seven managed to get the total up to 101, which gave them a lead of 41. England's best bowlers were Lawrence with 9 for 36 and Caffyn with 7 for 36. The visitors' batting was now fully expected to make up for its limp first-innings performance.

This time Lawrence and Bennett opened. But Lawrence was quickly caught off the wily George Moore, who was to bowl right through the innings again. Then Gilbert trapped Bennett, and Moore picked up the prize wicket of Caffyn. Either side of lunch, Mortlock (20) and Griffith (38) steadied the innings, putting on 35 for the fourth wicket, but they were the only batsmen to reach double figures as the All England innings raced to a second embarrassing conclusion for 75. Only Wells among the Englishmen was bowled out (by Conway) throughout the match, fourteen catches being held by the colonials.

Already there were rumbles of suspicion and displeasure among those who had put money on the Englishmen to win this match or to remain unbeaten on the tour. Surely they wouldn't be so foul as to 'throw' a match? The upright character of the captain suggests that no such thing were possible, but gossip is sometimes unstaunchable.

George Moore finished with 6 for 39 (10 for 61 for the match), and Gilbert, his captain, was credited with good deployment of his fieldsmen – not unduly difficult to achieve, perhaps, with 20 of them at his disposal. The United team were thus left in need of 35 for a famous victory, and with stumps having been drawn at 5.40 pm as the final English wicket fell, they had all night to think about it.

HH trusted Caffyn and Sewell, his sharpest bowlers, to save the match, and wickets toppled one after the other. But the runs were found, and with Park (3) and Brodie (0) at the wicket, the New South Wales & Victoria 22 sealed their triumph by 12 wickets, Cosstick yet again doing himself proud, top-scoring with nine priceless runs. Caffyn's 6 for 16 had been in vain.

Immediately, the theorising began. Was all the travelling weakening the Englishmen? Not only were there unpalatable suggestions in some quarters that the match might have been thrown: were they over-indulging off the field of play? Years later, in his book, Billy Caffyn confessed that 'scarcely a day passed without our being entertained to champagne breakfasts, luncheons and dinners', and when thinking back to this match, he wrote that 'we once more had high jinks at Sydney'. Might this have contributed to his dual batting failure? If so, the 'relaxation' did his bowling no harm: he took 13 for 52 in the match.

The Englishmen, it was reported, took their defeat 'in the most kindly manner . . . no losing of temper, no manifestation of annoyance'. It was a major milestone in Australian cricket history: the first victory by a colonial team, albeit with odds, over a representative English team. February 15, 1862 thus became a red-letter day. The *Sydney Morning Herald* recognised the significance: 'A new cricketing era has doubtless commenced throughout this and the sister colony of

OUTER DOMAIN, SYDNEY, February 13, 14, 15, 1862

Toss won by All England   Umpires: P.C.Curtis & W.Mudie

ALL ENGLAND XI

G.Bennett	run out (Cosstick/Gilbert)	7	c Curtis b Gilbert		4
R.Iddison	st Thomson b Gilbert	14	[7] c Curtis b G.Moore		0
G.Griffith	c Gregory b Gilbert	11	[5] c Gregory b G.Moore		38
W.Mortlock	c Gilbert b G.Moore	4	[3] c Newcombe b G.Moore		20
W.Caffyn	run out (Gilbert)	6	[4] c Smith b G.Moore		1
E.Stephenson	st Thomson b Gilbert	0	[11] not out		1
*H.H.Stephenson	c Cosstick b G.Moore	4	[10] c Newcombe b G.Moore		4
G.Wells	c G.Moore b Gilbert	2	b Conway		0
T.Sewell	c Gregory b G.Moore	1	[6] run out		6
C.Lawrence	not out	4	[2] c – Huddlestone b G.Moore		0
T.Hearne	c Curtis b G.Moore	7	[9] c Curtis b Conway		1
Extras		0			0
Totals		**60**			**75**

Fall: 1/21 2/22 3/27 4/42 5/42 6/42 7/46 8/47   1/2 2/8 3/11 4/46 5/68 6/69 7/69
       9/51 10/60   8/70 9/73 10/75

Bowling	Balls	Runs	Wickets		Balls	Runs	Wickets
Gilbert	84	38	4	Gilbert	80	31	1
G.Moore	83	22	4	G.Moore	122	39	6
				Conway	44	5	2

TWENTY-TWO OF NEW SOUTH WALES & VICTORIA

A.L.Park	run out (H.H.Stephenson)	20	[9] not out		3
- Brodie	c Bennett b Sewell	7	[11] not out		0
F.Rowley	st H.H.Stephenson b Iddison	3			
- Smith	b Lawrence	4			
- Curran	b Lawrence	10			
J.Huddlestone	st H.H.Stephenson b Caffyn	11	[3] c & b Caffyn		6
J.L.Kettle	b Caffyn	2	[5] b Caffyn		2
N.F.D.Thomson	c & b Caffyn	5	[2] c E.Stephenson b Caffyn		1
S.Cosstick	c Iddison b Caffyn	10	[4] b Sewell		9
H.C.E.Newcombe	lbw b Lawrence	1	[6] c E.Stephenson b Sewell		4
T.Huddlestone	b Lawrence	0	[7] c Wells b Caffyn		0
S.G.Hopkinson	run out (E.Ste'son/H.H.Ste'son)	5			
G.T.Curtis	b Lawrence	0	[8] c Wells b Caffyn		0
- Gregory	b Lawrence	5			
*G.H.B.Gilbert	c Iddison b Caffyn	0	[1] b Caffyn		2
T.Moore	st H.H.Stephenson b Caffyn	6			
J.Clarke	c Wells b Lawrence	0			
J.Moore	c & b Lawrence	3			
G.Elliott	run out	2			
J.Boak	c Griffith b Caffyn	3			
J.Conway	not out	2	[10] c Wells b Sewell		3
G.Moore	c Iddison b Lawrence	0			
Extras lb 2		2	lb 5		5
Totals		**101**	9 wkts		**35**

Fall: 1/13 2/22 3/27 4/41 5/56 6/58 7/64 8/74 9/74   1/2 2/9 3/11 4/24 5/27 6/27 7/27
       10/75 11/75 12/76 13/81 14/81 15/87 16/91   8/27 9/32
       17/91 18/94 19/97 20/99 21/101

Bowling	Balls	Runs	Wickets		Balls	Runs	Wickets
Sewell	40	9	1	Caffyn	72	16	6
Griffith	28	8	0	Sewell	72	14	3
Iddison	20	10	1				
Lawrence	128	36	9				
Caffyn	116	36	7				

TWENTY-TWO OF NEW SOUTH WALES & VICTORIA WON BY 12 WICKETS

Victoria, and the prevalent mania will probably rage with greater or less violence for some time to come. From this date cricket becomes the leading national pastime of Australia.'

And the 'prevalent mania' rages still, almost a century-and-a-half later.

The All England cricketers attended a performance of *Rip Van Winkle* and *Mazappa*, a burlesque, for their benefit at the Victoria Theatre, which was packed out. With the Governor and the Mayor of Sydney and a gaggle of VIPs in the audience, H.H.Stephenson, standing with his team on stage, read a farewell address, for they would not be returning to Sydney. There were several other speeches, before an adjournment to Tattersall's for some 'parting bumpers' to be exchanged with their host of friends.

The journey to Tasmania was to be via Melbourne, and their sailing from Sydney was well enough publicised for there to be thousands of people to see them off not only at Circular Quay but from vantage points all along the harbour. As their trusty vessel moved seawards, rockets and blue lights burst into the night sky, and not every onlooking eye was dry. The All England visit had been symbolic, as – from the viewpoint of their emigrant cousins and brothers – are all tours by cricketers from home. Friendly folk left behind; more awaiting up ahead.

Hobart at the time the first English cricketers landed there.

CHAPTER 10

Apple Isle and Goldfields

HAVING safely negotiated the turbulent Bass Strait crossing from Melbourne to what was earlier named Van Diemen's Land, *Royal Shepherd* let her passengers ashore at Launceston, forty miles up the River Tamar, on the north coast, where an enthusiastic crowd – and the inescapable brass band – greeted them. The English cricketers responded to the crowds in the street by appearing on the balcony of their haven, the Launceston Club Hotel in Brisbane Street, where a public dinner was laid on for them, presided over by the Mayor. They had loosened up with some practice at the local ground, watched by several hundred fascinated locals. From here, it was a case of crossing the triangular island of Tasmania in one of Page's coaches, a journey of some 150 miles, starting at 5 o'clock next morning, with keen greetings at all the hamlets along the way. Their progress was smooth, thanks to a comfortable coach and a road which was almost completely macadamised. A floral welcoming arch had been erected at Melton Mowbray, where there was fruit and wine refreshment for them, and at Oaklands they were presented with an illuminated address. Further honours came their way at O'Brien's Bridge. People really did care.

Once in Hobart, the cricketers were surrounded by a sizable portion of the stable population of 89,000. A welcoming deputation, with the Rifle Corps band, the 22 Tasmanian cricketers, and all manner of curious followers, had met them at New Town, several miles out, where they arrived nearly two hours late that evening and had a fine meal at the Horse & Jockey. Then they were escorted into Hobart, along Elizabeth and Liverpool Streets, thoroughfares thick with jubilant people, passing under more welcoming arches, until finally reaching the comfort of their short-term home, the Union Club Hotel in Murray Street. Soon the English cricketers were unpacking their bags with relief and washing the dust from their persons.

Only eight Aboriginals remained in Tasmania now, and soon there would be none, and what was later dubbed 'the Apple Isle' was still strongly identified with the horrific harshness of the notorious penal settlement at Port Arthur. Hobart, nestling by the waters of the Derwent and beneath the often mist-shrouded Mount Wellington, appealed to some if not to all, as shown by one visitor's verdict in the mid-1850s – 'an opulent city' with 'an amount of animation and even gaiety in the streets . . . that proves exhilarating to a stranger' – against another's in the late 1860s: 'perhaps twice as large and straggling as Dorchester, Ipswich or Bury, but ten times more stagnant, dull and lifeless'.

The match had taken some setting-up. At first, Spiers and Pond's terms had seemed well beyond the cricket community's ability to meet them. They had asked £1000 plus travelling and subsistence expenses, saying that they had cleared £450 at Beechworth and saw no reason why the Hobart match, with entrance money and income from the booths, should not result in a surplus of £1500 for the Tasmanians. Thomas Westbrook, trustee of Hobart Cricket Ground and a batsman and point fieldsman of note, seemed prepared somehow to raise the necessary funds, but a meeting on January 24 concluded that the demand was too high. John Davies, proprietor of the *Mercury* newspaper, sailed to Melbourne to present the promoters with a counter-offer of £500 plus all expenses. A component of the consortium's funding plan was a promise from a gentleman named Gardiner to give half the takings from a special performance by the American Circus, which was now in Hobart. This, it was thought, would add £70 or so to revenues. In the event, it amounted to £22.

With their tour itinerary still far from full and settled, Spiers and Pond suddenly came back with a fresh idea. Why not let them take all the revenues during the three-day match while they took care of their own travel costs, the locals paying all theirs for ground, players and policing? The deal was agreed.

With Hobart and Launceston being firmly independent of each other in cultural terms, a diplomatic mix of 11 players from each area made up the 22 – all amateurs – under the leadership of the strong-willed, bearded William Holden Walker, who could hit the ball as hard as any batsman in Australia or keep wicket or bowl clever lobs. (Roundarm bowling was still regarded with scepticism in Tasmania.) Born in Islington, Walker had come to the new world as recently as 1859, and was a solicitor in Launceston. The northern players, housed at the Ship Hotel, were to wear all white, while the Hobart men had shirts of scarlet, thereby precluding any full sense of unity.

H.H.Stephenson won the toss and gave the Twenty-two of Tasmania first innings on a fast pitch which soon showed as unreliable, even dangerous; so much so that HH refrained from using his fastest bowlers, Sewell and Griffith. The Lower Domain ground, cleared in 1832 by Hobart Town CC, was in a hollow in what was known as the Government Paddock, and on the western side ran a carriageway up to Government House. So marked was the slope from the Queen's Battery side to the other that a ball rolled far enough for the batsmen to run seventeen in the days before boundaries were introduced. The high ground beyond, of course, gave opportunity for many people to watch matches without paying admission. Following a merger between Hobart CC and Derwent CC, the militia took over the ground in 1839. With the opening of the Tasmanian Cricket Association ground on a higher plateau in 1881-82, the Lower Domain fell gradually into disuse, having long been prey to military exercises and public trampling. Today it is barely discernible through a thick spread of buildings, roads and car parks.

It was a beautiful sight on February 21, 1862, though the promoters were disappointed at the moderate turnout, attributed mainly to the fact that last-minute letters and parcels had to be finalised before the mail steamer left for England. That country's cricketers emerged from their tent near the Battery, while the Tasmanian openers, Tom Westbrook and left-hander Henry Dumaresq, both Apple Islanders by birth, came from a tent on the opposite side, to the left of the grandstand. It was Charles Lawrence's turn to act as umpire, his colleague being

Three Tasmanians who upheld the island's honour against All England: Henry Dumaresq (standing), Tom Whitesides, the only batsman to reach fifty in any match against the tourists, and W.H. Walker (spotted shirt) the captain.

Courtesy of Ric Finlay

W.T. Hewitt, and before the first ball was bowled by Caffyn, a charming little ceremony was transacted. The local players gave three cheers for the visitors, Stephenson's men reciprocating.

Before the Mayor of Hobart and civic and church dignitaries, play got under way just after noon. Dumaresq took a single in the second over, bowled by Bennett, but after HH and his long-stop had conceded some byes as the ball misbehaved, Bennett slipped one through Dumaresq, and the expected slide was under way. Walker, the captain, ran himself out. Soon it was five down for 21; then six for 22, before Robert Still and John Tabart added 20, each hitting two stirring fours. Iddison replaced Bennett for a time, sharing the attack from his end through the innings with Caffyn bowling unchanged from the other.

Cox also proudly hit two fours before Bennett bowled him. He was the third and last to register double figures, a feat that, in the context of contemporary cricket, almost brought hero status with it. Watson's downfall came with a lovely leaping catch at long-off by Mudie, and a batsman with the very Tasmanian name of Boon barely got off the mark.

By the lunch interval the score had advanced to 97 for the loss of 17 wickets, and soon after the accomplishment of reaching 100, the innings of the Tasmanian 22 ended for 109, if the *Sydney Mail* be believed, the *Melbourne Argus* more credibly giving 107. Iddison's underhand slows brought him 8 for 32, Bennett finished with 6 for 27, Caffyn 5 for 37. It was 4 o'clock, and a quarter-of-an-hour later All England began their reply, intent on showing that the recent Sydney performance was a passing aberration. Iddison and Ned Stephenson opened to the bowling of Still and Perry.

Runs came steadily until Iddison (10) was caught-and-bowled at 34. And then Griffith got to work, smashing a square-cut for four and hoisting another ball into the grandstand for a five, only to be run out for 11: 56 for 2. Caffyn's polished strokeplay and 'Yorkshire' Stephenson's obstinacy then carried All England to a stumps score of 81 for 2, a prospect which drew a bigger crowd on the second day, a day of delightful weather and fervent hopes that the Tasmanians would acquit themselves well.

Toss won by All England   Umpires: W.T.Hewitt & C.Lawrence

TWENTY-TWO OF TASMANIA

T.Westbrook	b Bennett	1	[7] run out		0
H.R.G.Dumaresq	b Bennett	5	run out		18
*W.H.Walker	run out	7	[5] b Sewell		7
C.T.H.Perry	b Caffyn	0	[12] c E.Stephenson b Bennett		8
H.G.Spicer	b Caffyn	2	[8] b Iddison		3
I.Brooks	b Bennett	0	[11] st H.H.Stephenson b Iddison		1
R.S.Still	b Iddison	13	[15] st H.H.Stephenson b Iddison		0
J.L.B.Tabart	b Caffyn	15	[1] run out		10
T.Whitesides	c Griffith b Bennett	7	[4] b H.H.Stephenson		50
C.H.Taylor	lbw b Bennett	1	st H.H.Stephenson b Iddison		0
T.Cox	b Bennett	11	[6] b Caffyn		2
C.Watson	c Mudie b Iddison	9	[14] lbw b Iddison		2
- Mace	c Mortlock b Iddison	0	[9] c Wells b Iddison		0
G.Boon	b Iddison	3	[18] b Iddison		9
T.F.Patterson	b Caffyn	5	[21] not out		1
W.Sidebottom	b Caffyn	2	[3] run out		2
G.Dargaville	b Iddison	5	[13] c Wells b Iddison		9
H.E.Lette	c Hearne b Iddison	3	[19] c Bennett b Iddison		2
G.Marshall	run out	0	[16] b Iddison		0
W.A.B.Jamieson	hit wkt b Iddison	3	c Wells b Caffyn		6
B.Watson	b Iddison	3	[17] b Iddison		0
G.Orford	not out	1	b Caffyn		3
Extras	b 9 lb 2	11	b 4 lb 3 w 1		8
Totals		**107**			**141**

Fall: 1/8 2/19? 3/19 4/19 5/21 6/22 7/42 8/52 9/53   1/14 2/18 3/53 4/63 5/68 6/79 7/85 8/85
10/55 11/72 12/74? 13/80 14/84 15/86 16/90   9/85 10/92 11/103? 12/110 13/117 14/117
17/97 18/97 19/99 20/104 21/107   15/117 16/117 17/? 18/? 19/132 20/136 21/141

Bowling	Balls	Runs	Wickets			Balls	Wides	Runs	Wickets
Caffyn	180	37	5		Caffyn	189	0	39	3
Bennett	104	27	6		Iddison	136	0	63	11
Iddison	66	32	8		Bennett	68	0	15	1
					Wells	24	0	1	0
					Sewell	48	1	13	1
					H.H.Stephenson	40	0	2	1

ALL ENGLAND XI

R.Iddison	c & b Still	10	[8] not out		3
E.Stephenson	c Jamieson b Spicer	60	[4] c Lette b Walker		0
G.Griffith	run out	11	[5] c Perry b Spicer		36
W.Caffyn	b Spicer	17	[6] c Westbrook b Spicer		0
W.Mortlock	c B.Watson b Spicer	0			
W.Mudie	b Spicer	7			
*H.H.Stephenson	b Walker	2	[1] not out		23
T.Hearne	not out	35	[2] c Tabart b Spicer		2
G.Bennett	b Spicer	2	[7] b Walker		2
T.Sewell	lbw b Walker	0	[3] c Lette b Walker		0
G.Wells	run out	8			
Extras	b 6 lb 1 w 16 nb 1	24	b 4 w 4 nb 1		9
Totals		**176**	6 wkts		**75**

Fall: 1/34 2/56 3/92 4/94 5/108 6/113 7/148   1/10 2/10 3/10 4/60 5/61 6/68
8/152 9/161 10/176

Bowling	Balls	Wides	Runs	Wickets		Balls	Wides	Runs	Wickets
Still	84	8	37	1	Spicer	92	4	36	3
Perry	44	2	10	0	Walker	88	0	30	3
Spicer	144	3	60	5	*Walker bowled 1 no-ball*				
Boon	12	3	1	0					
Walker	88	0	43	2					

Walker bowled 1 no-ball
Bowling plus extras makes 175

ALL ENGLAND XI WON BY 4 WICKETS

Play began at 11.15, and by 1 o'clock England had been bowled out for 176, a lead of only 69. Stephenson had gone on to a most valuable 60, strong defence blending with some resounding hits, and Tom Hearne's unbeaten 35 (three fours) from No.8 had ensured a reasonable lead. But apart from Caffyn's 17 there was little else from the bat. Spicer, a roundarmer who bowled Caffyn, Mudie and Bennett, came away with the bowling honours, securing 5 for 60 off 36 overs, while Walker's underhand 'twisters' as well as his wicketkeeping made an impression. The Tasmanians earned praise for their fielding on this rough ground.

The match had come alive, and the man from the *Argus* found the inspired prose for the occasion, the Derwent's blue waters 'glittering in the sunshine like a mirror of burnished steel' and, against the bright sky, Mount Wellington 'towering aloft like a giant guardian of the fair city'. The 'gay uniforms' of the southern cricketers contrasted finely with the 'white dresses' worn by the northerners and the Englishmen, dated language more in need of translation than most.

At 1.20 pm, the Tasmanian 22 began their second innings, Tabart this time accompanying Dumaresq, and if there is little that is unique in cricket, the loss of the first three wickets in an innings all to run-outs is unusual. Tabart, Sidebottom and Dumaresq all fell this way, making it 53 for 3. The sixth wicket to fall, Westbrook's, was also to a run-out; but the runs were accumulating, and the man chiefly responsible was 25-year-old Tom Whitesides, a Hobart-born right-hander, who held out for almost four hours for a score of 50 which amazingly was to remain the only half-century made against All England from one end of their tour to the other. He reached the boundary three times and also picked up a three, seven twos and 21 singles, his tenacity and skill being rewarded with a prize bat which was still in the proud possession of the family over a century later. It took one of H.H.Stephenson's slightly grotesque breakbacks, pitched short, to terminate his monumental innings four minutes from the end. Whitesides, who became secretary of the Southern Tasmanian Cricket Association in 1866, was to live until 1919, dying at the age of 83, a month after Billy Caffyn.

Hearne had taken ill during the second afternoon, and was replaced in the field by one of the local players, though he was well enough to bat in the second innings. By the close the Tasmanians, at 111 for 12, were 42 ahead, and the final day – after a Sunday of rest – afforded an intriguing prospect.

It began with environmental problems, for the temperature was cruelly high, and smoke from nearby bushfires caused discomfort for the 3000 around the ground who had paid their one-and-sixpence. To general relief, a sea breeze sprang up around noon to make life easier, but by then the Tasmanian innings was over, the last nine wickets having mustered only 30 runs. Iddison had another field day to finish with 11 for 63. H.H.Stephenson, too, did well, making three stumpings ('a cat watching a mouse' was the popular impression) off Iddison apart from bowling top-scorer Whitesides and finishing with one wicket for 2 off 10 overs. And now, at last, he was to make runs.

All England's target was 73, and HH took Hearne in with him to open. The Middlesex man was soon caught at long leg for 2, and excitement rose as Walker claimed both Sewell and Ned Stephenson without addition, so that England were 10 for 3. Griffith then took the wobbly situation by the scruff of the neck, smiting 36 very quickly, with two hits to the boundary and one well over it. The score had grown by 50 when Spicer had him caught, adding Caffyn straight after for the Surrey star's first duck of the tour: 61 for 5. Bennett's demise made it 68 for 6, but the reassuring, almost biblical figure of HH stood tall and patient, and with his chunky, red-faced Yorkshireman Iddison with him, he saw his side to a four-wicket victory at 3 o'clock, soon after the lunch-hour. It left Tasmanians well pleased with their men's performance while perhaps wondering if the travelling and incessant hospitality had indeed taken just a little of the edge off England's play. Perhaps, too, without any form of communication, some of them were seriously missing their families so far away. Who can say?

The match having concluded early, it was decided to play on until evening, the exhibition overs carrying England's total to 185 and ensuring that the crowd had its fill. 'We shall be like Charles XII in his wars with Russia,' wisely proclaimed the *Mercury*, 'who learnt more in defeat than in victory.'

Next day there was a pick-up match for the benefit of the English team. Elevens led by the two Stephensons hit just over 200 runs while 25 wickets were taken, local hero Whitesides now failing. Mixing the teams was a convivial gesture, and the young Tasmanians will have treasured the opportunity. But HH declined to treat it like a beer match, bowling Lawrence (3 for 30) and Iddison (7 for 52) right through the innings of 86. Ned Stephenson then used only Caffyn and Sewell, apart from a couple of overs from Wells and Hearne at the end. Before they ran out of time, Iddison picked up three more wickets. People had come to watch him bowl, no doubt, whereas they could see the local lads in club games any old weekend.

HH and his men had their constitutions further tested by a public dinner at the end of the main match, at Basstians Hotel, presided over by Colonial Secretary Henty, and which concluded at 10.30. After the benefit match, there was another procession, led by the Battalion band, back to their hotel, where crowds gathered to bid them farewell. They knew well by now what it felt like to be loved and admired.

Thirty members of Oaklands CC had signed a letter eagerly suggesting an All England fixture against a team of 22 from the north and south of Tasmania, but the tour schedule was too tight.

Returning to Melbourne, the tourists next braced themselves for a special contest which had been suggested in newspaper columns some time earlier. Why not pit the best cricketers in the colony and these fine Englishmen against each other in a mixed 11-a-side match? Not only would such a match celebrate Surrey's role in making this historic tour possible, but it would enable Melbourne cricket-lovers to see how England's champions dealt with each other's skills, something not possible when they were opposed merely to the local and 'inferior' cricketers.

Spiers and Pond liked the idea, so the return match with a Victorian 22 was postponed to the end of the tour, and with free use of the Melbourne Cricket

LOWER DOMAIN, HOBART, February 25, 1862
Exhibition match

E.STEPHENSON'S XIII

W.Caffyn	c Griffith b Iddison	29		
T.Westbrook	b Iddison	2	b Stephenson	1
- Mace	b Iddison	9		
G.Bennett	b Lawrence	22		
T.Whitesides	c Lawrence b Iddison	3		
T.Sewell	b Iddison	0		
J.L.B.Tabart	b Iddison	0	b Stephenson	4
G.Wells	b Lawrence	3	st Stephenson b Iddison	0
T.Hearne	c Stephenson b Lawrence	11		
C.T.H.Perry	not out	2	not out	4
*E.Stephenson	c Sidebottom b Iddison	0		
- Watson	b Iddison	5		
- Davies	st Stephenson b Iddison	6		
Extras b 3 w 1		4	b 2	2
Totals		**85**	5 wkts	**22**

Bowling	*Balls*	*Runs*	*Wickets*		*Balls*	*Runs*	*Wickets*
Lawrence	86	30	3	H.H.Stephenson	32	2	2
Iddison	83	52	7	Iddison	32	18	3

Bowling plus extras makes 86

H.H.STEPHENSON'S XI

W.H.Walker	b Sewell	2	*Bowling*	*Balls*	*Runs*	*Wickets*
W.Mudie	c & b Sewell	6	Caffyn	100	36	4
G.Dargaville	b Sewell	2	Sewell	104	47	5
C.Lawrence	c Wells b Caffyn	17	Wells	8	2	0
W.Sidebottom	b Sewell	0	Hearne	4	1	0
R.Iddison	lbw b Sewell	0	*1 wicket was unattributed*			
H.E.Lette	b Caffyn	0				
G.Griffith	b Caffyn	12				
H.G.Spicer	b Caffyn	0				
W.Mortlock	not out	25				
*H.H.Stephenson	c Perry b ?	22				
Extras b 11 lb 3		14				
Total		**100**				

MATCH UNFINISHED (Drawn)

Ground still available to them, they scheduled the event, with teams designated 'Surrey' and 'The World'. They would have been gratified to have known that many years later it would be the one match of the tour to be given first-class status, only the 13th such match ever in Australia.

On the eve of the match, news of Prince Albert's death reached far-distant Melbourne at long last, bringing with it extensive shock and sadness. The colony clothed itself in mourning. As there were also rumblings of war, the Governor of Mauritius having made some alarming statements, it was perhaps time to seek refuge in a cricket match.

The Surrey XI comprised H.H.Stephenson (captain), Mortlock, Griffith, Caffyn, Mudie and Sewell from the touring team, joined by local players Sam Cosstick, Jerry Bryant and Gid Elliott, all Surrey-born Victorians, and C.O.Blanchard, a Surrey-born colt, and Fred Christy, about whom little is known (he may have been a Surrey Club player – or was it his brother, as *Bell's Life* suggested?). Hammersley declined a place, being out of practice.

The World XI was led by steady Tom Hearne and included Wells, Ned Stephenson, Bennett, Iddison and Lawrence, together with George Marshall, Jack Huddlestone, James Moore (but not the successful brother George), Jack Conway and Dick Wardill from local ranks. (The ill-fated Wardill's younger brother Ben, now only nineteen, was to enjoy a much more comfortable life, serving as a popular Melbourne CC secretary for 31 years from 1879 and managing Australian tours of England.)

From Saturday's first-day attendance of 4500 (the grandstand was deserted at the start), the figure dwindled on the Monday and Tuesday to 2500 and 1000, there being little cricket to follow by the third morning. Allowing for Monday's being a working day, the modest Saturday figure suggests that Melbourne might have had its fill of big cricket for the time being. Equally, the regional format, as has been shown in modern times, did not have the same appeal. The absence of booths and flags rendered the occasion so much less picturesque than those of the preceding month.

The Man of the Match would unquestionably have been George 'Farmer' Bennett, whose 3½-hour innings of 72 (three fours), a masterpiece of defensive batting, was followed by long, fruitful spells of crafty high-flighted slow bowling that brought him figures of 7 for 30 and 7 for 85 and set up the World XI's six-wicket victory.

And yet the innings of the match was played by Surrey's Caffyn, whose 75 not out in the follow-on contained eleven sweetly-stroked fours. He was at the crease for just over 2½ hours, and drew from the *Age*'s correspondent the description 'brilliant', an adjective used much more sparingly in those days than in ours.

Hearne batted upon winning the toss from HH, and in the four hours' play the World completed their innings by stumps for a solid 211. Wells and Wardill opened, 'Tiny' making a chanceless 48, which was to be his highest score of the tour. He was heartily cheered by 'English lungs' (*Argus*) on his way back to the dressing-room when Caffyn bowled him, having made the first claim upon the 'ten-guinea stakes' (performance prize). One of his hits carried the boundary, and there were four others for four, one running between Griffith's legs at cover point. The fieldsman seemed to enjoy the inevitable chaffing that followed.

At lunch, D.S.Campbell, who presided, proposed a toast to Surrey County Cricket Club, coupled with Messrs Marshall and Burrup, which was responded to by none other than F.C.Christy, HH's guest player.

Wells and Bennett took the World to 90 for 3 before Marshall helped Bennett put on 72, major interest seeming to lie with the ten-guinea prize. Would Wells be overtaken by Marshall, who was batting so robustly? HH had a bowl and made

MELBOURNE CRICKET GROUND, March 1, 3, 4, 1862

Toss won by The World   Umpires: J.C.Brodie & J.A.Smith

THE WORLD XI

G.Wells	b Caffyn	48	[5] not out		27
R.W.Wardill	c Mudie b Caffyn	7	[4] b Griffith		12
E.Stephenson	b Griffith	4	st Stephenson b Griffith		2
G.Bennett	c Cosstick b Griffith	72			
G.Marshall	c Mudie b Stephenson	45			
R.Iddison	c Stephenson b Griffith	28			
C.Lawrence	c Elliott b Griffith	0	[2] run out		15
*T.Hearne	b Bryant	1	[1] b Bryant		5
J.Huddlestone	b Bryant	0	[6] not out		17
J.Moore	b Griffith	0			
J.Conway	not out	0			
Extras	b 1 lb 3 w 1 nb 1	6	b 6 lb 2		8
Totals		**211**	4 wkts		**86**

Fall: 1/18 2/22 3/90 4/162 5/209 6/209 7/210   1/15 2/24 3/24 4/45
      8/210 9/211 10/211

Bowling	Balls	Wides	Runs	Wickets		Balls	Runs	Wickets
Caffyn	104	1	63	2	Griffith	65	37	2
Griffith	140	0	52	5	Bryant	72	17	1
Bryant	52	0	22	2	Sewell	20	13	0
Sewell	12	0	12	0	Caffyn	12	11	0
Mudie	4	0	3	0				
Mortlock	20	0	13	0				
Cosstick	24	0	8	0				
H.H.Stephenson	36	0	32	1				

Stephenson bowled 1 no-ball

SURREY XI

*H.H.Stephenson	c Iddison b Lawrence	4	[7] c Bennett b Iddison		3
W.Mortlock	b Iddison	15	[5] b Bennett		4
G.Griffith	c Wardill b Bennett	39	[6] b Bennett		13
W.Caffyn	c & b Bennett	13	not out		75
S.Cosstick	lbw b Bennett	22	[3] b Bennett		15
J.M.Bryant	c & b Bennett	1	[8] b Conway		24
W.Mudie	c Stephenson b Bennett	14	[1] c Marshall b Iddison		13
T.Sewell	st Stephenson b Bennett	4	[2] c & b Bennett		10
C.O.Blanchard	c Lawrence b Bennett	0	[10] c Wardill b Bennett		11
G.Elliott	not out	0	[9] c Huddlestone b Bennett		7
F.C.Christy	run out (Iddison/Stephenson)	0	b Bennett		0
Extras	b 2 w 1	3	b 2 lb 1 w 1		4
Totals		**115**			**179**

Fall: 1/16 2/28 3/55 4/85 5/94 6/100 7/113 8/113   1/20 2/40 3/40 4/48 5/67 6/70
      9/115 10/115   7/133 8/144 9/179 10/179

Bowling	Balls	Wides	Runs	Wickets		Balls	Wides	Runs	Wickets
Iddison	120	1	53	1	Iddison	144	0	65	2
Lawrence	56	0	29	1	Bennett	162	1	85	7
Bennett	70	0	30	7	Wells	16	0	10	0
					Lawrence	20	0	5	0
					Conway	24	0	10	1

THE WORLD XI WON BY 6 WICKETS

sure he was not, having the Victorian captain caught by Mudie at 'long slip' attempting a sixth four when three short of Wells's 48. The 200 came up with only four wickets down, but dramatic collapse followed as Griffith had Iddison caught off his glove by keeper HH to trigger the fall of the last six wickets – Bennett's included, for his admirable 72 – for a mere two runs. Griffith took the bowling honours with 5 for 52.

At noon on the Monday, Surrey began their reply, with HH and Mortlock opening to the bowling of Iddison and Lawrence, the latter soon having their tour skipper caught at point by the former. Iddison then bowled Mortlock (15) with a shooter, and wickets fell steadily thereafter, seven of the eight to Bennett's slows, the other to a run-out. First, Caffyn spooned a return catch; then 'colonial slogger' Cosstick's bright 22 closed with an lbw verdict; Griffith's 39, which saved the innings from total eclipse, ended with a magnificent outfield catch by Wardill, who then dropped Mudie. Ned Stephenson, showing a different style behind the stumps to that of HH, stumped Sewell and caught Mudie (for a 'pretty' 14), and with 115 on the board Surrey were 96 behind on first innings and following on, the World XI now being 3 to 1 favourites. Bennett's marvellous 7 for 30 came from 17.2 four-ball overs.

Sewell and Mudie opened the second Surrey innings at 3.30 pm, but the first six wickets – including Sewell's for 10 after he had backed himself to reach double figures – went down for 70, threatening a finish inside two days. But Caffyn, 33 not out, and Bryant, 18 not out, held out against bowling that was starting to wilt from the day-long effort. At 110 for 6, Surrey were ahead by the slight margin of 14 runs.

The third day was hot, with a northerly blowing, and with Bennett and Iddison bowling for once none too impressively, the score rose to 133 before Conway got a shooter through his Victorian team-mate Bryant's defences. Caffyn now punished Conway with some glorious shots, but was left high and dry with 75 as Surrey fell away for 179, Bennett completing his second seven-wicket haul of the match, this time for 85 off 40.2 overs. Blanchard, the novice, followed his fine performance in the field with a conscientious innings of 11. Caffyn received a memorable reception.

The World XI needed 84 for victory, and Hearne himself went in with Lawrence, only to be bowled by Bryant for 5 third ball after the hour's break for lunch. Lawrence (15) was run out 'in a very stupid manner', and then the Stephensons had a split-second encounter, HH stumping Ned for 2. When Griffith bowled Wardill for 12 there was just a glimmer of hope at 45 for 4. But Wells batted commandingly again and put on 41 with Huddlestone to carry their team across the line, the winner coming in the untidy shape of a bye. The only mystery concerned the match scores, which showed discrepancies in every available version. Bennett and Caffyn each received a ten-guinea purse from Melbourne CC for unquestionably top-scoring.

Now it was time for the Englishmen to see Victoria's famed goldfields, which were still active, though the great rush of the 1850s had subsided somewhat. First it was Ballarat's turn to work itself into a new kind of frenzy as

Sturt Street, Ballarat at the time the English cricketers came to town.

the great cricketers approached. The tourists' coach, doing about 8 mph on the flat, took them by way of Geelong, and was met at Buninyong by a great cluster of fans, with the centrepiece a Cobb & Co coach drawn by six horses, British flag flying from the front and Federal American flag at the rear. Inside and on top were the Twenty-two who were to represent Ballarat. The English cricketers hove into view and were soon surrounded by the welcoming party, shaking hands with the cricketers they already knew (some of the grips of the horny-handed diggers were over-exuberant and painful), principally the four who were to guest for Ballarat and strengthen the side, Bryant, Morres, Butterworth, and the ubiquitous Cosstick. There were actually six proposed guest players present, but H.H.Stephenson objected to the inclusion of that many, so George Marshall and Jack Huddlestone were stood down.

'Brown with our southern sun,' observed the *Argus*, 'begrimed with our all-pervading dust, these out-and-out English-looking cricketers seemed to enjoy the fun of the thing amazingly.' They and their opponents tucked into supplies of apples and ginger-beer before proceeding to Ballarat, greeted all along the way from roadsides and at junctions, gently tapping time to the band's *Rule Britannia* and *See the Conquering Hero Comes*. Bunting and flags were draped all over the town as they braked outside the North Grand Hotel and were plied with champagne, and a welcoming address by the chairman of the Eastern Municipality, before pushing on to their accommodation at the Café Royal in Sturt Street.

Work was still going on down at the ground, for the 300ft curved grandstand was not quite finished. It was designed to hold almost 2000, and had a promenade at the back where men could smoke without missing a view of the cricket. Underneath were the two dressing-rooms and luncheon room. On this ground, the

Eastern Oval, under the celebrated Brown Hill, with a solitary tree on its summit, many a keen tussle had taken place between Ballarat and Melbourne teams. *Bell's Life* put the town's recent history into an elegant nutshell: 'Where a few years ago diggers' tents, shanties and sly grog shops existed, when Golden Point and the Gravel Pits lead were in their full glory, now stands the city of Ballarat, with its fine spacious streets, handsome buildings, the metropolis of the western goldfields . . . Warrenheep and Buninyong Mount frown darkly in the distance, and tall chimneys rising into the air in various directions point out the localities of the different quartz-crushing machines.'

The paper further remarked that ground improvements would ensure that Yarrowee Creek, if it should overflow, would never again flood the cricket ground with stormwater and sludge.

All the same, following overnight rain, play could not start until 1.45 pm. Sensibly, a public holiday had been declared in the town, and as the ground dried out and spectators poured in at a shilling a head (1/6d extra for the grandstand) the Englishmen and their opponents practised in the outfield, letting youngsters join in and winning praise for the manner in which the 'healthy, lithe, active, and even playful character of the Eleven's disportments must have delighted those who took pleasure in "muscular Christianity".'

Griffith bowled to Bryant, who was soon out, but his opening partner, Sweeney, the Ballarat 22's captain, dropped anchor, and was to bat for an hour-and-a-quarter for 22, being the sixth out at 52 when Caffyn hit the middle stump. Two wickets later, Stephen Thomas Clissold entered. He was now Ballarat's police magistrate, but in 1843 he had played for Eton against Harrow, returning to Lord's a year later in Cambridge colours and playing in a second Varsity match in 1846 at the Magdalen ground, taking six wickets in the Oxford innings to go with his rowing Blue. Bennett caught him at slip off Caffyn for 1.

Costick now came to liven things up. A complex series of run awards had been agreed on the shorter grandstand side of the ground, but Sam left no doubt with a colossal hit over the flag-adorned stand. A whack into the stand followed, for a statutory three runs, and then another. Fourteen wickets were down before the hundred came up with a Costick hit that parted the ranks of standing spectators and finished up in Merry's hotel, just beyond the square-leg boundary. And then he was caught for 31, comfortably the highest score of the Ballarat innings, which was soon over for 122, a par kind of total. Iddison, Caffyn and run-outs had accounted for most of the wickets, and the crowd went home happy and looking forward to seeing the Englishmen at the crease tomorrow.

The ground was packed on the second day, over 5000 being present at the peak, many of them females. Hundreds more townsfolk looked in from the high ground outside, though the authorities managed to keep the railway embankment fairly clear.

Tom Sewell and the other umpire, Biers, supervised the pitch preparation while Sweeney took his time about placing his regiment around the field. Then, close to noon, Mudie and Bennett came out to open the England innings. There really was no such thing as an established opening pair.

A lithograph gives some impression of the gathering for the Ballarat match.

All England batted through the day, ending on 136 for 8, Griffith, not for the first time, providing most excitement with his left-hand power hitting. Not until the fourth over did Mudie make the first run, and soon Bryant bowled him middle stump. Bennett and Griffith then had a stand, the 'Lion Hitter' thrilling the occupants of the grandstand by landing one blow off slow bowler Sanders onto its roof. Sweeney's wicketkeeping and Butterworth's efficiency at long-stop were noted, but high hits often had fieldsmen bumping into each other, and the odd bruise developed.

Bennett was out for 13 when Cosstick snapped his middle stump, and the same keen bowler had Griffith (34) taken in the deep by Magistrate Clissold of Eton and Cambridge. Morres, the smooth-actioned fast bowler, took the first of his four wickets by bowling Caffyn for 8, then had Wells caught for 2

H.H.Stephenson came in to loud cheering, and facing a bit of a crisis. Runs had been hard to come by for the skipper on this tour, but now he carefully played himself in, taking a few singles from the draw shot. Iddison batted for almost an hour for 14, which included one massive hit for six – the shot of the match – to the railway embankment. Sanders, the bowler, soon got his revenge when Morres held a nice one-handed catch. Mortlock failed to score, and when Butterworth ran Lawrence out for a duck, to make it 91 for 8, the captain must have been reassured at the sight of the trusty Hearne coming in next. Together they saw out the day, Hearne, benefiting from a let-off, having made 30, HH, after nearly two hours at the wicket, 20, the total 136 for 8, a lead of 14. Honour was satisfied all round.

HH was not to add to his score on the Saturday, the final day, but Hearne went on to an unbeaten 37, and Ned Stephenson, in at No.11, made 11, taking All England to 155, ahead by 33. It remained for the Ballarat 22 to bat through the day, and this they did.

EASTERN OVAL, BALLARAT, March 6, 7, 8, 1862
Umpires: Mr Biers & T.Sewell

TWENTY-TWO OF BALLARAT
122 (S.Cosstick 31, D.Sweeney [captain] 22, Braithwaite 11, Butterworth 10, 7 ducks, 6 run-outs; Griffith 32 balls, 15 runs, 1 wicket; Iddison 148 balls, 50 runs, 7 wickets; Caffyn 116 balls, 35 runs, 6 wickets; Bennett 16 balls, 2 runs, 0 wickets; Lawrence 20 balls, 12 runs, 1 wicket; 8 byes) and **107** (J.M.Bryant 20, H.Smith 17; Caffyn 173 balls, 23 runs, 4 wickets; Iddison 136 balls, 50 runs, 7 wickets; H.H.Stephenson 99 balls, 25 runs, 4 wickets; Wells 64 balls, 6 runs, 1 wicket: 3 wickets unattributed)

ALL ENGLAND XI

W.Mudie	b Bryant	4	*Bowling*	*Balls*	*Wides*	*Runs*	*Wickets*
G.Bennett	b Cosstick	13	Sanders	95	0	31	1
G.Griffith	c Clissold b Cosstick	34	J.M.Bryant	90	0	20	1
W.Caffyn	b Morres	8	S.Cosstick	135	3	39	2
G.Wells	c Greville b Morres	2	T.F.Morres	140	1	41	4
R.Iddison	c Morres b Sanders	14	B.Figgis	20	3	4	0
W.Mortlock	c Cosstick b Morres	0	*Morres bowled 1 no-ball*				
*H.H.Stephenson	c Butterworth b Morres	20	*Bowling plus extras makes 147*				
C.Lawrence	run out (Butterworth)	0					
T.Hearne	not out	37					
E.Stephenson	run out	11					
Extras b 4 w 7 nb 1		12					
Total		155					

Fall: 1/? 2/? 3/54 4/58 5/66 6/66 7/91 8/91 9/136? 10/155

MATCH UNFINISHED (Drawn)

Bryant made 20, Smith 17, with the rest contributing their morsels. The overall score was 107, and All England were detained in the field well beyond the point where victory hopes were sustainable. It would probably have made no difference had there been a sizable purse at stake. Iddison took at least seven more wickets, Caffyn and HH at least four each, the statistical fogginess caused by the sole reporter's refusal to record lbws (there were three) with any bowler-identification. By the time Allan Lamb scored 143 against Victoria on this Eastern Oval in 1990, the ground and surrounds would have been completely unrecognisable to the 1862 pioneers.

That evening the players attended a benefit show for them at the Theatre Royal, not far away from the Victoria Theatre, a renowned venue since the scandalous Lola Montez performed her lewd dances there five years earlier, to the delight of the cheering miners and the professed distaste of the town's elders. When the editor of the *Ballarat Times* objected in print to her visit to the city, she tracked him down to the United States Hotel next door and horse-whipped him.

Ballarat was a lot calmer on the night of the farewell to the English cricketers, though the gestures of appreciation were just as sincere and noisy as they had been elsewhere. The Theatre Royal, opened only two years previously, had a revolving stage, and the Marsh family often put on 'beautiful tableaux' enacted by a 'family' consisting of 26 'stunning girls'. Patrons drank at the pub next door or upstairs at the Café Royal, where the English cricketers were now staying.

All was fairly decorous the night before the Englishmen departed. Before a packed theatre, Tom Hearne, probably deadpan, received his prize bat for the match top score of 37 not out, and Cosstick, undoubtedly more animated, gladly took his for that lively innings of 31. H.H.Stephenson delivered a measured speech of thanks, still professing reluctance in spite of all the practice over these weeks. 'I would rather play three games of cricket than make one speech,' he modestly said. 'I am no orator, and on occasions like these I am easily bowled out.' He then warmed to his mission: 'In truth, ladies and gentlemen, the farther we travel from home the more perfectly at home do we feel. The more we see of the colonies and their inhabitants, the better we like them. Our tour has been a succession of fetes and a succession of astonishments. We expected to find Ballarat a great encampment, but it turns out to be a great city. We expected to find everything rough and primitive, but it proves to be far advanced, and as comfortable as Europe.'

How would they tell England of their admiration and express their gratitude? 'Ladies and gentlemen: I know of but one way, and that is by speaking the honest truth about you when we return, and by telling the people in the old country how much we were delighted with all we saw in the new one.'

Road conditions dictated that they should return to Melbourne on the Sunday and set out for Bendigo (Sandhurst) in a fresh direction on the Monday morning. After a gruelling journey, the Englishmen looked over the cricket ground at Back Creek and were astonished to find that scarcely any grass grew on it. It had been fairly recently levelled and cleared of tree-stumps, Bendigo United CC having been formed only a year previously. There had been cricket in the district for a decade, mainly rough-and-tumble affairs between teams of gold prospectors, with some heated contests between the Australian Club and the Albion (English-born). And the establishment of the Melbourne-Bendigo rail link in 1862 was to necessitate a further transfer to the Upper Reserve. The Back Creek ground on which the first English team played survived and in due course was named after Australia's 1890s captain Harry Trott.

On that semi-bald oval, Stephenson and his men took first innings after the usual vociferous town welcome. Unfortunately, the fine weather which had followed them through the tour was now temporarily lost in a fierce southerly wind that made playing and watching anything but a pleasure. The dust swirled everywhere, reducing vision, concealing the cricketers 'as completely as a London November fog could have done'. Since the grandstand faced south, its occupants 'came down with faces changed in hue, throats furred and habiliments calling loudly for a good brushing'.

The attendance was considered worthwhile when the match began, after the players had warmed up with some hitting and catching. A policeman was the sole casualty, taking a ball thumped by Griffith painfully on the arm. At noon the bell rang and the action got under way, Mortlock and Hearne opening for All England. Among the youngsters watching was a 14-year-old named Harry Boyle, who one day would not only invent the 'suicide' short-leg fielding position and bowl out W.G.Grace but would also stun the Mother Country by running all over MCC on

147

a sensational day at Lord's in 1878, bowling his medium-pace variables in tandem with 'Demon' Spofforth. That well and truly put Australia on the cricket map. The pair were also to orchestrate Australia's staggering seven-run Test victory at The Oval in 1882 from which grew the Ashes legend.

For the time being, the young Sydney-born Boyle, living with his parents at Peg Leg Gully, was so inspired by what he saw from Stephenson's men that he and a few mates cleared some ground close by at Sydney Flat – sometimes working by moonlight – and started up a boys' cricket team. Another lad who would rise to Test cricket – moreover for both his native England and Australia – was Billy Midwinter. Now aged ten, the strapping 'Sandhurst Infant' had been brought to the goldfields by his parents in 1860 – they lived in a shack in California Gully – and he was most likely watching the English playing in Bendigo this day. By 1883, Midwinter regarded himself as 'Australian to the heart's core', and objected strongly to being classified as 'Anglo-Australian'. Yet another lad with a future who was probably in attendance this day was W.L.Murdoch, who had been born in Sandhurst in 1854 and was destined to become the best batsman in Australia.

Shum soon hit Hearne's middle stump with a shooter, but Mortlock and Bennett made a stand of 27, balls often reaching the crowd, shots for which the umpire called three runs. When Bennett's bat broke at the handle, they all had drinks. Soon Mortlock (25) was caught, but catches continued to be floored. It was a mixed blessing for the onlookers when Griffith was caught in the deep for only 8. No more wickets fell before lunch, an interval graced, as usual, with effusive speeches.

George Marshall, denied a game at Ballarat, made sure of one with the Bendigo 22, and in the afternoon he took the ball and started to work his way to a final analysis of 6 for 40, beginning with Lawrence, caught for 18, and then 'Farmer' Bennett, caught for a splendid 56, only the sixth half-century for All England on the tour – and Bennett's second.

Bendigo began to think the unthinkable, for England were half out for 117, and then Marshall bowled Iddison. But Caffyn was on his way to another masterly performance, 57 this time, and HH was about to make his highest score of the tour, 47. They batted through to the end of the first day, stealing runs, sometimes cracking big hits, either way confusing the field and causing errors on the ground and in the air. They finished at 186 for 6, Caffyn 29, Stephenson 21, and continued next day until Marshall broke through, getting them both and Sewell too as England amassed 246, their best total since Beechworth two months before.

Now, as was widely expected, the real fun began. As one incompetent after another took his turn at the crease, almost sadistically the English bowlers overwhelmed them. Shum (12) and Hewitt (11) alone of the 22 reached double figures; Marshall made 6; there were seven ducks. All out for 81 in 74 overs by the end of the second day, Bendigo were to follow on. Stephenson used only three bowlers (how those not used must have fretted): Bennett took 13 for 40, Caffyn 8 for 29, and somehow Iddison failed to strike in his six overs. What must have

BACK CREEK, BENDIGO, March 11, 12, 13, 1862

Toss won by All England   Umpires: E.Stephenson & unknown

ALL ENGLAND XI

W.Mortlock	c Barrett b Mace	25	*Bowling*	*Balls*	*Wides*	*Runs*	*Wickets*
T.Hearne	b Shum	4	A.Shum	240	0	55	2
G.Bennett	c Mackay b Marshall	56	Crofts	116	4	43	0
G.Griffith	c Hewitt b Thompson	8	Mace	140	3	50	1
C.Lawrence	c Bruce b Marshall	18	J.B.Thompson	36	0	33	1
W.Caffyn	c Hunt b Marshall	57	G.Marshall	95	0	40	6
R.Iddison	b Marshall	4	Hewitt	8	3	2	0
T.Sewell	b Marshall	2					
*H.H.Stephenson	lbw b Marshall	47					
G.Wells	b Shum	1					
W.Mudie	not out	1					
Extras	b 12 w 10 nb 1	23					
Total		**246**					

TWENTY-TWO OF BENDIGO

81 (A.Shum 12, Hewitt 11, 4 byes, 2 leg-byes, 7 ducks; Bennett 148 balls, 40 runs, 13 wickets; Caffyn 124 balls, 29 runs, 8 wickets) and **102** (J.B.Thompson 19, W.Bruce 16, Ratcliffe 13, 8 byes, 1 leg-bye, 6 ducks; Bennett 132 balls, 41 runs, 10 wickets; Caffyn 28 balls, 16 runs, 2 wickets; Iddison 52 balls, 24 runs, 4 wickets; Lawrence 48 balls, 12 runs, 4 wickets)

ALL ENGLAND XI WON BY AN INNINGS & 63 RUNS

Lawrence played Captain Skene (who was allowed 10 fieldsmen) at single-wicket afterwards. Neither player scored a run from the bat, but Skene lost the match when he bowled a wide.

gone through the minds of the onlooking boys Boyle, Midwinter and maybe Murdoch too?

On the third morning, quite early, the English cricketers went to the Catherine Reef United Claimholders' mine, and were unlikely to have come away empty-handed. Then, from the 11 o'clock start, they made short shrift of the Bendigo 22 in their second innings. In 76 overs this time they mopped up the 21 wickets, Bennett taking 10 for 41 with his effortless slows to give him a match haul of 23 wickets for 81 runs to go with his knock of 56. Iddison and Lawrence picked up four wickets apiece, Caffyn two. Bendigo mustered 102 to lose by an innings and 63, Thompson, Bruce and Ratcliffe alone getting to double figures. Mace, who is thought to have been the Kit Mace who played for the Victorian 18 in the opening tour match, and might also have played against All England in Hobart, managed only 4 and 9. His acquaintance with Iddison, also from Bedale, Yorkshire, quite possibly led to Mace's travelling with the English team. Bendigo's misery was best summed up by the count of thirteen ducks in the match and the fact that 25 of their men were bowled out.

The big match having ended well before nightfall, there was a bonus for those of the 2000 spectators who remained: a single-wicket challenge between Charlie Lawrence and the local champion, Captain Skene of the Bendigo Volunteer Rifle Corps. The prize was a gold nugget ring, and although Lawrence allowed his opponent ten fielders, he won. Neither batsman scored a run in either of his innings, but Skene fluffed his chance by bowling a wide.

Next day the All England team were in Castlemaine, about 30 miles south of Sandhurst/Bendigo, for the penultimate match of the tour. It was to cause a fair degree of uproar.

News was about to come through of the destruction of Charleston Harbour by the navy of the Northern States, which caused *The Times* to cry: 'This great act of malignity has filled every civilised country with astonishment.' England's touring cricketers felt similarly about the pitch prepared for them at Wattle Flat.

When their displeasure became known after the match, they were inevitably considered poor losers, although many critics were inclined to attribute their failure to the high living which supposedly had absorbed them from the moment they stepped off SS *Great Britain* all those weeks ago. A reader of *Bell's Life* probably aired the view of the majority when he wrote: 'An observant Press has informed us how they breakfasted, where they lunched, what they subsequently had for dinner, and in what privileged company they supped. We have had one long clatter of knives and forks followed by the usual popping of corks. No human digestions, unaccustomed to public eating and drinking, could stand this.' And this appeared a month *before* the 'disaster' at Castlemaine!

What gave the people of Castlemaine special satisfaction was the fact that all 22 of their players were local men, even Ben Butterworth and Charles Makinson, the Victorian representative cricketers, the famed long-stop having lived in the town for some time and Makinson being a resident of Saradale, ten miles away.

HH and his crew left Bendigo on the morning of the match and reached Castlemaine ahead of schedule, so that the band had not yet tuned up, nor had the customary hordes of welcoming townspeople assembled in full force. Mr Robertson's plan to drive his coach, pulled by eight magnificent greys, to meet the cricketers out of town was also spoiled. The Englishmen rattled along Harcourt Road, colours flying, and soon drew up at the Queen's Hotel, to be greeted by the committee. After a break to refresh themselves, off they went to the cricket ground at Wattle Flat, where the grandstand was already half-full with 500 people. The 3000 in attendance that day were kept happy between cricket episodes by the band of the Volunteers.

There were furrowed brows when the furrowed surface was inspected, and if HH, as he chose to bat first, knew full well that pitches often play better than appearances suggest they might, such was not the case here. The Englishmen were made to hop about, and took a bruising. The bowler who did the damage in the first innings was J.W.Amos, a roundarm medium-pacer who usually did little with the ball. He hardly needed to. The pitch did it for him today.

The first wicket went to Brooker, left-arm round, fastish and a little on the wild side. He bowled Mudie for 1. Then Amos's seven-wicket rampage began. Had Roger Iddison not held on for 36 resolute, priceless runs there is no telling how acute would have been England's embarrassment. Wells and Bennett made 4 apiece, Ned Stephenson a duck, and when Amos bowled Caffyn for 17 (everyone had just been stunned when the reliable Butterworth, Castlemaine's captain, dropped him), the local writer went overboard: his bowler 'at last convinced this formidable opponent that Fryer's Creek bowling was not to be held cheaply'. The ball 'neither ripped, touched, or twisted, but went straight in and demolished the middle stump instantaneously'.

HH made 2, Hearne none, giving the exultant Amos his seventh wicket, and Maynard, on for Brooker, evicted the dangerous Griffith and Lawrence. All England had somehow totalled 80, which included five wides and three byes, and were determined now to make life impossible for their inexperienced opponents.

At lunch, served in Dolphin's booth next to the grandstand, Captain Harrison proposed the loyal toast, observing that no cheering would follow in view of the bereavement 'so lately' suffered by Her Majesty. After toasting the All England XI, he expressed the hope that they would have a pleasant voyage home, and 'would represent the colony as it was, without exaggeration for or against us'. The band played *For They Are Jolly Good Fellows*. England's captain apologised for his team's poor performance so far that day, then uninhibitedly referred to the rough state of the ground. A couple more toasts, a response from Mr Pond, and the fraught contest continued.

By the 6 o'clock close, Twenty-two of Castlemaine had lost 17 wickets for 49, 'Ben' Griffith having got among them almost vengefully with his 'fast-killing' style. Jemmett's 17 and Amos's 10 were the best scores; no-one else was to exceed 5. Even the local paper conceded that it was ridiculous.

On the Saturday morning, all was excitement. Vehicles brought the thousands to Wattle Flat, 'a few crazy carriages' coming to grief in the pandemonium in the pot-holed streets leading to the ground. Castlemaine's last four wickets fell for five runs, giving England a welcome first-innings lead of 26, and Griffith came away with bizarre figures of 13 for 18 off 26 overs. Iddison, coming on late, took 4 for 1.

The pitch was beyond redemption, and All England's second innings was quickly destroyed by Brooker, the left-arm fast man. He did not open the attack. Amos and Maynard (3 for 30) did so. The reversible batting-order principle applying, Sewell and Lawrence opened, but Sewell was caught for a duck off Maynard, who also bowled Griffith for 8 and had Iddison caught for 11. Then Brooker replaced Maynard and began his blitz by firing a shooter through Ned Stephenson (12). Amos, a little less effective after being injured while batting, dispatched Caffyn for a duck, having him caught at point off a 'bumper', before Brooker torpedoed the rest, bowling Hearne for his second duck just before the pause not only for luncheon but for breath all round.

There was no phoney diplomacy by H.H.Stephenson in his speech, which was delivered quietly. After the customary cordialities, he referred again to the bad pitch, after which Butterworth, with Lancashire bluntness, stated that no pains or expense had been spared in preparing the ground, and he regretted that it did not meet with the approval of the visitors.

Wells managed to hit a rare four, but Brooker then had top-scorer Lawrence caught by Butterworth for 15. Next ball, Brooker bowled Bennett, and those who had been lucky enough to get 10 to 1 on England were feeling nervous.

Dolphin brought off a special catch to inflict a duck on Mudie, and when HH was caught for 3, his side had totalled only 68 (including a bye and seven wides),

WATTLE FLAT, CASTLEMAINE, March 14, 15, 17, 1862

Toss won by All England   Umpires: W.Mortlock & unknown

ALL ENGLAND XI

W.Mudie	b Brooker	1	[10] c Dolphin b Brooker	0
G.Wells	c Brooker b J.W.Amos	4	[8] not out	11
R.Iddison	c Makinson b J.W.Amos	36	[4] c Makinson b Maynard	11
G.Bennett	b J.W.Amos	4	[9] b Brooker	0
E.Stephenson	c Oddy b J.W.Amos	0	b Brooker	12
W.Caffyn	b J.W.Amos	17	c Oddy b J.W.Amos	0
*H.H.Stephenson	c Dolphin b J.W.Amos	2	[11] c Lewis b Brooker	3
T.Hearne	b J.W.Amos	0	[7] b Brooker	0
G.Griffith	c Lewis b Maynard	5	[3] b Maynard	8
C.Lawrence	c Makinson b Maynard	2	[2] c Butterworth b Brooker	15
T.Sewell	not out	1	[1] c Lockyer b Maynard	0
Extras	b 3 w 5	8	b 1 w 7	8
Totals		**80**		**68**

Bowling	Balls	Wides	Runs	Wickets		Balls	Wides	Runs	Wickets
J.W.Amos	89	1	13	7	J.W.Amos	77	5	24	1
Brooker	75	3	52	1	Maynard	38	2	30	3
Maynard	15	1	7	2	Brooker	35	0	6	6

TWENTY-TWO OF CASTLEMAINE

R.Dann	c E.Stephenson b H.H.Stephenson	0	[6] c Lawrence b Bennett	4
J.Taylor	b Griffith	5	[4] b Griffith	0
M.Amos	run out	0	[15] lbw b Lawrence	0
S.D.Jemmett	b Griffith	17	[7] b Griffith	0
J.Brooker	b Griffith	3	[11] c Iddison b Lawrence	1
W.Lewis	b Griffith	2	[12] b Lawrence	1
R.Culmer	b Griffith	0	[9] b Griffith	2
J.S.Oddy	c Mudie b Sewell	0	[1] c Iddison b Griffith	0
J.Dolphin	b Griffith	1	[18] not out	6
C.Makinson	b Griffith	0	[5] b Griffith	36
A.Drinkwater	c Iddison b Griffith	0	[8] b Griffith	3
J.W.Amos	b Griffith	10	[13] b Griffith	2
*B.Butterworth	b Sewell	1	[2] c Mudie b Iddison	2
F.F.Morris	b Griffith	0	c Wells b Lawrence	0
G.A.Wilson	b Griffith	1		
T.Bond	b Griffith	0	[17] c Wells b Lawrence	3
G.C.Maynard	b Griffith	2	[10] lbw b Lawrence	3
R.Manning	not out	3	[3] b Griffith	11
H.C.Staveley	b Iddison	1	[16] lbw b Lawrence	1
E.Bull	b Iddison	0		
W.Lockyer	c Wells b Iddison	1	[19] lbw b Griffith	0
T.W.Adams	b Iddison	0	[20] not out	0
Extras	b 4 lb 1 w 2	7	b 12 lb 7 w 2	21
Totals		**54**	18 wkts	**96**

Bowling	Balls	Wides	Runs	Wickets		Balls	Wides	Runs	Wickets
Griffith	104	0	18	13	Griffith	161	1	28	9
H.H.Stephenson	29	1	19	1	Iddison	40	0	9	1
Sewell	49	1	9	2	Lawrence	93	0	22	7
Iddison	27	0	1	4	Caffyn	41	1	7	0
					Bennett	8	0	9	1

TWENTY-TWO OF CASTLEMAINE WON BY 3 WICKETS

leaving Castlemaine to get 95 if they were to pull off a wondrous victory. Brooker was aglow with figures of 6 for 6 off 8.3 slightly terrifying overs, and there was much praise for Butterworth's pick-ups and throws from the vital long-stop position: there had been only four byes in the two English innings, when many more could have been expected on the uneven surface.

Butterworth and Oddy opened Castlemaine's innings, but an Iddison catch quickly made Oddy the first of six duck-makers, three of whom secured pairs. Three more wickets fell quickly before Dann stayed with Makinson, who got eight runs from one hit: a five plus three overthrows, the sort of inferior cricket which brought charges of too late a night for the Englishmen the night before. (HH told an interviewer some years later that he favoured cold tea during a match – but not thereafter!)

Stephenson swung his bowling around, but Castlemaine made it to stumps at 40 for 4, Makinson 19, Dann 4; another 55 needed; the town all a'tremble. And everyone had plenty of time to ponder the situation, for tomorrow was Sunday, a day of rest. Tonight, there was to be another banquet.

About fifty sat at the Malakoff Hotel, in a room into which much effort had been expended by way of decoration. Captain Bull presided, and the speeches were of the usual kind, his own being cordial, confirming how keen were settlers everywhere to be thought well of and for good impressions to be conveyed to the old homeland. HH rose, his players wondering whether he would launch a broadside at the pitch. He spoke of certain warnings they had received before sailing, and of how the tour so far had brought them little but pleasure. It had been a time of 'jollification' to them – rather too much so, perhaps, occasionally. There were laughs and cheers throughout his address, and he sat down, to the relief of the committee, without speaking of his disappointment at the condition of the ground. Then Will Mudie sang a song for them.

HH rose again to toast his opponents, and made a lavish reference to Butterworth's skills and qualities as a gentleman. The Lancashire lad must surely have blushed, but when he stood, he reiterated his claims about the huge efforts put into the ground preparation, and expressed sorrow that the Englishmen might have felt the way they did. Among the remaining speakers were Mallam and then Spiers, with Robertson, who was one of those who had opened up contact between towns in the interior, saying how proud he was to have driven the English cricketers to the ground, and how much he hoped they would tell the people at home how efficiently they had been conveyed around the colonies in Cobb & Co coaches.

The gathering dispersed just before midnight, and when the final day's cricket began around 12.30 on St Patrick's Day, the streets of Castlemaine and surrounding townships were practically deserted. People crammed into Wattle Flat Reserve, filling the stand and lining the ropes in thick groups. Others camped on the high ground outside. Fifty-five needed; 17 wickets in hand. Surely it could be done?

For half-an-hour there was no breakthrough. Dann was twice 'caught' off 'bum [*sic*] balls', and there were leg-byes. Then Dann's agonisingly long but valuable innings of 4 was ended by a glorious catch by Lawrence, who ran and took the ball one-handed. Jemmett, the first-innings top-scorer, entered – only to be bowled middle stump immediately by Griffith. Caffyn now softened up Drinkwater, who had to lie down for a few minutes after being hit, and was then skittled by one of Griffith's probing left-arm fastish deliveries.

Makinson, who had registered a pair in the opening match of the tour at the MCG, was still the backbone, and had taken his score to 36 when Griffith bowled him too. His monumental innings owed everything to a missed catch before he had scored, but that was forgotten in the sustained, rapturous reception as he walked sadly back. The pressure was still growing: Lawrence got Maynard, Griffith hit the stumps again to get Culmer, and Brooker was caught off Lawrence, who then bowled Lewis. Castlemaine were letting it slip.

Twelve runs needed, nine wickets left. The Englishmen, in all they did, seemed determined to save the game. Nerves tingled during the 45-minute luncheon interval, when HH told the gathering that the match was still anybody's; the Eleven would be doing their very best.

Griffith instantly bowled one Amos, and Lawrence, having had Morris taken to a simple catch and beaten Staveley with a leg in front, had the other Amos lbw too. Men watching eased their own nerves by yelling cautions to the batsmen. Bond hit a three, as did Dolphin. The job was almost done. But then Lawrence dismissed Bond, and Griffith, also fighting hard, had Lockyer leg-before. With only three wickets in hand, Castlemaine needed two to win.

With Adams as his partner, little Dolphin now drove Lawrence for the runs that secured victory, and the ground rocked with roars of excitement as thousands of bearded miners cheered as they had never cheered before (apart from those rare questers who had struck gold in a big way). Dolphin was carried from the field on the shoulders of laughing, red-shirted, white-trousered team-mates, and for almost a quarter-of-an-hour the public acclamation continued: 'it might have been supposed that a very extensive Bedlam had broken loose'.

Whether or not the Englishmen lost because they had overindulged, or missed a vital catch, mattered not at all. Unimagined delight had been brought to this quiet bush town by eleven famous cricketers from afar and the local heroes who beat them. In truth, it was a rehearsal for all the volcanic vocalising that lay ahead over the decades and perhaps centuries to come as Australia beat England and England beat Australia (slightly less often, certainly, but perhaps all the sweeter for that).

Castlemaine, according to neighbouring Victorian cricket clubs, was an important cricket centre, and thought 'no small beer' of itself. If this meant conceit or bombast, the victory over All England could only worsen the condition. It probably mattered little that soon after the conclusion, Griffith, Lawrence and Iddison defeated Eleven of Castlemaine in a single-wicket contest, their fast bowling proving too much in a game where runs could be scored only in front of the wicket. After that, there was more entertainment when a foot-race was held, won by a Castlemaine player, and a ball-throwing contest, which was won by England.

Off to the theatre all the players went that evening, to listen to Messrs Poussard and Douay play a piece especially composed for the occasion. Then the curtain was raised, to reveal all the cricketers from both teams on stage. Felix Spiers presented the top-scorers, Makinson and Iddison, with prize bats, both responding pleasantly, and Ben Butterworth read from an address to be presented to the English cricketers. It was an erudite and heartwarming document, the work, perhaps, of a cricket-loving solicitor. It referred in part to their 'scientific' play, and the example set to local youngsters of 'complete discipline and good humour'.

H.H.Stephenson gave thanks and called for three cheers for the winning Twenty-two of Castlemaine. He kept it to himself that he and his players regarded the ground on which they had just been vanquished as the worst, without exception, that they had ever played upon. Next morning they boarded the coach for Melbourne for their final match.

As for the area's newspaper, the *Mount Alexander Mail*, not being satisfied with a ten-page match preview, it now gave its readers a post-match edition entirely devoted to the great victory.

A hundred years later, while Ted Dexter's England side were in Victoria, playing at Bendigo, the team's vice-captain, Colin Cowdrey, fresh from a record 307 against South Australia, and the acting manager, MCC secretary S.C.'Billy' Griffith (no relation of the 1862 player), travelled to Castlemaine and unveiled a commemorative plaque to mark the centenary of this match. Among the 350 people present was a grandson of Dann, the opening batsman in 1862. But of the arena there was now little to be seen. Wattle Flat was overgrown and almost back to its original bushland condition.

CHAPTER 11

The Last Leg

TOUR-WEARY, and knowing that home was still a two-month journey away by sea and land, the English cricketers braced themselves for the final match, which was to start in Melbourne three days after the Castlemaine reversal. Even Mr and Mrs 'Tiny' Wells, who had planned to stay in Australia, were beginning to wonder if that was what they really wanted. Spiers and Pond, hoping to enlarge on their stupendous profit of £11,000, offered an enticement of £1200 (£100 per man) for the team to stay for an extra month, but were turned down because of the players' commitments in England . . . much to the annoyance of Charlie Lawrence.

In his unpublished memoirs, written with a firm pen in a black-covered exercise-book, Lawrence was to claim that the sponsors told him in London years later that revenue exceeded the total tour expenses of £39,000 by *£19,000,* almost twice the accepted profit figure. As for the offer to stay the extra four weeks, while acknowledging that the organisers' motive was primarily for the team to 'make money for Spiers and Pond' themselves, Lawrence, who was due to stay on anyway, made his views clear: 'I wanted all of us to remain for another season on our own account for I felt sure we should have done equally as well but they would not agree with my idea and returned home leaving me behind for I thought I should soon make a fortune for I had an idea or a presentiment after I had seen the blacks throw the boomerang and spears that if I could teach them to play cricket and take them to England I should meet with success.'

It seems from this that Lawrence suggested to the English players that they should while away the Australian winter (note the use of the word 'remain') and then mount their own second tour of Australia, pocketing profits just as vast as Spiers and Pond's had been. Even the family men in the party must have been tempted.

As it was, further benefits were now about to come their way. Spiers and Pond gave the Englishmen half the receipts from this final match at the MCG, a considerable sum, and Melbourne Cricket Club generously handed the tourists a bonus of 100 sovereigns to go with the hoard of gifts collected along the way.

Spiers and Pond were less generously disposed towards the club however. Even though they were Melbourne CC's caterers, and had been given free use of the ground from which they had reaped such huge profits, they quibbled over a bill for £175 for ground repairs at the end of the 1861-62 season.

LAMBING FLAT: Highway Robbery by Gardiner and His Mates. Such was the main news as the English cricketers prepared for their last match. The Melbourne 22 looked a strong combination, and with the Castlemaine result in mind, hopes were high that the visitors might be beaten, a result which would give cricket in the colonies its greatest fillip yet.

At the start of Thursday's play only fifty or so spectators were in the ground, and if the attendance built up to over 2000 by 4 o'clock, with some of the non-payers peering from the high ground outside clambering over the fence when the police were not looking, there was a marked decline in atmosphere when compared to the earlier Melbourne matches. Inside the ground, there was little decoration, and only one booth, George Marshall's. The only sideshows were a catch-ball machine and a 'knife-and-ring' man. As the match was, in part, for the benefit of the Englishmen, Spiers and Pond had put an admission of half-a-crown on the gate, which served as a further deterrent.

Ned Stephenson was umpire for this final match, acting with Jack Smith, and All England took the field after HH lost the toss to George Marshall, re-elected as the Victorians' captain. Griffith began proceedings, and in the second over, bowled by Bennett (with his 'half slows'), Brodie was run out by an accurate throw from Hearne. The first decent hit was made by Bryant, to cries of 'Bravo, Jerry!' from the pavilion, but Griffith soon had Hope, Bryant and Thompson out, and the sense of panic was only slowly dispersed by Hamilton, who made 17 before being run out after slipping, and Huddlestone, whose gallant effort looked likely to bring him only the second half-century taken off English bowling. After Sam Cosstick was run out without scoring, Wardill helped Huddlestone take the total past 80 before Huddlestone, attempting another stylish stroke, glided down the pitch to Iddison, missed, and was deftly stumped by HH for 44. Victoria were 82 for 7.

Dick Wardill was caught at midwicket for 10, and on the stroke of lunch Makinson, the batting hero of Castlemaine, was bowled by Iddison for the fourth of the nine ducks in the innings.

Dr Sewell presided at the luncheon, and HH, replying to the toast to All England, mentioned that it was only a few days before they would be sailing home, but they hoped they would return and play many more times against the colonial cricketers.

Skipper Marshall drove well to get the score moving that afternoon, bringing up the hundred with an on-drive and reaching the boundary by the old water-jump near the grandstand with an off-drive. Hopkinson then played on to Iddison: 105 for 10; and after Morres had struck a four, Marshall lofted Caffyn only for Hearne to run in and take an excellent catch. Guinness, recently arrived from England, one of the late recruitments when some of the best goldfields cricketers had to withdraw, used his wrist in 'a most extraordinary manner' but not well enough to elude Iddison in the long-field. The collapse was on.

HH made another stumping to send Castlemaine captain Butterworth on his way for 6, and then Drinkwater, another country player, was out in a curious way, taking a long time to take guard, then instead of eyeing the bowler he seemed to be watching the pavilion. Iddison, never one to miss a trick, bowled him first ball.

The end soon came, the last 11 wickets falling for 25 runs, Blanchard run out unnecessarily going for an overthrow. Iddison took 9 for 37, Caffyn 5 for 24. The Victorian 22 had lasted 84.3 overs in making 140 by 5 o'clock, and in the half-hour remaining England lost Bennett to Bryant, to finish at 19 for 1.

Drinkwater, it was remarked, appeared to be as good a fielder as batsman after letting a hit from Bennett pass between his legs for two runs.

The second day, again with fewer than 3000 in the ground at best, was marked by dreadful Victorian fielding. There were 22 in the field, not 18 as in the tour opener, and yet run-getting seemed less difficult. Marshall was even called to account for poor field-setting. Butterworth, Blanchard, Wardill, Thompson, O'Mullane and Cosstick all did themselves credit as fielders and catchers, but the others were bitterly disappointing, putting catches down, Huddlestone's at square leg to let off Caffyn being the most important. Griffith was not only dropped by Guinness and Bryant, but Handfield stood and watched a catch go past him.

Wells was run out by Sam Cosstick's throw, but from 41 for 2, All England in the shapes of Caffyn and Mortlock took matters seriously. There was many a maiden over, but the third-wicket stand laid the necessary foundation before Caffyn was bowled by Marshall for 45 soon after the century had been posted. H.H.Stephenson put himself in next, and displayed fine form, finding the boundary and running twos from his renowned leg-side drives and seeing his side past the Victorian total before Mortlock hit a high one off Morres and was caught for a praiseworthy 53. 'Stonewall' had seldom failed his captain on this tour.

The total had climbed to 189 before Griffith was well caught-and-bowled by Cosstick for 23, ending the day's play, with All England five down, 49 ahead, and the skipper, batting pride restored, 31 not out.

The third day, a Saturday, at least had some atmosphere. The attendance grew to upwards of 8000, a few having knocked a fence down and rushed through, leaving the policemen helpless to check them. And they saw the England innings subside fast, thanks initially to HH's run-out for 35 by Sam Cosstick's smart pick-up and throw. No-one else reached double figures, Cosstick's sharp spell accounting for Lawrence and Hearne, both caught at slip, and he bowled Mudie to come away with a proud 4 for 46.

Still, with a score of 218 and a lead of 78, All England were in command, and when, after a 20-minute interval, they came out to bowl, it was soon a source of wonder how skilfully Stephenson deployed his fieldsmen, who seemed so few after the Victorians, just on two dozen of them, had vacated the field. For the remainder of the third day, HH used only Griffith and Iddison, and they nearly finished the match off by the close, when the Victorians were 89 (11 ahead) for the loss of 16 of their wickets. Roger Iddison had another personal feast, taking 12 of them.

Marshall, the captain, took Drinkwater in with him for the second innings, and if a cricketer can be said to redeem himself with a mere six runs, Drinkwater did that, batting calmly and sensibly while the early wickets fell. But when he sallied forth to Iddison and was stumped by HH and Wardill was bowled by a Griffith shooter, the score was a menacing 24 for 5, made worse by Hopkinson's dismissal just before the 2.30 lunch adjournment, which stretched out to an hour-and-a-half because of a meeting to decide on the appointment of a professional to Melbourne CC. The crowd meanwhile made do with watching the cricketers at practice.

Professor Irving had presided over the luncheon, and the English captain's theme was the great welcome given his team everywhere, people sometimes walking six miles along bush roads just to greet them. He had seen improving cricket standards, and felt that if they were to come back in a year or two it would be 'to be beaten'.

With Bryant caught at slip by Sewell, in came Makinson, who soon executed what the *Argus* reporter viewed as the 'hit of the season'. He lined up one of Iddison's slows and struck it powerfully to leg, over the chain fence and all the way to the entrance gate for a five. It was a rare moment of joy for the locals. More wickets clattered, including Sam Cosstick's to complete his pair, and eventually Makinson's for 20 as he went out to Iddison and was deceived and bowled. The innings defeat was avoided, but the slender lead was 11 runs at close of play on the Saturday, the latter stages interrupted only by the 5 o'clock arrival of the Governor, for whom the England XI stopped play to give three cheers.

After a Sunday of relaxation, England needed five more wickets and a few runs to end the tour. It looked straightforward. But it wasn't to be.

There was a piquant sadness in the air on the final morning. For Melbourne cricket-lovers, it was like 'the last performances of favourite actors', with universal regret touching those who had got to know the visiting cricketers personally. Over 7000 people turned out to watch.

At noon, James Thompson (12) and Adam Hope resumed Victoria's innings, but the latter completed his pair without ceremony, giving Iddison his 13th wicket and taking the Yorkshireman (alone) beyond 100 tour wickets. Thompson had support from a'Beckett (10), who was finally bowled by Lawrence after the first change of bowling. That made it 112 for 18, the end surely imminent.

But O'Mullane scrounged 12 not out, Thompson, who took a few blows from Griffith and Caffyn and was to be substituted by Raleigh when the Victorians fielded, raised his score to 25 before Bennett took a running catch, and in a pulsating nine minutes at the crease Conway thrashed 24 runs, five of which came from a hit even bigger than Makinson's. When all was done, the Victorian 22 had mustered 151 and stretched their lead to 73.

In terms of the long Anglo-Australian cricket history that lay ahead, All England's tough final day was something of a pointer. Not only did the Victorian innings drag on well beyond expectation, but now, in the 57 overs faced by England in the time remaining, wickets tumbled, four to Conway's fast bowling. The target of 74 was not quite reached, and the score at stumps was tantalising in the extreme. But no agreement could be reached for extending the match to the Tuesday, and patriots from both sides were inclined to claim moral victory.

With Drinkwater injured, McHarg had been a second substitute in the field for Victoria, but Butterworth, whose hand was damaged soon after the final England innings began, refused to leave the field, perhaps sensing he might be part of something marvellous, like being in a winning team two matches running.

Sewell and Griffith (belting the ball to leg) gave England a flying start, and soon after lunch the total had shot to 26, over a third of the target, before Griffith was caught off Morres. Bennett's 18 and Sewell's 13 took All England much

MELBOURNE CRICKET GROUND, March 20, 21, 22, 24, 1862

Toss won by Victoria

Umpires: J.A.Smith & E.Stephenson

TWENTY-TWO OF VICTORIA

Player	Dismissal	Runs	2nd innings	Runs
J.M.Bryant	c Mudie b Griffith	5	[8] c Sewell b Griffith	7
- Brodie	run out (Hearne)	0	[3] b Iddison	1
A.Hope	b Griffith	0	[18] b Iddison	0
T.F.Hamilton	run out	17	[12] c Mortlock b Iddison	0
J.B.Thompson	b Griffith	1	[13] c Bennett b Caffyn	25
J.Huddlestone	st H.H.Stephenson b Iddison	44	[7] c Griffith b Iddison	7
S.Cosstick	run out	0	[11] b Griffith	0
R.W.Wardill	c Sewell b Iddison	10	[6] b Griffith	4
S.G.Hopkinson	b Iddison	8	[5] b Iddison	10
C.Makinson	b Iddison	0	[9] b Iddison	20
*G.Marshall	c Hearne b Caffyn	18	[1] c Hearne b Iddison	3
T.F.Morres	b Iddison	6	[14] c Griffith b Iddison	0
- Guinness	c Iddison b Caffyn	1	[4] b Iddison	0
C.O.Blanchard	run out	6	[15] c Lawrence b Iddison	4
B.Butterworth	st H.H.Stephenson b Iddison	6	[16] c & b Iddison	1
A.Drinkwater	b Iddison	0	[2] st H.H.Stephenson b Iddison	6
E.Mortimer	c & b Caffyn	0	[10] c Griffith b Iddison	8
- Handfield	c Lawrence b Caffyn	0	[22] c Griffith b Caffyn	1
- a'Beckett	c Griffith b Iddison	0	b Lawrence	10
J.Conway	c Caffyn b Iddison	5	[21] b Caffyn	24
G.J.P.O'Mullane	not out	4	[20] not out	12
G.Cosstick	c Mortlock b Caffyn	0	[17] b Griffith	1
Extras b 3 lb 5 w 1		9	b 3 lb 4	7
Totals		**140**		**151**

Fall: 1/1 2/6 3/7 4/? 5/? 6/? 7/82 8/87 9/? 10/105
11/115 12/118 13/118 14/128 15/128 16/129
17/129? 18/129? 19/136 20/136 21/140

1/3 2/? 3/? 4/19 5/24 6/24? 7/35 8/52?
9/63 10/67? 11/68 12/69 13/69? 14/80
15/? 16/89 17/89? 18/112 19/? 20/? 21/151

Bowling	Balls	Wides	Runs	Wickets		Balls	Wides	Runs	Wickets
Griffith	72	1	26	3	Griffith	144	0	45	4
Bennett	84	0	23	0	Iddison	156	0	68	13
Lawrence	16	0	11	0	Caffyn	46	0	18	3
Sewell	20	0	10	0	Lawrence	32	0	13	1
Iddison	84	0	37	9					
Caffyn	63	0	24	5					

ALL ENGLAND XI

Player	Dismissal	Runs	2nd innings	Runs
G.Bennett	b Bryant	9	[3] c Butterworth b Bryant	18
G.Wells	run out (S.Cosstick)	17	[7] b Conway	1
W.Caffyn	b Marshall	45	[5] c Makinson b Conway	2
W.Mortlock	c S.Cosstick b Morres	53	c O'Mullane b Bryant	1
*H.H.Stephenson	run out (S.Cosstick)	35	[8] not out	1
G.Griffith	c & b S.Cosstick	23	[1] c sub (Raleigh) b Morres	15
R.Iddison	b Bryant	9	[6] b Conway	6
C.Lawrence	c Morres b S.Cosstick	0		
W.Mudie	b S.Cosstick	2	not out	0
T.Hearne	c Bryant b S.Cosstick	3		
T.Sewell	not out	6	[2] c O'Mullane b Conway	13
Extras b 9 lb 1 w 6	16		b 2 lb 2 w 1 nb 1	6
Totals		**218**	7 wkts	**63**

Fall: 1/? 2/41 3/106? 4/148 5/189 6/206
7/206? 8/? 9/210? 10/218

1/26 2/48 3/49 4/54 5/56 6/62 7/63

Bowling	Balls	Wides	Runs	Wickets		Balls	Wides	Runs	Wickets
Morres	132	4	33	1	S.Cosstick	16	1	8	0
Bryant	148	0	32	2	Conway	116	0	24	4
O'Mullane	68	0	40	0	Bryant	52	0	15	2
Handfield	16	0	7	0	Morres	44	0	10	1
G.Cosstick	20	0	11	0	*Morres bowled 1 no-ball*				
S.Cosstick	124	0	46	4					
Conway	32	2	4	0					
Marshall	40	0	29	1					

MATCH UNFINISHED (Drawn)

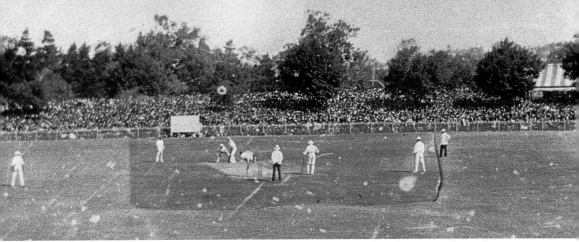

By 1895 – with the thrilling Ashes decider in progress – the elm trees planted at the MCG by the English cricketers in 1862 (far side of the ground) were close to maturity – but were not to survive long into the 20th Century.

closer, but then wickets began to topple as the Victorians, especially Conway, bowled as if their lives were at stake. For once the fielders backed them to the hilt. Mortlock, Iddison, Caffyn and Wells all succumbed to the pressure, and by the time Mudie joined his captain at the wickets, time had run out. All England were 63 for 7, 11 runs short of victory. In the face of much curiosity, and to the chagrin of most, the match was declared unequivocally finished and drawn.

H.H.Stephenson again put diplomacy to one side and expressed a certain grievance and frustration that the match could not be played out. His letter to the *Argus* drew a response from Marshall, the Victorian captain, who pointed out that some of his players had had to return to work on Tuesday, and in any case the agreed finish was advertised as being Monday evening. He was 'hurt and annoyed' at insinuations from elsewhere (in particular from D.S.Campbell, past president of Melbourne CC) that he had wanted to play on a fifth day probably because he had big money on his team to pull off a victory. If so much time had not been wasted over the luncheon interval, he wrote, the match would have reached a conclusion. And the Englishmen would hardly have presented him with a gold ring the following evening if they had regarded him as a 'black sheep', concerned only with winning a bet.

Soon after play had ended, the English cricketers planted commemorative elm saplings around the outskirts of the Melbourne ground, with 'patronymics [labels crediting each cricketer by name] at the stems'. These trees, selected by Dr Mueller at the Botanical Gardens, were to flourish in remembrance of the trailblazing tour, towering tall by the time A.E.Stoddart's English team played there a third-of-a-century later. In 1911, however, the trees were felled, creating room for an additional 5000 spectators. Historical relics of beauty and significance were thus sacrificed in the name of progress, and Tom Horan, in his column in *The Australasian,* lamented the fact that 'the ruthless destroyers of our elms never dreamed of giving the "elmers" a bit of wood to turn into anything in the nature of a keepsake or as a reminder of the many pleasant hours they passed beneath the rustling leaves'.

BATTING AVERAGES: all 15 matches (*including Surrey v World, exhibition and scratch matches, but excluding single-wicket matches*)

	Matches	Innings	Not Out	Runs	Ducks	Highest	Average
W.Caffyn	15	21	2	455	2	79	23.95
G.Griffith	15	22	1	480	0	61	22.86
W.Mortlock	12	16	2	313	2	76	22.36
G.Bennett	15	19	1	312	2	72	17.33
H.H.Stephenson	15	22	4	248	1	47	13.78
R.Iddison	15	20	1	250	3	36	13.16
E.Stephenson	13	18	2	203	4	60	12.69
G.Wells	14	20	3	197	3	48	11.59
T.Hearne	14	18	2	172	3	37*	10.75
W.Mudie	12	17	4	134	2	27*	10.31
T.Sewell	14	20	5	135	4	41	9.00
C.Lawrence	14	18	1	119	6	20	7.00

BOWLING AVERAGES: all 15 matches (*including Surrey v World, exhibition and scratch matches, but excluding single-wicket matches. Balls bowled and runs conceded in Bathurst 2nd innings unknown but wickets included – bar one unattributed. In scratch match Feb 12, balls bowled and runs conceded unknown but wickets included. Three wickets were unattributed in Ballarat's 2nd innings, but balls and runs included*)

	Balls	Runs	Wickets	Best	Average
G.Wells	244	30	11	8-10	2.73
T.Sewell	1144	277	55	15-27	5.04
G.Griffith	1344	361	70	13-18	5.16
G.Bennett	1385	433	81	13-40	5.35
C.Lawrence	658	239	40	11-38	5.98
W.Caffyn	1877	530	84	10-37	6.31
H.H.Stephenson	328	105	16	7-23	6.56
R.Iddison	1982	741	112	13-68	6.62
T.Hearne	4	1	0	-	-
W.Mortlock	20	13	0	-	-
W.Mudie	36	25	0	-	-

As for the magnificent MCG grandstand, the most impressive in the world when it was built in time for the Grand Match in 1862, insured for only £3000 against building and development costs of £6000, it burned down in 1884.

The last hours in Melbourne – in Australia – were a time for all kinds of courtesies and gifts, with appearances required of the English cricketers at several venues, beginning with Marshall's in Swanston Street, where Melbourne CC secretary Dick Wardill handed them the 100 sovereigns subscribed by members, and a Mr Henderson gave them £45 collected by non-members, apologising for the fact that it wasn't more. HH presented George Marshall, the Victorian captain, with the gold ring, and after many kind words all round, they moved on to Marsh's Royal Lyceum Theatre, where they appeared on the flag-bedecked stage during the interval, Miss Louise appearing after the anthem to recite some humorous verse which included reference to 'Father' Hearne's captaincy of 'The World'. Felix Spiers presented Mortlock with a bat for top-scoring in the final match, and Tom Huddlestone received another on behalf of his brother Jack.

Next stop was the Theatre Royal, where, after the opera *Martha* had been performed, the band played *Le Bon Voyage Valse* and *The All England Eleven Polka*. The players appeared on stage, and their captain made a speech, insisting still that he was no orator, and that he felt more at home on turf than on the stage. In fact he would rather face the swiftest bowler than advance to these footlights to confront such a brilliant assemblage. 'We came here as strangers,' he said touchingly, 'but we shall go away like people who are departing from home.' He thanked Spiers and Pond, and announced that they had just paid an extra £540 to get the team back to England in time for the new season. The players then stepped forward, one by one, Spiers and Pond too, to take the final plaudits after so many.

At last, on Wednesday, March 26, the cricketers packed their bags for the marathon voyage home, a copy each of Sands & McDougall's *Victoria Illustrated* being among the last of the gifts received. The final utterances were made at their erstwhile home, the Café de Paris, before they boarded the special carriages of the midday train which would take them down to the wharf, H.H.Stephenson having been moved by a testimonial presented to him on behalf of the cricket community of Victoria. After it was read out, he responded, saying how proud he was, and paying tribute to his men, who had 'all behaved like good soldiers, and were always ready and willing to obey the word of command'. Afterwards he presented Mallam with a gold chain and pin.

Ben Butterworth got up and said nice things about Messrs Spiers and Pond; Pond acknowledged HH's co-operation and suggestions throughout their travels; Spiers presented the captain with a watch, to which HH remarked that if there was a chance of a man being killed with kindness, he thought he would soon drop. An address to show their appreciation of Spiers and Pond's promotion and, not least, the benefit in the final match was signed by all the English players and conveyed at the very end to the two men who had been their employers these past five months.

At Sandridge, they were taken out to the deeper water by the launch *Sophia*, and after the final handshakes they hauled themselves aboard the P & O vessel RMS *Northam*, which had reached Hobson's Bay thirteen days earlier, under the command of Captain Potts. In due course, the anchor was weighed, and movement was discerned. Seawards she moved. 'And the last was seen by the Victorians of the All England Eleven.'

CHAPTER 12

The Consequences

S O ENDED the great venture. Not only had the gamble paid off handsomely, but when its consequences are weighed it may be recognised as the most significant step cricket has ever taken. One small step for Stephenson . . . . Had the reception to the English team been no more than lukewarm then any second tour would surely have been a long time coming. But there was a second tour two years later, and after hesitation and hiatus for a further ten years, another after that, led by W.G.Grace. At Melbourne, three years further on, came Test match cricket. And finally, the marriage of the two cricket-crazy countries was fully consummated with Australia's first tour of England in 1878, and the creation of the Ashes tradition two tours later – though the first few northern excursions were nothing like as cheerful as those to the Antipodes. Lord Harris said of the 1880 Australian gamble that they had 'asked no-one's goodwill in the matter'. He branded the tour 'a discourteous way of bursting in on our arrangements'.

WG's elder brother E.M.Grace, the first amateur to tour, kept a diary on the 1863-64 expedition, lengthy and well-written, with an acute insight into Australian feelings about the link with the Mother Country. He saw Australia as a 'golden land' where there was 'less ignorance, less superstition, and more enterprise'. Having acknowledged that 'there are some, no doubt, who would desire nothing more than a separation from England, because they look forward, under such a possibility, to a scramble for power &c', 'The Coroner' explained that 'everything which keeps them united to Britain and to Britain's green and to Britain's people, everything which binds them in any way close to those they left behind, is regarded with feelings of no ordinary pleasure'.

These sentiments were to prevail, at least among Australia's British stock, for many years, intensified by the side-by-side participation in the Boer wars and the Great War, imperilled by the dark doings in the Bodyline Tests of 1932-33, restrengthened during the Second World War, and ultimately and inevitably diluted by Australia's sudden assertion of what might be termed its realisation of having grown up. It so happened that this first showed almost exactly 100 years after the Stephenson tour. As the almost unthinking respect so long directed towards Britain started to fade, a petrol company took as its slogan 'Be Australian: Buy Australian', a novel urging that had people blinking. Then, one afternoon on the Hill at the Sydney Cricket Ground, as England laboured to dismiss Norm O'Neill and Peter Burge, a barracker bellowed out a mysterious (to the majority of us) message: 'Yeah, Dexter, what about the Common Market!' Something had changed forever.

Australia's enduring cricket strength developed from the hesitant beginnings of the Stephenson tour, when, as Lawrence noted, advancement was being held back by poor pitches and lack of tuition. Both problems were soon remedied, in the same determined pioneering spirit that opened up the wide brown continent itself.

W.J.Gordon wrote 25 years after the Stephenson tour that 'the matches were show matches, mere exhibitions of the game' with wins that were 'but of moderate merit' against nervous colonials who proved easy prey. When these remarks are aligned with HH's assertion that the colonial bowlers had little variation or method – 'wanted in science' – when compared (a little unfairly) with masters of old William Clarke and William Lillywhite, there was scope for pessimism. Australia might after all have had as grey a cricket future as America. But at the conclusion of the 1861-62 tour 'one of the most eloquent of public writers in Australia' (in *Baily's Magazine*) touched the pure truth when he wrote that 'if our youth learn that to become really great, whether as cricketers or as politicians, they must pitch their standard higher than that of the men whom they see around them, the visit of the All England Eleven will have been productive of more good than the discovery of an additional goldfield, or the passage of a new land bill'. As a later rather successful Australian batsman, D.G.Bradman, was to put it, the aim always was to show that he was a better batsman than his opponent was a bowler. The spindly little joey that was Australian cricket in the 1860s grew into an increasingly muscular kangaroo as the years passed.

Presciently, the *Argus* had surmised after the opening match of the tour that this cricket display would be 'the theme of tradition from father to son'. By tour's end, the paper believed that the scientific skill of the English cricketers had given a strong impetus to the game, particularly in Victoria. Melbourne's thickly-populated lanes and alleys were now alive with boys playing cricket: 'We have seen wickets pitched in Russell Street, and miniature Caffyns and Bennetts deftly at work in lanes and rights-of-way, with a pertinacity superior to all the vigilance of the policeman'. Nor should it be overlooked that the tour created local heroes: Jack Conway, George Marshall, Sam Cosstick, George Gilbert, Ben Butterworth, Jack Huddlestone, Charlie Makinson, John Kettle, who made an admirable 39, Tom Whitesides, the Tasmanian who registered the only fifty against the tourists, steady Alfred Park, old George Moore, Macartney's gran'dad, young Tress, who took 8 for 70 for Bathurst, and a chap who proclaimed to posterity that not all Aussies are physical giants: to shrieks of excitement the diminutive Dolphin hit the winning runs at Castlemaine.

All this from what was originally a 'mere mercantile speculation'.

Twenty years after the tour, remarks in *Boyle & Scott's Australian Cricketers' Guide* encapsulated its far-reaching success and sheer significance while dismissing the objection that visits by England diminished the domestic programme: 'To excel in any art, the pupil must have the advantage of the very best masters of that art.' Having improved their play, Australia's best were then able to tour the Mother Country, thus reaping social and commercial benefits which, if missed, would have been 'an incalculable loss to the Australian colonies'. Those visits had done more to bring Australia 'under the notice of the British public than all the advertising mediums which could possibly be adopted'. If tours ceased, the friendly relations between the two countries would be 'ruthlessly torn asunder', and the great benefits, well beyond cricket, would be a national loss to Australia.

The playing successes of the tour were Caffyn, Griffith, Mortlock and Bennett with the bat, and Iddison, Caffyn, Bennett, Griffith and Sewell with the ball. H.H.Stephenson excelled as wicketkeeper, and his namesake also had his moments as a batsman. Poor seasick Hearne had little to show for his efforts, and much the same had to be said of Mudie and Wells, while Lawrence, ever thoughtful, rose to the occasion once in a while. Billy Caffyn's 79 in the opening match remained the highest of England's eight half-centuries. It was not until Parr's tour two years later that the first representative English century was scored in Australia (by the fringe-bearded Bob Carpenter of Cambridgeshire: a nine-hour 121 against Ballarat). Not until 1877 was an Australian to make the first hundred off English bowling: Charlie Bannerman's 165 retired hurt in the first of all Test matches.

Apart from Carpenter's 1864 century, the performance of Cris 'Spider' Tinley must have left observers wondering if colonial cricket had actually slipped backwards since the Stephenson tour two years earlier. With almost cruel intent, in the first six matches in Australia Tinley took *138* wickets with his slow bowling, at 3.01 apiece, his 21 for 56 at Castlemaine, together with Hayward's 15 wickets, emphatically avenging England's humiliation there in 1862. The 1863-64 side, as it happened, made a profit of £6000 but were 'far from being as popular as the first team under Stephenson', as Victorian Cricket Association secretary E.E.Bean averred in 1924: 'This was due to the parsimonious manner in which Parr's team treated their brother professionals in Victoria.'

With 'Tiny' Wells returning to England later and Charlie Lawrence taking up his coaching engagement in Melbourne, Heathfield Harman Stephenson had only nine of his team with him on the journey home. It was an uneventful voyage on placid seas, and as if to show they were not fatigued from playing, there was cricket on deck, to the annoyance of some of the ladies, even though the cricketers used soft balls made for them by the sailors.

As RMS *Northam* ploughed up the Red Sea, Ned Stephenson made his memorable remark about its colour. They left the ship (there was no Suez Canal until 1869) and made their way overland to England, stopping off in Paris, where, according to Harry Sydney's songs at the welcoming dinners in London soon afterwards, three of the cricketers were delayed, though whether by social commitments or because they were mugged remains unclear:

In safety the others reached Paris; / But three of the ten had to stop,
For a very cute fellow who there is, / On the Yorkshireman managed to drop.

'Farmer' Bennett is later mentioned as having been 'left behind', but neither Iddison nor Ned Stephenson is identified as the Yorkshireman.

The bulk of the team reached England on May 12, 1862, having been away for 206 days. (The next trip to Australia took Parr and his men away for 243 days.) Now the task of refamiliarisation with families and neighbours began. The tourists were royally toasted – the Surrey players at least – at the club's annual dinner three days later, at the Bridge House Hotel, where Harry Sydney sang his song, all nine eight-line verses of it. Part will suffice, merely to clear Mr Sydney of any suspicion of genius:

Bennett, Iddison, Mortlock, and Sewell,
Yorkshire Stephenson, Mudie, and Hearne,
Caffyn, Ben, and the Captain, now you will
Congratulate on their return.

Surrey CCC threw another banquet the following night, this time a benefit for the players at Weston's Music Hall in Holborn, where Harry Sydney was at it again:

N stands for the Nuggets, quite plentiful they say;
O is for The Oval, so noted for good play;
P for Pond and Partner, who so liberal have been;
All cricketers are loyal, and Q stands for their Queen.

Soon they were back to business on rich green English springtime turf, HH for the All England XI in Sheffield and then at Rossall within the week, six others for the United All England in Southsea, and then, on May 26, six of them for Surrey against Yorkshire (with Iddison and Stephenson) at The Oval, where Caffyn and Sewell destroyed the Northerners' second innings. Curiosity must have been rife among opponents and followers, and often the pioneer tourists will have been called upon to roll out their stories of the amazing expedition to Australia. And so it would be for the rest of their days – granted that 'Old Ben' Griffith, in his bitter melancholy, may have been an exception.

As for the two men whose financial speculation had made the tour possible, their lives were about to alter greatly. Having led Melbourne's progress towards European-style wining and dining, and with over 100 employees on their books, Felix Spiers and Christopher Pond decided they needed fresh fields to conquer, so they sold up and moved back to their native England. Melbourne society, which they had served so profitably and well, was sorry to see them go. In London they built the Criterion Theatre and Restaurant on the site of the White Bear Inn (1685) on the south-eastern side of Piccadilly Circus. Designed by Thomas Verity, who also designed the monumental Lord's pavilion, the Criterion complex cost £80,000. At the end of their historic tour of 1882, the Australians were feted at a banquet at the Criterion, with none other than the former Governor of Victoria, Sir Henry Barkly, in the chair.

The partners also took over the Gaiety Restaurant and made it a popular gathering-place, and set up the Viaduct Hotel, Holborn, catering for passengers of the London, Chatham & Dover Railway, paying the railway company six percent of the cost of building and ten percent of profits. There were other railway catering deals, and they even set up a café at the International Exhibition in Paris.

The busy-minded Pond died in 1882, and a limited liability company was set up, with the calm, phlegmatic Spiers as chairman until his retirement in 1905.

Silver-mounted emu egg presented by Spiers and Pond to Surrey secretary William Burrup in appreciation of his assistance in assembling the touring team. It is now at Lord's.   *Courtesy of MCC*

Spiers then lived in Paris, where he died in the summer of 1911. A solid bronze bust of Pond, by Boehm, was placed in the Criterion Theatre (a listed building now) after his death. In 1995, Grand Metropolitan, successors to the original company set up by Spiers, presented MCC with the illuminated address which had been given to the partners at the end of the 1861-62 tour, and it is now held at Lord's.

Relics from the tour surface occasionally. Spiers and Pond were generous, albeit that they could afford to be. A four-piece silver-plated tea service which they gave to mark their gratitude for services rendered by G.J.Shoosmith was sold for £682 at a Phillips auction in London in 1995, while in the MCC Collection at Lord's are two silver-mounted emu eggs, the former presented to W.B. – or B.W. – Mallam, the latter to William Burrup, both for their efforts in assembling a team of good English cricketers. And a notebook covering part of the tour, compiled by a contemporary but anonymous reporter, was secured by Melbourne Cricket Club for £2000 at Knight's auction in Leicester in May 1999.

As for commemorations, fifty years on, the Victorian Cricket Association staged a smoking concert, by invitation only, at the Masonic Hall, Collins Street, Melbourne on December 30, 1911, which was the opening day of the second Australia v England Test match of the series. That morning, at the MCG, S.F.Barnes had famously taken 5 for 6 in his first 11 overs, and after the Sunday of rest, on the second day J.W.Hearne, a cousin removed of old Tom from the first tour (who had been dead eleven years by now), was to make a century while still a month short of his 21st birthday. There was much music at the concert, with songs from the famed tenor John McCormack, and from several others, including Rufus Ferguson of the Melba Grand Opera Company, humour blending nicely with the serious items. Lord Denman, the Governor-General, was there, as were Prime Minister Andrew Fisher and some State ministers. Judge Moule was among fellow Test veterans in Tom Horan, Jack Blackham and Frank Allan, alongside the current teams, whose skippers were Clem Hill and Johnny Douglas. There were men in that room who had not only seen WG play on his first (1873-74) tour, but had witnessed too some of H.H.Stephenson's cricket. The English captain on

Programme for the commemorative gathering in Melbourne 50 years on from the first tour.

this 1911-12 tour was P.F.Warner, but he was too ill to play after the opening match and too poorly to go to this concert. Still, he reflected in his book on the tour: 'How different was that first team, with their bearded, whiskered faces and solidly built frames, from the slim, youthful, almost boyish-looking cricketers of today. At that time Australia had everything to learn from Stephenson and his men, and right well did they learn their lesson – too well we Englishmen are apt to think at times.' How, he wondered, could a nation of five million produce cricketers to hold their own with the cricketers of the Mother Country with its 40-odd million? It was another of those questions that echo down the years.

Jack Hobbs, on his second Australian tour, enjoyed the concert. He noted that there were over 500 in attendance, including some who had played not only in the first Test, in 1877, but in the first intercolonial matches in the 1850s. The lengthy ovation given to Blackham, with handkerchiefs waving, must have been the greatest ever received by 'the world's greatest wicketkeeper'. It clearly and understandably affected him. Cotter, Armstrong and Kortlang then went round with hats and collected £56.4.2d for the financially-straitened old keeper.

By late 1911, only two of HH's party survived, and both, Caffyn and Lawrence, were depicted on the rear of the concert programme: 'Both 83 and still batting'. Ill-health prevented the eager Lawrence from attending, but he sent a letter from his Melbourne home explaining that in his 84th year his interest remained just as keen as in 1849 when he bowled out the entire All England XI in Edinburgh. His message caused laughter and cheers.

The centenary of the 1861-62 tour was not so precisely or resoundingly marked. Shell and Qantas produced pamphlets; a Sydney bank housed an exhibition; a few cursory newspaper and magazine articles appeared; but plans – which included an Australia v Rest of the World match – that Melbourne CC were putting together for 100th anniversary celebrations for 1961-62 were blotted out by the Australian Cricket Board's announced intention of calling the 1962-63 Ashes series the Centenary Series. It so happened that this England team was the last to sail to Australia, even part of the way (Aden to Fremantle). The era of the Jumbo jet aircraft was dawning.

So the Melbourne Cricket Ground was the venue again, 101 years on, and England won the Test match, as in 1911. Fred Trueman took eight wickets, David

Sheppard and Colin Cowdrey made centuries, and Ted Dexter, the captain, scored 93 and 52.

E.M.Wellings was among the English journalists covering the '62-63 tour, and in his book he described the scene with typically trenchant words: having acknowledged that Stephenson and his men had played on 'the pleasant meadow which had since grown into a vast stadium, in which cricket's record crowd of nearly 91,000 had been housed two years earlier when Australia and West Indies played', he lamented that a century ago 'it looked more like a cricket ground than it does today'. All the building development had 'deprived it of its historic cricketing atmosphere', and half the occupants of the Press-box could not see the solitary scoreboard. Moreover, the seats in that Press-box 'would not fetch tuppence in a jumble sale'.

Before play began on the first morning there was a compressed re-enactment of the Grand Match of 1862, which lasted about an hour. Efforts were made to replicate the scores, and among the current and past players dressed in period costume were the falsely-bewhiskered Bill Ponsford, Lindsay Hassett, Ray Lindwall, Bill Johnston and Jack Iverson. H.H.Stephenson was played by recently-retired England express bowler Frank Tyson, who, unlike HH, had settled in Australia.

The so-called Centenary Series of 1962-63 and the Ashes Test series during the remainder of the 1960s were often tedious, but the 1970s and 1980s were to bring livelier cricket. In the ten years since 1989, however, the balance of power has shifted to Australia so decisively and English cricket has suffered such loss of both confidence and esteem that many devotees have been left to wonder if the 1862 pattern has mystically been turned upside-down 137 years on.

The reader has sat through numerous toasts by H.H.Stephenson and his star-struck hosts. So, as the story ends, let us raise a few bumpers of our own: firstly to those smart businessmen, the 'cake and pie' people, Spiers and Pond, and their Mr Mallam, for their faith, their persistence and their successful application of, in today's jargon, venture capital; secondly, to H.H.Stephenson, for his dignity in command and for the example and inspiration he and his trailblazing cricketers cast all around them in the awakening country; and thirdly, to the legend of Anglo-Australian cricket, which will surely survive without recourse by England to turning back the clock, reversing the odds, and fielding a force of eighteen players to Australia's eleven.

THE END
(and yet, as they say in the movies, just a beginning)

BIBLIOGRAPHY

Alverstone, Lord & Alcock, C.W. *Surrey Cricket: Its History & Associations* Longmans, Green, 1904

Amey, Geoffrey *Julius Caesar – the Ill-Fated Cricketer* unpublished manuscript, 1987

Ashley-Cooper, F.S. *Edward Mills Grace: Cricketer* Chatto & Windus, 1916

Ball, Adrian *Is Yours An SS Great Britain Family?* Kenneth Mason, 1988

Batchelder, Alf {article} *The Yorker* Melbourne Cricket Club Library, 1999

Bay Books {publishers} *Australians From Everywhere*

Bettesworth, W.A. *Chats on the Cricket Field* Merritt & Hatcher, 1910

Bouwman, Richard *Glorious Innings* Hutchinson, 1987

Bowen, Rowland *Cricket: A History of Its Growth & Development Throughout the World* Eyre & Spottiswoode, 1970

Boyle & Scott's Australian Cricketers' Guide for 1881 and 1882

Brownlee, W.Methven *W.G.Grace: A Biography* Iliffe, 1895

Caffyn, William {ed. Mid-On} *Seventy-One Not Out* Blackwood, 1899

Cashman, Richard & others *The Oxford Companion to Australian Cricket* OUP, 1996

Christen, Richard *Some Grounds to Appeal* published privately, 1995

Clarke, A.E. *East Melbourne Cricket Club: Its History 1860 to 1910* Robertson, 1910

Corlett, Ewan *The Iron Ship* Conway, 1990

Cricket Scores and Biographies various volumes

Daft, Richard *Kings of Cricket* Arrowsmith, 1893

Davies, David *The Last of the Tasmanians* Muller, 1973

Derriman, Philip *True to the Blue* Richard Smart, 1985

Down, Michael & West, Derek *Sketches at Lord's* Collins, 1990

Dunstan, Keith *Saint Ned* Methuen, 1980

Dunstan, Keith *Sports* Cassell, 1973

Dunstan, Keith *The Paddock That Grew* Cassell, 1962

Fairfax, William {ed.} *The Australian Cricketer's Guide 1858-59*

Farnsworth, Keith *Before and After Bramall Lane* published privately, 1988

Finlay, Ric *Island Summers* St David's Park, 1992

Flanagan, Martin *The Call* Allen & Unwin, 1998

Fraser, Bruce {ed.} *The Macquarie Book of Events* Macquarie Library, 1983

Frith, David *By His Own Hand* Stanley Paul, 1990

Goulstone, John *The 1789 Tour* International Research Publications, 1972

Griffin Press {publishers: 1979} *Australia's Yesterdays*

Griffiths, G.J. *King Wakatip* McIndoe, 1971

Griffiths, G.J. *The Maces of Macetown* published privately, 1969

Harris, John & Wust, Ken *Bendigo District Cricket 1853-1990* Crown Castleton, 1991

Hearne, J.W.'Jack' *Wheelwrights to Wickets* Boundary Books, 1996

Hedley, Harry W. {ed.} *At the Wickets: NSW v Victoria 1856-1888* Centennial, 1888

Hobbs, J.B. *Recovering the Ashes* Pitman, 1912

Horan, T.P. {'Felix'} {ed. Crowley, B.M. & Mullins, Pat} *Cradle Days* Macmillan, 1989

Hutchison, G.A. *Cricket: A Popular Handbook of the Game* Religious Tract Society, 1887

Lillywhite, Frederick *The English Cricketers' Trip to Canada and the United States* F.Lillywhite, 1860

Macartney, C.G. *My Cricketing Days* Heinemann, 1930

Mancini, A. & Hibbins, G.M. *Running with the Ball* Lynedoch, 1987

McKernan, Michael {ed.} *The Makers of Australia's Sporting Traditions* Melbourne University Press, 1993

Mills, Vic *Cricketing Pioneers* unpublished manuscript, 1982

Mynah {publishers: 1996} *Australia Through Time*

O'Dowd, Kevin *Geelong's Blazing Century* published privately, 1989

Patterson, William Seeds *Sixty Years of Uppingham Cricket* Longmans, Green, 1909
Piesse, Ken {ed.} *The Great Australian Book of Cricket Stories* Currey O'Neil, 1982
Pycroft, Revd James *The Cricket-Field* St James's Press, 1922
Rienits, Rex & Thea *A Pictorial History of Australia* Hamlyn, 1969
Scott, Jas {ed. Cashman, Richard & Gibbs, Stephen} *Early Cricket in Sydney* NSW Cricket Association, 1991
Storey, Graham *The Letters of Charles Dickens, Vols 9 & 10* OUP, 1998
Thomas, Peter *Yorkshire Cricketers 1839-1939* Derek Hodgson, 1973
Tyson, Frank *The History of the Richmond Cricket Club* Richmond CC/Hudson, 1987
Warner, P.F. *England v Australia* Mills & Boon, 1912
Webber, J.R. *The Chronicle of WG* Association of Cricket Statisticians & Historians, 1998
Webster, Ray {ed. Miller, Allan} *First-Class Cricket in Australia: Vol.1 1850-51 to 1941-42* privately published, 1991
Wellings, E.M. *Dexter versus Benaud* Rigby, 1963
West, G.Derek *The Elevens of England* Darf, 1988
Willey, Keith *Our Australian Heritage* PR Books, 1989

NEWSPAPERS & PERIODICALS
Australia's Heritage (Hamlyn Partwork); Ballarat Star; Bathurst Free Press & Mining Journal; Bell's Life; Brisbane Sunday Mail; The Cabinet; Cricket: A Weekly Record of the Game; The Cricket Quarterly; The Cricket Statistician; Illustrated London News; The Journal of the Cricket Society; Melbourne Argus; Melbourne Herald; Mount Alexander Mail; Sun-Herald; Sydney Mail; Sydney Morning Herald; Wisden Cricket Monthly